CIMA

Certificate in Business Accounting

BA2: Fundamentals of Management Accounting

Course Book

For exams from January 2024

BPP

Exam

CW01668538

Seventh edition 2023

ISBN 9781 0355 0851 8

(Previous ISBN 9781 0355 0259 2)

e-ISBN 9781 0355 0867 9

(Previous e-ISBN 9781 0355 0309 4)

ISBN (for internal use only) 9781 0355 0782 5

British Library Cataloguing-in-Publication Data

A catalogue record for this book is available from the British Library

Published by

BPP Learning Media Ltd

BPP House, Aldine Place

London W12 8AA

learningmedia.bpp.com

Printed in the United Kingdom

Your learning materials, published by BPP Learning Media Ltd, are printed on paper sourced from sustainable, managed forests.

IFRS

AICPA & CIMA
Registered Tuition Provider

Contents

Welcome to BA2 Fundamentals of Management Accounting

Description of the exam

This subject deals with the fundamental knowledge and techniques that underpin management accounting. It identifies the position of the management accountant with organisations and the role of CIMA. The subject portrays the role of management accounting in the contexts of commercial and public sector bodies and its wider role in society.

The identification and classification of costs and their behaviour provides the basis for understanding and applying the tools and techniques needed to plan, control and make decisions. Budgetary control requires the setting of targets and standards which then allow the performance of organisations to be reported and analysed by the calculation of variances. Investment appraisal, break-even analysis and profit maximisation are used to inform both long- and short-term decision making.

Syllabus Areas and their weighting

Weight	Syllabus topic
10%	A. The Context of Management Accounting
25%	B. Costing
30%	C. Planning and Control
35%	D. Decision Making

The Objective Test exam

Format	Computer Based Assessment
Duration	2 hours
Number of questions	60
Marking	No partial marking – each question marked correct or incorrect. All questions carry the same weighting (ie same marks)
Weighting	As per Syllabus Areas All component learning outcomes will be covered
Question types	Multiple Choice Multiple Response Number Entry Drag and Drop Hot spot Item Sets
Booking availability	On demand
Results	Immediate

Verb hierarchy

LEVEL 3

LEARNING OBJECTIVE

APPLICATION

How you are expected to apply your knowledge

VERBS USED	DEFINITION
Apply	Put to practical use
Calculate	Ascertain or reckon mathematically
Demonstrate	Exhibit by practical means
Prepare	Make or get ready for use
Reconcile	Make or prove consistent/compatible
Solve	Find an answer to/prove with certainty
Tabulate	Arrange in a table

LEVEL 2

LEARNING OBJECTIVE

COMPREHENSION

What you are expected to understand

VERBS USED	DEFINITION
Describe	Communicate the key features of
Distinguish	Highlight the differences between
Explain	Make clear or intelligible/state the meaning or purpose of
Identify	Recognise, establish or select after consideration
Illustrate	Use an example to describe or explain something

LEVEL 1

LEARNING OBJECTIVE

KNOWLEDGE

What you are expected to know

VERBS USED	DEFINITION
List	Make a list of
State	Express, fully or clearly, the details/facts of
Define	Give the exact meaning of

Learning outcomes

A. The Context of Management Accounting (10%)

On completion of their studies, students should be able to:

Lead	Component	Level
1. Explain the purpose of management accounting and the role of the Management Accountant.	(a) Explain the need for management accounting	2
	(b) Explain the characteristics of financial information for operational, managerial and strategic levels within organisations	2
	(c) Explain the role of the management accountant	2
	(d) Explain the relationships between the management accountant and the organisation's managers	2
2. Explain the role of CIMA as a professional body for Management Accountants.	(a) Explain the role of CIMA in developing the practice of management accounting	2

B. Costing (25%)

On completion of their studies, students should be able to:

Lead	Component	Level
1. Demonstrate cost identification and classification.	(a) Explain the classification of costs in relation to output	2
	(b) Explain the classification of costs in relation to activity level	2
	(c) Calculate appropriate costs having identified cost behaviour	3
	(d) Explain the classification of costs in relation to decisions	2
2. Apply absorption costing and marginal costing.	(a) Prepare overhead cost statements	3
	(b) Calculate the full cost of products, services and activities	3
	(c) Calculate the marginal cost of products, services and activities	3
	(d) Reconcile the differences between profits calculated using absorption costing and those calculated using marginal costing	3
	(e) Apply cost information in pricing decisions	3

C. Planning and Control (30%)

On completion of their studies, students should be able to:

Lead	Component	Level
1. Prepare budgets for planning and control.	(a) Explain why organisations prepare forecasts and plans	2
	(b) Prepare functional budgets	3
	(c) Explain budget statements	2
	(d) Identify the impact of budgeted cash surpluses and shortfalls on business operations	2
	(e) Prepare a flexible budget	3
	(f) Calculate budget variances	3
2. Apply variance analysis to reconcile budgeted and actual profits in a marginal format.	(a) Explain why planned standard costs, prices and volumes are useful	2
	(b) Calculate variances for materials, labour, variable overheads, sales prices and sales volumes	3
	(c) Prepare a statement that reconciles budgeted profit with actual profit calculated using marginal costing	3
	(d) Explain why variances could have arisen and the inter-relationships between variances	2
3. Calculate appropriate financial and non-financial performance measures.	(a) Explain the need for appropriate performance measures	2
	(b) Calculate appropriate financial and non-financial performance measures in a variety of contexts	3
4. Prepare accounts and reports for managers.	(a) Explain the integration of the cost accounts with the financial accounting system	2
	(b) Prepare a set of integrated accounts, showing standard cost variances	3
	(c) Prepare appropriate accounts for job and batch costing	3
	(d) Prepare reports in a range of organisations	3

D. Decision Making (35%)

On completion of their studies, students should be able to:

Lead	Component	Level
1. Demonstrate the impact of risk.	(a) Explain the concepts of risk and uncertainty	2
	(b) Demonstrate the use of expected values and joint probabilities in decision making	3
	(c) Calculate summary measures of central tendency and dispersion for both grouped and ungrouped data	3

Lead	Component	Level
	(d) Demonstrate the use of the normal distribution	3
2. Demonstrate the use of appropriate techniques for short-term decision making.	(a) Apply breakeven analysis	3
	(b) Demonstrate make or buy decisions	3
	(c) Calculate the profit maximising sales mix after using limiting factor analysis	3
3. Demonstrate the use of appropriate techniques for long-term decision making.	(a) Explain the time value of money	2
	(b) Apply financial mathematics	3
	(c) Calculate the net present value, internal rate of return and payback for an investment or project	3

Exam technique overview

The best approach to the CBA

You're not likely to have a great deal of 'spare time' during the CBA itself so you must make sure you don't waste a single minute.

You should:

(a) Work through the whole exam, answering any questions you think you can answer correctly in a reasonably short time. If you find on occasion that you are not very confident with your answer, click the 'Flag for Review' button before moving on.

(b) Click 'Next' for any that have long scenarios or are very complex and return to these later.

(c) When you reach the 60th question, use the Review Screen to return to any questions you skipped past or any you flagged for review

Here's how the tools in the exam will help you to do this in a controlled and efficient way:

The 'Next' button

What does it do? This will move you on to the next question whether or not you have completed the one you are on.

When should I use it? Use this to move through the exam on your first pass through if you encounter a question that you suspect is going to take you a long time to answer. The Review Screen (see below) will help you to return to these questions later in the exam.

The 'Flag for Review' button

What does it do? This button will turn the icon yellow and when you reach the end of the exam questions you will be told that you have flagged specific questions for review. If the exam time runs out before you have reviewed any flagged questions then they will be submitted as they are.

When should I use it? Use this when you've answered a question but you're not completely comfortable with your answer. If there is time left at the end then you can quickly come back via the Review Screen (see below) but if time runs out at least it will submit your current answer. Do not use the Flag for Review button too often or you will end up with too long a list to review at the end. Important Note – scientific studies have shown that you are usually best to stick with your first instincts(!)

The Review Screen

What does it do? This screen appears after you click 'Next' on the 60th question. It shows you any Incomplete Questions and any you have Flagged for Review. It allows you to jump back to specific questions OR work through all your Incomplete Questions OR work through all your Flagged for Review Questions.

When should I use it? As soon as you've completed your first run through the exam and reached the 60th question. The very first thing to do is to work through all your Incomplete Questions as they will all be marked as incorrect if you don't submit an answer for these in the remaining time. Importantly, this will also help to pick up any questions you thought you'd completed but didn't answer properly (eg you only picked two answer options in a multi-response question that required three answers to be selected). After you've submitted answers for all your Incomplete Questions you should use the Review Screen to work through all the questions you Flagged for Review.

Errata

BPP Learning Media do everything possible to ensure the material is accurate and up to date when sending to print. In the event that any errors are found after the print date, they are uploaded to the following website: https://www.bpp.com/learningmedia/Errata

The different Objective Test Question Types

Passing your CBA is all about demonstrating your understanding of the technical syllabus content. You will find this easier to do if you are comfortable with the different types of Objective Test Questions that you will encounter in the CBA, especially if you have a practised approach to each one.

You will find yourself continuously practising these styles of questions throughout your Objective Test programme. This way you will check and reinforce your technical knowledge at the same time as becoming more and more comfortable with your approach to each style of question.

Multiple choice

Standard multiple choice items provide four options. One option is correct and the other three are incorrect. Incorrect options will be plausible, so you should expect to have to use detailed, syllabus–specific knowledge to identify the correct answer rather than relying on common sense.

Multiple response

A multiple response item is the same as a multiple choice question, except more than one response is required. You will be told how many options you need to select.

Number entry

Number entry (or 'fill in the blank') questions require you to type a short numerical response. You should carefully follow the instructions in the question in terms of how to type your answer – eg the correct number of decimal places.

Drag and drop

Drag and drop questions require you to drag a 'token' onto a pre-defined area. These tokens can be images or text. This type of question is effective at testing the order of events, labelling a diagram or linking events to outcomes.

Hot spot

These questions require you to identify an area or location on an image by clicking on it. This is commonly used to identify a specific point on a graph or diagram.

Item set

Two–four questions all relating to the same short scenario. Each question will be 'standalone', such that your ability to answer subsequent questions in the set does not rely on getting the first one correct.

Features in this Course Book

Key term

A key definition which is important to be aware of for the assessment

Formula to learn

A formula you will need to learn as it will not be provided in the assessment

Formula provided

A formula which is provided within the assessment and generally available as a pop-up on screen

Activity

An example which allows you to apply your knowledge to the technique covered in the Course Book. The solution is provided at the end of the chapter

Illustration

A worked example which can be used to review and see how an assessment question could be answered

Exam focus point

A high priority point for the assessment

1 Introduction to management accounting

Learning outcomes

Having studied this chapter you will be able to:
• Explain the need for management accounting
• Explain the characteristics of financial information for operational, managerial and strategic levels within organisations
• Explain the role of the management accountant
• Explain the relationships between the management accountant and the organisation's managers
• Explain the role of CIMA in developing the practice of management accounting

Chapter context

This chapter introduces the paper by looking at what management accounting is and the role of management accountants within organisations as well as the role of CIMA itself. There are a couple of relatively lengthy definitions in the middle of the chapter but the key thing at this stage is to be comfortable with the main areas of management accountancy in Section 1.

Syllabus context

This chapter is part of syllabus **Section A**, which looks at **'The Context of Management Accounting'**.

This syllabus area has a weighting of **10%** and is covered by **Chapter 1 only**.

In the exam, you will be expected to demonstrate competence in the following areas:

- The Global Management Accounting Principles.
- Characteristics of financial information.
- The CIMA definition of the role of the management accountant.
- The IFAC definition of the domain of the professional accountant in business.
- The positioning of management accounting within the organisation.
- The need for a professional body in management accounting.
- CIMA's role in relation to its members, students, the profession of management accounting and society.

Chapter overview

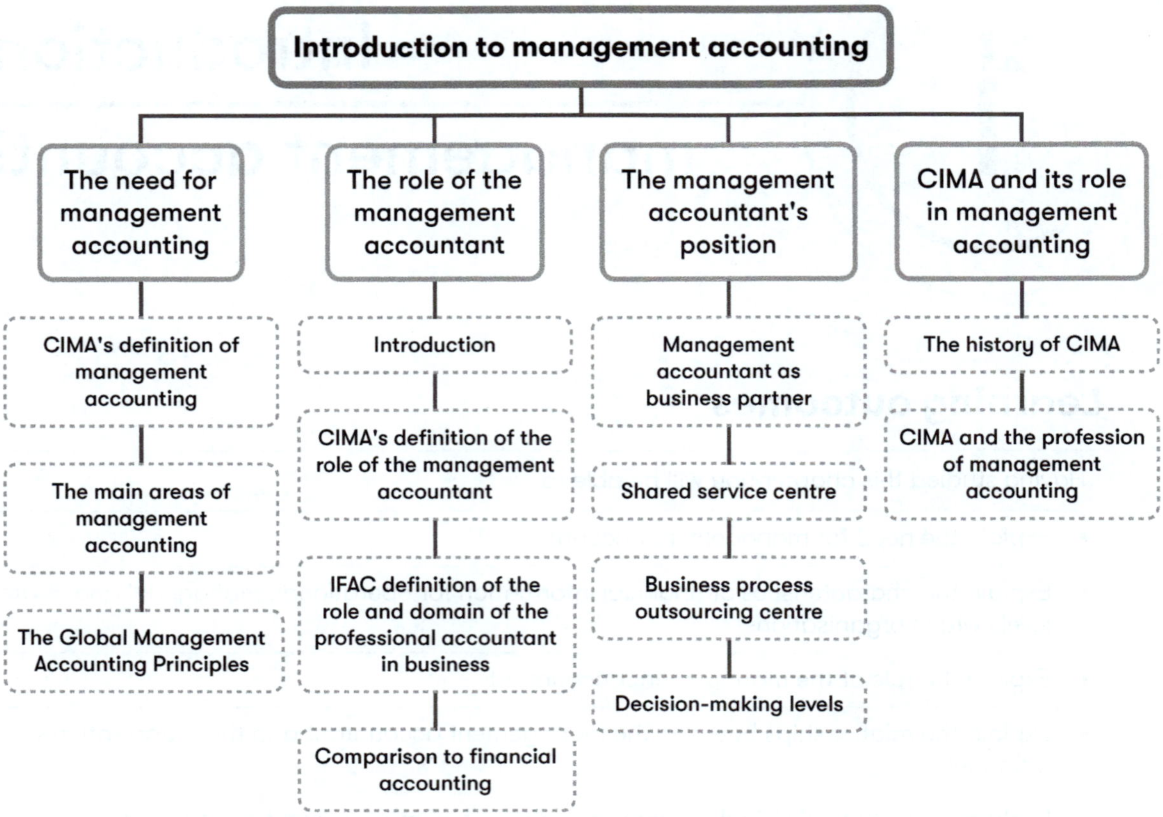

BPP

1 The need for management accounting

It is useful to start by looking at a definition:

1.1 CIMA's definition of management accounting

KEY TERM

Management accounting: 'The application of the principles of accounting and financial management **to create, protect, preserve and increase value** for the stakeholders of for-profit and not-for-profit enterprises in the public and private sectors. Management accounting is an **integral part of management.** It requires the **identification, generation, presentation, interpretation and use of relevant information'.**

(CIMA Official Terminology, 2005)

1.2 The main areas of management accounting

Following on from the above definition we could break down management accounting into five main areas:

(a) **Costing**

What is the cost of goods produced or services provided?

We need to know this to assess the profitability of products or services, to help set prices and to value inventory in the statement of financial position.

(b) **Planning**

Planning involves defining objectives and assessing future costs and revenues to set up a budget.

Planning is essential to help assess purchasing and production requirements of the business. It forces management to think ahead.

(c) **Control**

Once plans have been made, the company must ensure they are being followed and assess any inefficiencies in the business.

(d) **Decision making**

There are many decisions managers may have to make such as:

- What should we produce?
- How should we finance the business?
- Is a project worthwhile?

The finance function is often involved in assessing and modelling the expenditure and cash flow implications of proposed decisions.

(e) **Performance evaluation**

Employees and divisions can be assessed by comparing their performance against targets or budgets. Sometimes performance evaluation is classed as part of control; see (c) above.

1.3 The Global Management Accounting Principles

KEY TERM

Global Management Accounting Principles: CIMA, in a joint project with the AICPA, has developed four principles of management accounting to support organisations in benchmarking and improving their management accounting systems.

The principles help the public and private sectors make better decisions, respond appropriately to the risks they face and protect the value they generate. The four principles are:

(a) **'Communication provides insight which is influential'**

Objective. 'To drive better decisions about strategy and its execution at all levels.'

- Communication on strategy should involve all employees
- Communication should be adapted to suit the user's needs (eg no jargon)
- Good communication helps decision making

(b) **'Information is relevant'**

Objective. 'To help organisations plan for and source the information needed for creating strategy and tactics for execution.'

- Information is accurate, timely and collected from the best sources
- It is financial and non-financial
- It is quantitative (capable of being expressed in numbers) and qualitative (non-numeric)

(c) **'Impact on value is analysed'**

Objective. 'To simulate different scenarios that demonstrate the cause-and-effect relationships between inputs and outcomes.'

- Models should be used to estimate outcomes and measure impact of decisions
- Models can lead to improved prioritisation of undertakings (eg prioritising by value rather than by cost)

(d) **'Stewardship builds trust'**

Objective. 'To actively manage relationships and resources so that the financial and non-financial assets, reputation and value of the organisation are protected.'

- Competent people applying best practice
- Behaving with integrity, objectivity and accountability
- Considering economic, environmental and social risks

2 The role of the management accountant

2.1 Introduction

The management accountant assists in the management of an organisation by providing relevant information to help it achieve its objectives. The management accountant also helps to improve the systems that produce that information.

Although it is important to appreciate that businesses will have many objectives in order to satisfy various different groups (eg employees, customers, suppliers, the Government), the assumption that will usually be made in your studies is that companies wish to maximise the wealth of their shareholders. Usually this will be achieved by maximising profit. Not-for-profit organisations will have other objectives and different information needs.

Type of organisation	Objective	Information needed
Commercial Manufacturing and retail businesses, service providers.	Profit	Costs of running business functions. Profitability
Not-for-profit Providing services to society (eg charities and public services such as health and education)	Value-for-money, effectiveness, efficiency	Funds raised, donations made, services provided.

Note that society may also have a need for relevant information. For example, customers, employees, communities and shareholders may all be interested in the environmental and societal impact of organisations.

Management accountants undertake a wide variety of tasks and activities and their role isn't solely restricted to producing information in monetary terms.

For a more detailed description of the role of a management accountant it is worthwhile referring to some definitions:

2.2 CIMA's definition of the role of the management accountant

'Chartered Management Accountants help organisations **establish viable strategies and convert them into profit** (in a commercial context) or into **value for money** (in a not-for-profit context).

To achieve this they work as an integral part of multi-skilled management teams in carrying out the:

- Formulation of policy and **setting of corporate objectives;**
- Formulation of **strategic plans** derived from corporate objectives;
- Formulation of shorter-term **operational plans;**
- Acquisition and use of **finance;**
- **Design of systems,** recording of events and transactions and **management of information systems;**
- **Generation, communication and interpretation** of financial and operating **information** for management and other stakeholders;
- Provision of specific **information and analysis** on which **decisions** are based;
- **Monitoring of outcomes against plans** and benchmarks, and the initiation of responsive action for performance improvement;
- **Derivation of performance measures** and benchmarks, financial and non-financial, quantitative and qualitative, for monitoring and control; and
- **Improvement of business systems and processes** through risk management and internal audit review.

Through these forward-looking roles and by application of their expert skills management accountants help organisations improve their performance, security, growth and competitiveness in an ever more demanding environment.'

(CIMA Official Terminology, 2005)

CIMA's website says:

'Chartered management accountants:

- Advise managers about the financial implications of projects.
- Explain the financial consequences of business decisions.
- Formulate business strategy.
- Monitor spending and financial control.
- Conduct internal business audits.
- Explain the impact of the competitive landscape.
- Bring a high level of professionalism and integrity to business.'

(CIMA, 2016)

2.3 IFAC definition of the role and domain of the professional accountant in business

The International Federation of Accountants (IFAC) recognises that the roles of professional accountants who work in business are extraordinarily varied in terms of work, experience and responsibilities. IFAC (2005) describes a professional accountant in business as:

'Someone that first meets the standards of a professional, defined as:

- Having skills, knowledge and expertise tested by examination and continuously developed in a structured and monitored context
- Committed to the values of accuracy, honesty, integrity, objectivity, transparency and reliability
- Subject to oversight by a body with disciplinary powers

This is similar to other professionals that achieve accreditation through exam, and maintain expertise via a commitment to on-going continuing education.

Second, is recognised as being an accountant, defined as:

- Belonging to a recognised accountancy body upholding professional standards and approaches in the discipline of recording, analysing, measuring, reporting, forecasting and giving advice in support of financial, management and strategic decisions.

And third, is in business, defined as:

- Working in an organisational entity of any size and ownership structure, or alone, whether or not operating for profit, other than engaged in external audit
- An integral member of, or support to, the management team striving to create and sustain value for stakeholders'

IFAC (2005) has defined the domain of the professional accountant in business as:

- 'The **generation or creation of value** through the effective use of resources (financial and otherwise) through the understanding of the drivers of stakeholder value (which may include shareholders, customers, employees, suppliers, communities, and government) and organisational innovation
- The **provision, analysis and interpretation of information** to management for formulation of strategy, planning, decision making and control
- **Performance measurement and communication** to stakeholders, including the financial recording of transactions and subsequent reporting to stakeholders typically under national or international Generally Accepted Accounting Principles (GAAP)
- **Cost determination and financial control**, through the use of cost accounting techniques, budgeting and forecasting
- **The reduction of waste** in resources used in business processes through the use of process analysis and cost management
- **Risk management** and business assurance

IFAC also states that 'The roles that Professional Accountants in Business perform include implementing and maintaining operational and fiduciary controls, providing analytical support for strategic planning and decision making, ensuring that effective risk management processes are in place, and assisting management in setting the tone for ethical practices'.

2.4 Comparison to financial accounting

The management accounting and financial accounting systems in a business both record the same basic data for income and expenditure, but each set of records may analyse the data in a different way. This is because each system has a **different purpose.**

(a) **Management accounts** are prepared for **internal** managers of an organisation. Their purpose is to help with decision making and there are no rules on their format or content.

(b) **Financial accounts** are prepared for individuals **external** to an organisation eg shareholders, customers, suppliers, tax authorities and employees. Their purpose is to provide statutory information and their format is governed by rules and regulations concerning their content.

The data used to prepare management accounts and financial accounts is the same. The differences between the management accounts and the financial accounts arise because the data is analysed differently.

3 The management accountant's position

The management accounting function may sit in various positions depending on the structure of the business. For example, the management accounting function may be included as part of the finance function or as a separate business partner function, or it could even be a function which is outsourced.

3.1 Management accountant as business partner

As we have mentioned already, management accounting covers costing, planning, control, and decision making. However, traditionally management accountants focused on producing cost information only. They were able to use the same basic data as financial accountants and it therefore made sense for them to be based in the finance function.

Over time their role has widened to encompass the production of both financial and non-financial information. This, coupled with the fact that much of the basic information production can now be automated, has led to the argument that the management accountant should be based outside the finance function, acting as a business partner and adviser and working in cross-functional teams.

The accountant should:	The business manager should:
Demonstrate technical ability	Trust the accountant
Demonstrate business awareness	Discuss matters confidentially
Act with integrity	State what they require clearly
Act professionally	Respect the knowledge and experience of the accountant

When the management accountant acts as an adviser in cross-functional teams, the following advantages and disadvantages apply:

Advantages	Disadvantages
Increased knowledge in each business area	Reduce knowledge sharing
Relationships between accountants and the business areas are strengthened	Duplication of effort
Management accounting becomes part of the business area	Accountants become isolated from the other accountants
	Accountants have a reduced of vision of the whole organisation's goals

3.2 Shared service centre

Alternatively, the entire finance function may be placed in a shared service centre. This is a single location that provides all the accounting support for the whole organisation.

Advantages
Increased service quality
Reduced costs

Advantages
Consistency of management information

3.3 Business process outsourcing centre

A third option is for an organisation to outsource all or part of the finance function to an external supplier.

Advantages	Disadvantages
Reduced costs	Over-reliance on the external supplier
Increased capacity of the organisation's finance team (where only routine functions are outsourced).	Less control over the finance function
Access to specialists	Potential risk to confidential information
	Potential reduced quality of information

Activity 1: Structure of management accounting function

Info Co is currently considering how to structure its management accounting function.

Required

State one advantage and one disadvantage for each of the three approaches listed below.

1 Management accountant as business partner

2 Shared service centre

3 Business process outsourcing centre

Solution

3.4 Decision-making levels

However the finance function is structured, it is important that management accountants recognise that the **management information** needs of each manager will vary depending on their level within the organisation.

KEY TERM

> **Management information:** The information supplied to managers for the purpose of planning, control and decision making.

Decision making operates at three levels:

Level	Nature of tasks	Nature of information
Strategic	Developing long-term organisational goals and objectives. Unstructured. Major impact on the organisation.	Used by senior managers, unstructured, forward-looking and externally focused, qualitative and quantitative, relevant to long term, highly summarised, uses estimates, derived from internal and external sources, wide variety of information and formats.
Management (Tactical)	Implementing the strategy set efficiently and effectively. Medium term in timescale and medium impact on the organisation.	Used by middle management, routine reports, for example, showing budget v actual, relevant to short and medium term, summarised at a lower level, primarily generated internally.
Operational	Ensuring that specific tasks are being carried out in an efficient, highly structured and effective way. Short-term in timescale and small impact on the organisation.	Used by front line managers, detailed, structured, numerical and internally focused on the decision, relevant to immediate term, derived almost entirely from historical, internal sources.

Management information should be good information. It should be relevant, complete, accurate, understandable, authoritative, easy to use and timely. Its cost should also be less than the benefits it provides.

Information is data (such as statistics and facts) that has been processed into a form that has a meaningful use.

Activity 2: Decision categories

Categorise the following decisions as either strategic, management or operational:

	Strategic	Management	Operational
Whether to take out loans or issue shares to raise finance			
Which products to continue/discontinue			
How many production staff to employ			
Which geographic markets to operate in			
Which suppliers to use			

4 CIMA and its role in management accounting

CIMA is a global accounting body based in the UK. It is the world's largest professional body of management accountants. It has over 229,000 members and students in 176 countries.

4.1 The history of CIMA

(a) CIMA was founded in 1919 as the Institute of Cost and Works Accountants (ICWA). It specialised in the development of accounting techniques for use in the internal control of manufacturing, service and public sector operations.

(b) It changed its name from ICWA to the Institute of Cost and Management Accountants (ICMA) in 1972.

(c) It changed its name again in 1986 to the Chartered Institute of Management Accountants (CIMA) after the granting of a Royal Charter in 1975.

4.2 CIMA and the profession of management accounting

(a) CIMA is committed to upholding the ethical and professional standards and to maintain public confidence in management accounting.

(b) CIMA regulates the activities of its members by a code of practice, conduct and discipline committees and a continuing education scheme.

(c) It is the responsibility of each student and member to ensure they comply with both CIMA's regulations and any specific regulations and legislation as required by their country of residence.

(d) Members and students must uphold the Code of Ethics and refrain from any conduct which might discredit the profession. This code is based on five fundamental principles:

- Integrity
- Objectivity
- Professional competence and due care
- Confidentiality
- Professional behaviour

(CIMA code of ethics, 2015)

(e) Sources of ethical dilemmas:

- Desire to act in own interest
- Threats and intimidation
- Pressure from management or others
- Being asked to perform a role with insufficient resources

(f) Any complaints against CIMA students and members are investigated and, after this process, the conduct committee may recommend that no action is taken. Alternatively, the student or member may admit misconduct and accept a sanction. Serious complaints are passed to the disciplinary committee or the Financial Reporting Council.

(g) Possible sanctions against students and members guilty of misconduct include:

- Admonishment
- Reprimand
- Severe reprimand
- Fine
- Conditional membership or student registration
- Suspension
- Expulsion

Chapter summary

Introduction to management accounting

The need for management accounting

CIMA's definition of management accounting
- CIMA's definition

The main areas of management accounting
- Costing
- Planning
- Control
- Decision making
- Performance evaluation

The Global Management Accounting Principles
- 'Communication provides insight which is influential'
- 'Information is relevant'
- 'Impact on value is analysed'
- 'Stewardship builds trust'

The role of the management accountant

Introduction
- Types of organisation
- Objective
- Information needed

CIMA's definition of the role of the management accountant
- CIMA's definition

IFAC definition of the role and domain of the professional accountant in business
- IFAC's definition

Comparison to financial accounting
- Management accounting
- Financial accounting

The management accountant's position

Management accountant as business partner
- Management accountant
- Business partner
- Advantages and disadvantages

Shared service centre
- Advantages of shared service centres

Business process outsourcing centre
- Advantages and disadvantages of business process outsourcing centres

Decision-making levels
- Strategic
- Management (tactical)
- Operational

CIMA and its role in management accounting

The history of CIMA
- CIMA's history

CIMA and the profession of management accounting
- CIMA's role in regulating members

Key terms

Management accounting: 'The application of the principles of accounting and financial management **to create, protect, preserve and increase value** for the stakeholders of for-profit and not-for-profit enterprises in the public and private sectors. Management accounting is an **integral part of management.** It requires the **identification, generation, presentation, interpretation and use of relevant information'.**

(CIMA Official Terminology, 2005)

Global Management Accounting Principles: CIMA, in a joint project with the AICPA, has developed four principles of management accounting to support organisations in benchmarking and improving their management accounting systems.

Management information: The information supplied to managers for the purpose of planning, control and decision making.

Activity answers

Activity 1: Structure of management accounting function

1 **Management accountant as business partner**

Advantages – By working in the operational environment, the management accountant develops a better knowledge of the business and stronger relationships with the managers they work with. Information produced by the management accountant can then be tailored to the needs of individual managers.

Disadvantages – Duplication of activities (where the same reports may be prepared by several different accountants); focus is on individual departments rather than the whole organisation; accountants can become isolated from their finance colleagues.

2 **Shared service centre**

Advantages – Centralising the function gives lower overall cost than the 'business partner' approach, consistent reporting as the same reports are prepared for each department, and therefore higher quality information.

Disadvantages – Unresponsive to local requirements, remote from and lacking knowledge of the operating units.

3 **Business process outsourcing centre**

Advantages – Lower cost, access to the skills and knowledge of a specialist provider

Disadvantages – Loss of control, potential loss of confidentiality, inflexible once the contract has been signed

(Only one advantage and one disadvantage for each was required)

Activity 2: Decision categories

	Strategic	Management	Operational
Whether to take out loans or issue shares to raise finance	Yes	No	No
Which products to continue/discontinue	No	Yes	No
How many production staff to employ	No	Yes	No
Which geographic markets to operate in	Yes	No	No
Which suppliers to use	No	No	Yes

Test your learning

1 In general terms, financial accounting is for internal reporting whereas management accounting is for external reporting.

- ○ True
- ◉ False

2 Which one of the following is **not** usually considered to be one of the purposes of management information?

- ◉ Implementing
- ○ Planning
- ○ Control
- ○ Decision making

3 Fill in the gaps.

Management accounting is increasingly being viewed as supporting [management] rather than being part of the [finance.] function.

4 Fill in the gaps.

Management information is used for planning, control and [decision making.] .

5 Non-financial information is relevant to management accounting.

- ◉ True
- ○ False

2 Costing

Learning outcomes

Having studied this chapter you will be able to:
• Explain the classification of costs in relation to output
• Explain the classification of costs in relation to decisions
• Explain the need for appropriate performance measures

Chapter context

This chapter introduces some important concepts and terms that are fundamental for this paper, including the benefit of splitting total costs into different categories to help us run the organisation effectively.

Syllabus context

This chapter is part of syllabus **Section B**, which looks at **'Costing'**.

This syllabus area has a weighting of **25%** and is covered by **Chapters 2 to 5**.

In the exam, you will be expected to demonstrate competence in the following areas:

- Direct and indirect costs.
- Relevant and irrelevant costs.
- Characteristics of service industries.
- Responsibility accounting (authority, responsibility and controllability).

Chapter overview

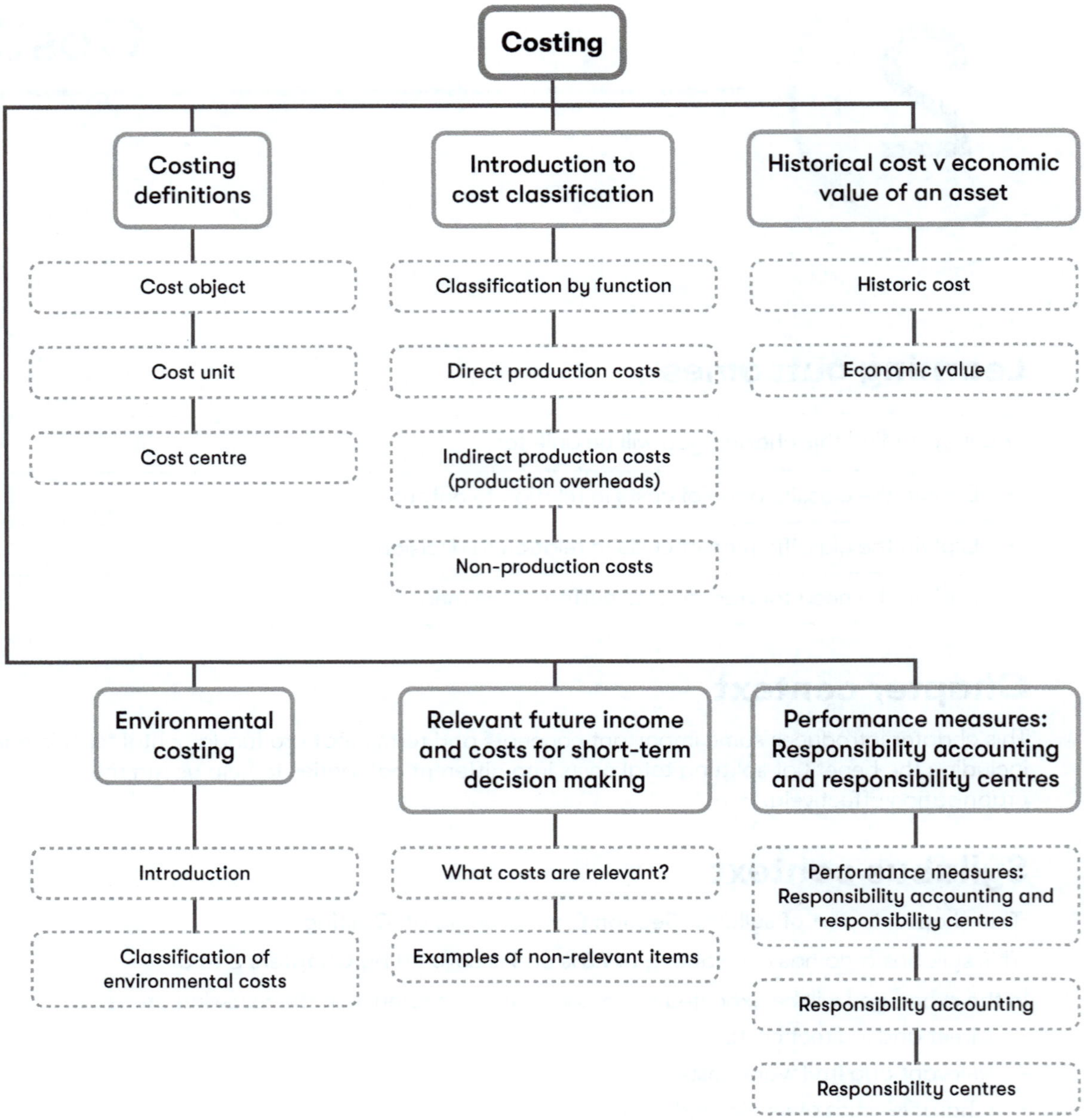

1 Costing definitions

1.1 Cost object

KEY TERM

Cost object: Anything for which cost data is desired eg products, product lines, jobs, customers or departments and divisions of a company.

1.2 Cost unit

KEY TERM

Cost unit: A unit of product or service in relation to which costs may be ascertained.

The cost unit should be appropriate to the type of business. For example, an audit firm could be trying to cost a complete audit, or one chargeable hour.

Activity 1: Cost units

Give appropriate cost units for the following:

Business	Appropriate cost unit
Car manufacturer	
Ball bearing manufacturer	
Builder	
Management consultant	

1.3 Cost centre

KEY TERM

Cost centre: A function or location for which costs are ascertained (and related to cost units for control purposes).

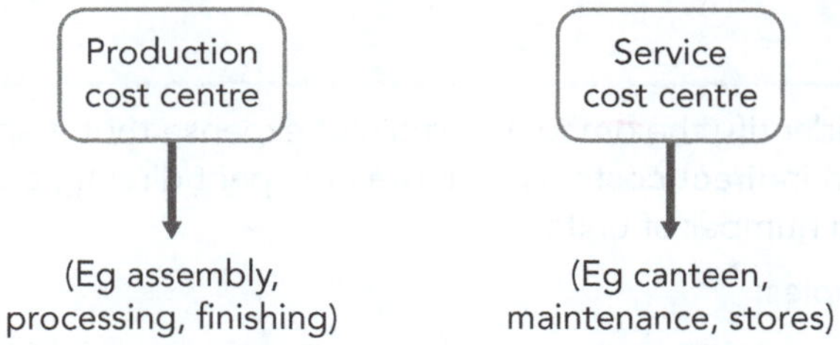

KEY TERM

Production cost centres: Those which are actively involved in the production process.

Service cost centres: Provide a service or back-up to the production departments.

2 Introduction to cost classification

Cost classification is the arrangement of cost items into logical groups. For example:

- Classification by **nature** (eg materials, wages)
- Classification by **function** (eg administration, production)
- Classification by **behaviour** (see Chapter 3) or **responsibility** (see Section 6)

One of the eventual aims is to determine the cost of making a product or providing a service.

2.1 Classification by function

	£
Production costs	X
Non-production costs	
Administration costs	X
Selling and distribution costs	X
Total cost	X

Production costs → **Direct** Prod'n cost / **Indirect** Prod'n cost

The management accounting techniques in this paper are mostly concerned with **production costs**.

2.2 Direct production costs

KEY TERM

Direct costs: Those costs which can be specifically identified with and allocated to a particular cost object. Usually the cost object will be a cost unit and therefore direct costs can be attributed in full to a particular unit of production.

Prime cost: The total of all direct production costs.

Note. Note that direct materials include **all material becoming part of the product** (unless used in negligible amounts and/or having negligible cost) – this includes packing materials. Direct labour is all basic hours or overtime expended on work on the product itself, including **altering** the condition, conformation or composition of the product, or inspecting, analysing or testing the product if this is specifically required for such production. Direct expenses are any expenses which are incurred on a specific product **other than direct material cost and direct wages.**

2.3 Indirect production costs (production overheads)

KEY TERM

Indirect production costs: Those costs which are incurred in the course of making a product/service, but which cannot be identified with a particular cost object (which is usually a cost unit).

It is usually easy to identify the amount of a direct expense that is spent on one unit, but it is more difficult to do so with **indirect costs** as they are not spent directly on one unit. They are usually spent in relation to a number of units.

Here are some examples:

Direct materials	Materials that are incorporated into the finished product (eg wood used in the construction of a table).
Indirect materials	Materials that are used in the production process but not incorporated into the product (eg machine lubricants and spare parts). Insignificant costs that are attributable to each unit are sometimes included in indirect materials for convenience (eg nails and glue).
Direct labour	Wages paid to those workers who make products in a manufacturing business (eg machine operators) or perform the service in a service business (eg hairdressers in a hair salon).

Indirect labour	Wages and salaries of the other staff, such as supervisors, storekeepers and maintenance workers.
Direct expenses	Expenses that are identifiable with each unit of production, such as patent royalties payable to the inventor of a new product or process.
Indirect expenses	Expenses that are not spent on individual units of production (eg rent and rates, electricity and telephone).

Activity 2: Direct and indirect costs

Jai starts a takeaway pizza business selling different types of pizzas (stone-baked and ordinary pizzas). He rents premises, hires a special oven for the stone-baked variety of pizza, employs an assistant to make the pizzas and a cleaner to clean the premises.

Required

Give some examples of direct and indirect production costs associated with the business.

Solution

Direct — indirect

Labour → Assistant — Labour → cleaner

Expenses → pizza oven — Expenses → Rent

materials → pizza ingredients. — materials → maintenence cleaning products ?

TOTAL PRODUCTION COST = PRIME COST + PRODUCTION OVERHEADS

Labour costs

The basic distinction for classification of labour costs is that labour costs of production workers are direct costs, and of other staff are indirect costs. However, there are two specific scenarios where the costs of production workers should be treated as indirect:

(a) Overtime premiums for general production (not a specific job)

(b) Idle time, where workers are being paid but no production is taking place

Activity 3: Direct or indirect?

Classify the following labour costs as either direct or indirect.

(1) The basic pay of direct workers (cash paid, tax and other deductions) is a(n) [D] cost.

(2) The basic pay of indirect workers is a(n) [I] cost.

(3) Overtime premium, ie the premium above basic pay, for working overtime is a(n) [I] cost.

(4) Bonus payments under a group bonus scheme is a(n) [I] cost.

(5) Social security (eg Employer's National Insurance) contributions is a(n) [d] cost.

(6) Idle time of direct workers, paid while waiting for work is a(n) ______ cost.

Illustration of cost classification

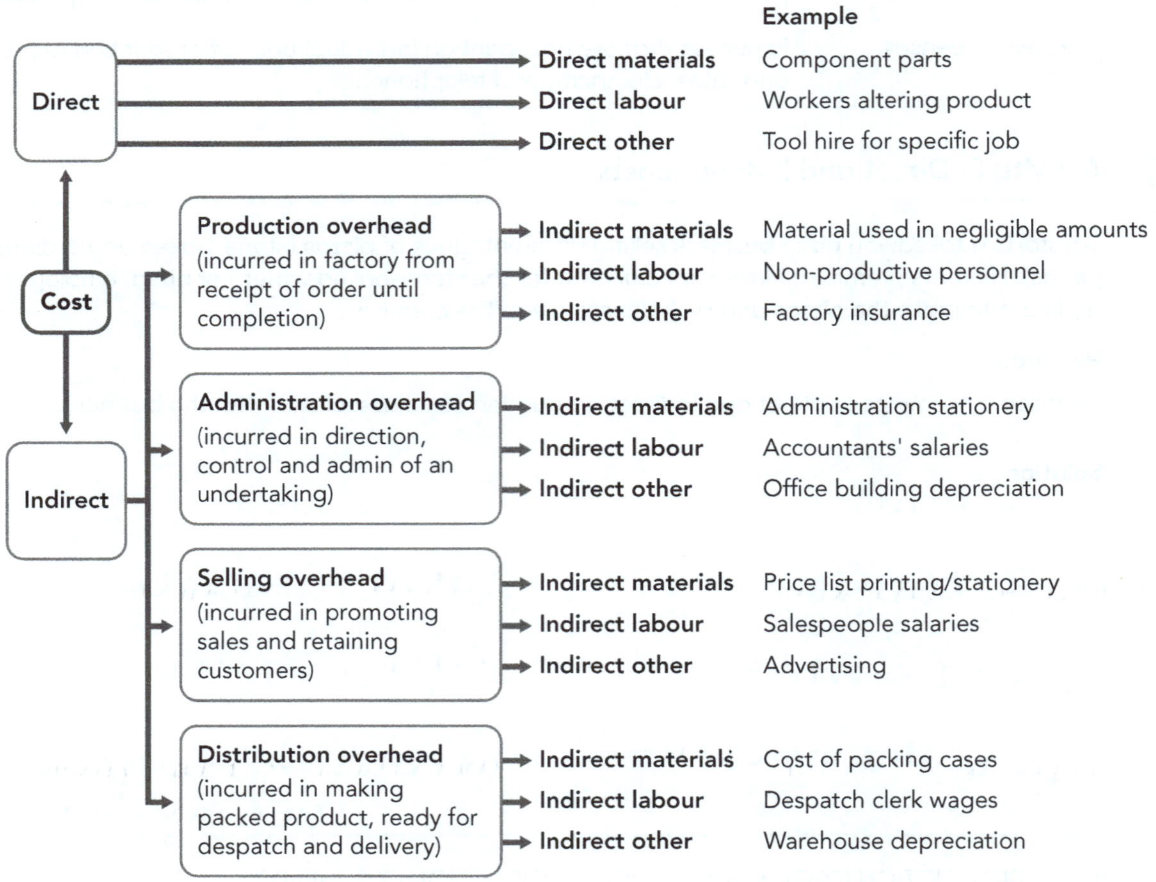

2.4 Non-production costs

As you know, total production cost = prime cost + production overheads. All other costs required to run the business are non-production costs.

Activity 4: Non-production costs

Give some examples of non-production costs.

Solution

TOTAL COSTS = PRODUCTION COSTS + NON PRODUCTION COSTS

3 Historical cost v economic value of an asset

3.1 Historic cost

In practice most organisations record assets at historical cost.

KEY TERM

> **Historic cost:** of an asset – the original cost to the organisation.

3.2 Economic value

However, assets can also be measured at their **economic value.**

KEY TERM

> **Economic value:** of an asset – the most someone is willing to give up in order to obtain the asset.

How much a person is willing to pay for the asset tells us the economic value.

4 Environmental costing

4.1 Introduction

Increasingly, businesses need to be aware of the environmental costs associated with business activities. In the past, environmental costs such as energy costs were treated as production **overheads** and effectively hidden from management scrutiny.

4.2 Classification of environmental costs

In order to manage environmental costs it can be useful to classify them into four categories.

KEY TERM

> **Environmental Prevention costs:** Costs incurred to prevent the production of waste that could cause damage to the environment.
>
> **Environmental Appraisal costs:** Costs incurred to assess whether a firm's activities comply with environmental laws and standards.
>
> **Environmental Internal failure costs:** Costs incurred after waste has been produced but not discharged into the environment.
>
> **Environmental External failure costs:** Costs incurred after waste has been produced and discharged into the environment. Some of these costs may be paid by society as a whole.

Case study

On 20 April 2010, multinational oil company BP's Deepwater Horizon rig exploded off the coast of the US state of Louisiana, killing 11 workers. BP chairman Carl-Henric Svanberg was invited to meet US President Barack Obama amid concerns that the company did not have enough cash to pay for the clean-up operation and compensation for those affected – and agreed to set up a claims fund of $20 billion. The reputation of the global BP brand was seriously damaged.

This is clearly an example of an external failure cost.

Activity 5: Environmental costs

MBash Co produces catalytic converters that are purchased by a wide range of motor manufacturers.

Required

Identify possible environmental costs that MBash may incur in each of the four categories.

spending money on more environmentally efficient machinery.
inspection costs
prevention → ensuring converter production doesn't emit pollution
appraisal costs → checking production complies w laws
cost disposal
internal → pollution produced - not discharged
external → discharged pollution from ; clean up costs

Solution

5 Relevant future income and costs for short-term decision making

5.1 What costs are relevant?

When providing management information for decision making, you must work out which costs and revenues are **relevant** to the decision.

In the context of short-term decision making, the **relevant cost** is contribution (the difference between selling price and variable costs – see Chapter 5). The fixed costs do not affect the decision made and are **irrelevant costs.**

KEY TERM

> **Relevant cost (sometimes known as an avoidable cost):** A future, incremental cash flow arising as a direct consequence of a decision.

(a) **Future costs.** A decision is about the future and it cannot alter what has already been done. Costs that have been incurred in the past are totally irrelevant to any decision that is being made 'now'. Such costs are **past costs** or **sunk costs.**

Costs that have been incurred include not only costs that have already been paid, but also costs that have been **committed.**

KEY TERM

> **Committed cost:** A future cash flow that will be incurred anyway, regardless of the decision taken now.

(b) **Cash flows.** Only cash flow information is required. This means that costs or charges that do not reflect **additional cash spending** (such as depreciation and notional costs) should be ignored for the purpose of decision making.

(c) **Incremental (sometimes called differential).** By this we mean the **increase** (only) in costs and revenues that occur as a result of the decision. For example, if an employee is expected to have no other work to do during the next week, but will be paid their basic wage (of, say, £100 per week) for attending work and doing nothing, their manager might decide to give them a job that earns the organisation £40. The net gain is £40 and the £100 is irrelevant to the decision because although it is a future cash flow, it will be incurred anyway whether or not the employee is given work. The £100 is not an extra cost.

KEY TERM

> **Opportunity cost:** The benefit which would have been earned but which has been given up by choosing one option instead of another.

Activity 6: Relevant costs

GA Co is considering whether to accept an order from a potential customer. The trainee accountant's estimate of the profit from the project is shown below:

	$
Revenue	27,000
Materials (Note 1)	(18,000)
Labour (Note 2)	(12,000)
Overheads (Note 3)	(10,000)
Profit/(loss)	(13,000)

Notes.

1 The materials include $10,000 of surplus inventory that GA Co has in its warehouse. It is not needed for any other production. This inventory has a scrap value of $2,000.

2 Labour includes 10% of the $50,000 salary of the production manager. The manager is an existing member of staff and has the time available to work on this order in addition to their other duties.

3 This is an apportionment of general overheads.

Required

Using **relevant cash flows** assess whether GA Co should accept this order.

Solution

5.2 Examples of non-relevant items

Here are some examples of non-relevant items that you may come across in the assessment:

Examples	Explanation
Non cash flow expenses	Eg depreciation, apportioned overheads
Sunk costs	Eg market research
Historic cost of material	If materials are used by a project then they will either: (a) Need to be replaced, so the **replacement cost** is the cash flow; or (b) They won't, so the cost is **zero** (or lost revenue if they could have been sold as scrap).
Cost of labour	If labour used by a project is **idle,** then the cost of using that labour is **zero.**

6 Performance measures: Responsibility accounting and responsibility centres

KEY TERM

Responsibility accounting: A system of accounting that segregates revenue and costs into areas of personal responsibility in order to monitor and assess the performance of each part of an organisation.

Responsibility centre: A department or function whose performance is the direct responsibility of a specific manager.

6.1 Responsibility accounting

Responsibility accounting attempts to associate costs, revenues, assets and liabilities with the managers most capable of controlling them. As a system of accounting, it therefore distinguishes between **controllable** and **uncontrollable costs.**

KEY TERM

Controllable cost: A cost which can be influenced by management decisions and actions.

Uncontrollable cost: A cost which cannot be affected by management within a given time span.

6.2 Responsibility centres

A responsibility centre will either be a **cost centre**, a **profit centre**, a **revenue centre** or an **investment centre**.

KEY TERM

Cost centre: Managers generally only have responsibility for controlling costs (ie they make decisions about expenditure only).

Profit centre: Any section of an organisation to which both revenues and costs are assigned, so that the profitability of the section may be measured.

Revenue centre: Any section of an organisation to which revenues are assigned, before they are analysed further.

The manager of the profit centre has some influence over both revenues and costs; that is, a say in both sales and production policies.

KEY TERM

Investment centres: Profit centres with additional responsibility for capital investment and possibly for financing.

Several profit centres might share the same capital items, for example the same buildings, stores or transport fleet, and so investment centres are likely to include several profit centres, and provide a basis for control at a very senior management level.

The financial performance measures used will differ between the different types of responsibility centre, and whether costs and/or revenues are controllable by a particular centre manager. This will be explored further later in this Course Book.

Chapter summary

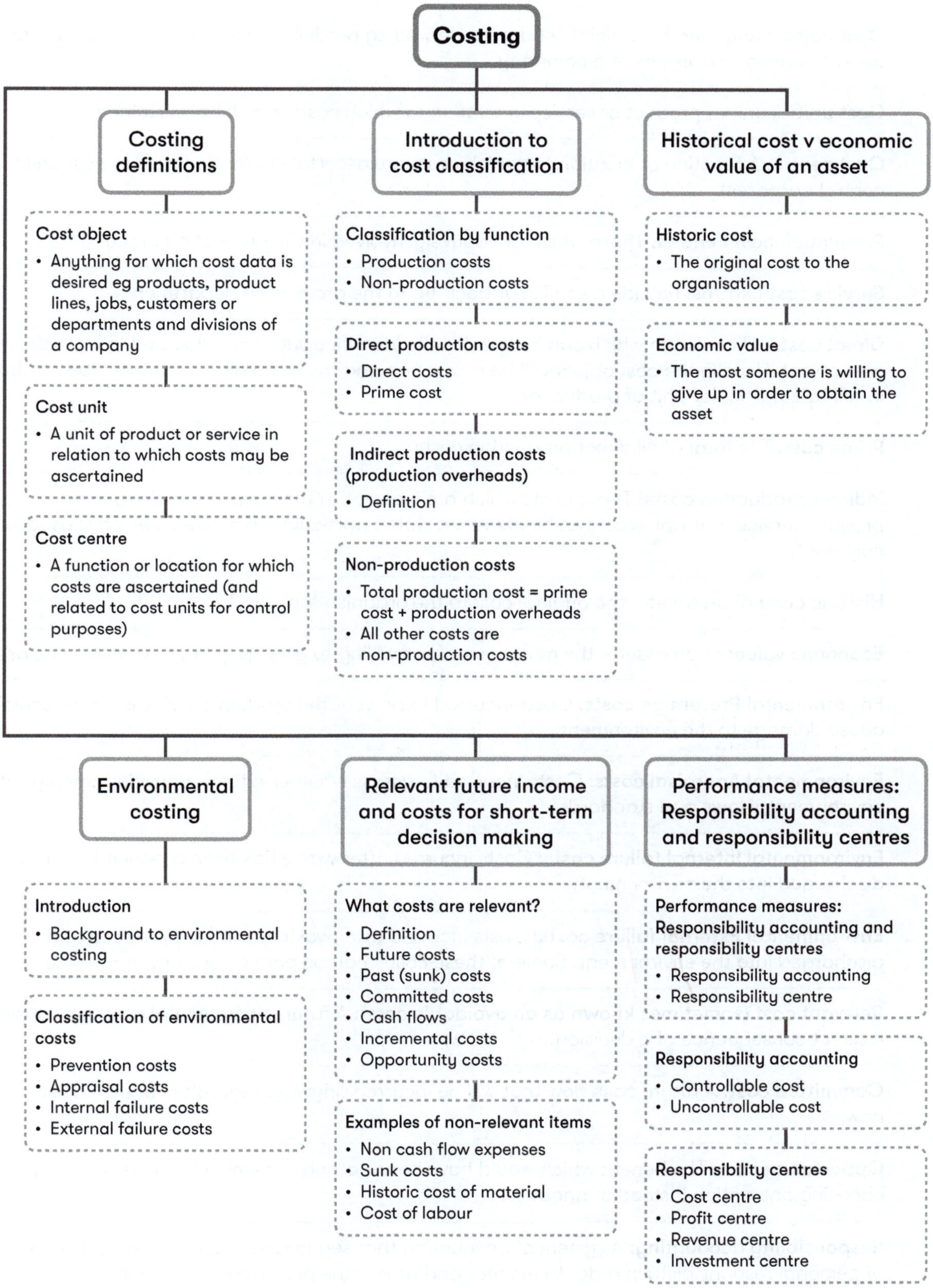

Key terms

Cost object: Anything for which cost data is desired eg products, product lines, jobs, customers or departments and divisions of a company.

Cost unit: A unit of product or service in relation to which costs may be ascertained.

Cost centre: A function or location for which costs are ascertained (and related to cost units for control purposes).

Production cost centres: Those which are actively involved in the production process.

Service cost centres: Provide a service or back-up to the production departments.

Direct costs: Those costs which can be specifically identified with and allocated to a particular cost object. Usually the cost object will be a cost unit and therefore direct costs can be attributed in full to a particular unit of production.

Prime cost: The total of all direct production costs.

Indirect production costs: Those costs which are incurred in the course of making a product/service, but which cannot be identified with a particular cost object (which is usually a cost unit).

Historic cost: of an asset – the original cost to the organisation.

Economic value: of an asset – the most someone is willing to give up in order to obtain the asset.

Environmental Prevention costs: Costs incurred to prevent the production of waste that could cause damage to the environment.

Environmental Appraisal costs: Costs incurred to assess whether a firm's activities comply with environmental laws and standards.

Environmental Internal failure costs: Costs incurred after waste has been produced but not discharged into the environment.

Environmental External failure costs: Costs incurred after waste has been produced and discharged into the environment. Some of these costs may be paid by society as a whole.

Relevant cost (sometimes known as an avoidable cost): A future, incremental cash flow arising as a direct consequence of a decision.

Committed cost: A future cash flow that will be incurred anyway, regardless of the decision taken now.

Opportunity cost: The benefit which would have been earned but which has been given up by choosing one option instead of another.

Responsibility accounting: A system of accounting that segregates revenue and costs into areas of personal responsibility in order to monitor and assess the performance of each part of an organisation.

Responsibility centre: A department or function whose performance is the direct responsibility of a specific manager.

Controllable cost: A cost which can be influenced by management decisions and actions.

Uncontrollable cost: A cost which cannot be affected by management within a given time span.

Cost centre: Managers generally only have responsibility for controlling costs (ie they make decisions about expenditure only).

Profit centre: Any section of an organisation to which both revenues and costs are assigned, so that the profitability of the section may be measured.

Revenue centre: Any section of an organisation to which revenues are assigned, before they are analysed further.

Investment centres: Profit centres with additional responsibility for capital investment and possibly for financing.

Activity answers

Activity 1: Cost units

Business	Appropriate cost unit
Car manufacturer	A single car
Ball bearing manufacturer	A box of ball bearings
Builder	A job
Management consultant	A project

Activity 2: Direct and indirect costs

Direct production costs

- Direct material – pizza dough and other ingredients
- Direct labour – wages paid to assistant making the pizzas
- Direct expenses – cost of hiring the pizza oven

Indirect production costs

- Indirect material – cleaning materials
- Indirect labour – cleaner's wages
- Indirect expenses – rent of premises

Activity 3: Direct or indirect?

(1) The basic pay of direct workers (cash paid, tax and other deductions) is a(n) [direct] cost.

(2) The basic pay of indirect workers is a(n) [indirect] cost.

(3) Overtime premium, ie the premium above basic pay, for working overtime is a(n) [indirect] cost.

(4) Bonus payments under a group bonus scheme is a(n) [indirect] cost.

(5) Social security (eg Employer's National Insurance) contributions is a(n) [direct] cost.

(6) Idle time of direct workers, paid while waiting for work is a(n) [indirect] cost.

Activity 4: Non-production costs

Non-production costs

- Advertising and marketing costs
- Administrative costs
- Selling and distribution costs
- Financing costs

Activity 5: Environmental costs

- **Prevention** – Costs incurred in designing the production process to reduce pollution and training employees in operating the process correctly

- **Appraisal** – Inspection of the catalytic convertors and the production process to ensure they comply with environmental legislation
- **Internal failure** – The cost of disposing of toxic materials and disposing of scrap
- **External failure** – The cost of clearing up toxic materials that have been discharged into rivers or into the atmosphere

Activity 6: Relevant costs

	$	Comment
Revenue	27,000	
Materials	(10,000)	The surplus inventory should be included at its scrap value (18,000 - 10,000 + 2,000).
Labour	(7,000)	The production manager's salary is not incremental.
Overheads		The overheads will be incurred whether or not the project is accepted.
Profit/(loss)	10,000	

The project generates a positive relevant cash flow of $10,000 (ie it will increase GA Co's bank balance by this amount) and therefore it should be accepted.

Test your learning

1 Fill in the blanks:

(1) A cost unit is a unit of product or service to which costs can be related. It is the basic control unit for costing purposes.

(2) A cost centre acts as a collecting place for certain costs before they are analysed further.

(3) A cost object is anything that users of accounting information want to know the cost of.

2 Choose the correct words from below.

In practice, most cost accounting systems use historical cost ▼ as a measurement basis.

Pull down list

- Cost value
- Economic cost
- Economic value
- Historical cost

3 Classification of expenditure into material, labour and expenses is an example of:

- Classification by nature
- Classification by function
- Classification by responsibility
- Classification by behaviour

4 There are a number of different ways in which costs can be classified.

(1) Direct and indirect (or overhead) costs

(2) Non-production costs costs (production costs, distribution and selling costs, administration costs and financing costs) functional

5 Which of the following would be classified as indirect labour?

- Assembly workers in a company manufacturing televisions ✗
- A stores assistant in a factory store ✓
- Plasterers in a construction company ✗
- An audit clerk in a firm of auditors ✗

6 What is the main aim of performance measurement?

- To obtain evidence in order to dismiss someone
- To establish how well something or somebody is doing in relation to a planned activity
- To collect information on costs ✗
- To award bonuses

7 A company has to pay a $1 per unit royalty to the designer of a product which it manufactures and sells.

Required

The royalty charge would be classified in the company's accounts as a:

- ◉ Direct expense
- ○ Production overhead ✓
- ○ Administrative overhead
- ○ Selling overhead

3 Cost behaviour

Learning outcomes

Having studied this chapter you will be able to:
• Explain the classification of costs in relation to activity level
• Calculate appropriate costs having identified cost behaviour

Chapter context

This chapter starts by covering an important way of classifying costs based on what happens when we increase or decrease output. We can split costs between those that stay the same as output increases (fixed costs) and those that change (variable costs). We then move on to look at how we can calculate the fixed and variable elements of an organisation's total costs.

Syllabus context

This chapter is part of syllabus **Section B**, which looks at **'Costing'**.

This syllabus area has a weighting of **25%** and is covered by **Chapters 2 to 5**.

In the exam, you will be expected to demonstrate competence in the following areas:

- Variable, semi-variable, stepped and fixed costs.
- The use of 'high-low', graphical and regression analysis methods to establish and predict total cost.

Chapter overview

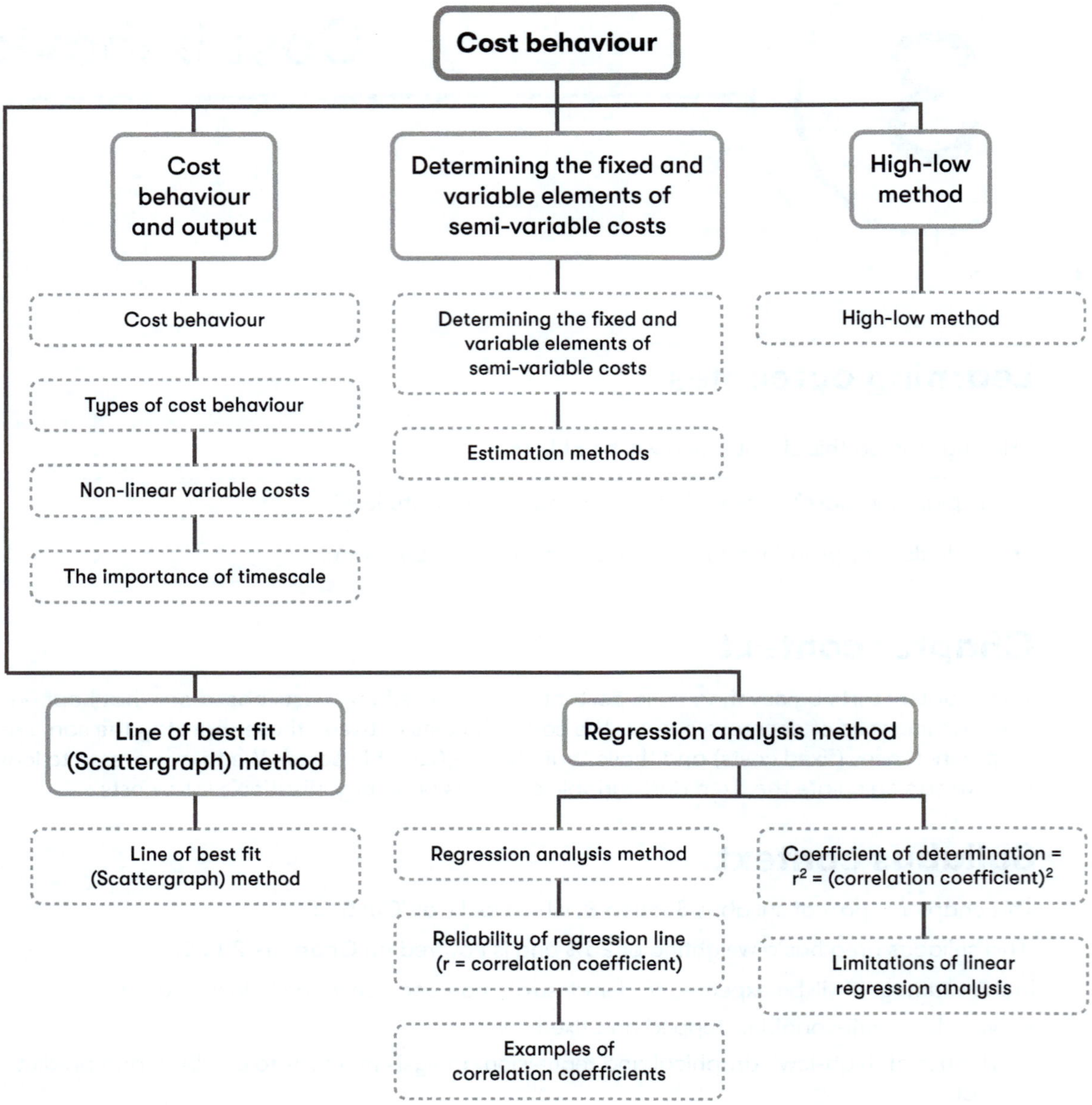

1 Cost behaviour and output

> **Cost behaviour:** The way in which a cost changes as activity level (volume of output) changes.

KEY TERM

A business needs to know how costs behave with output so that predictions of costs can be made.

It is expected that costs will increase as the level of activity increases, but the exact way costs behave with output may vary.

The level of activity refers to the amount of work done, or the number of events that have occurred. Depending on circumstances, the level of activity may refer to measures such as the following:

- The volume of production in a period → units produced.
- The number of items sold → sales.
- The number of invoices issued
- The number of units of electricity consumed – more units – more cost goes up.

For our purposes in this chapter, the level of activity will generally be taken to be the volume of production/output.

1.1 Types of cost behaviour

eg rent

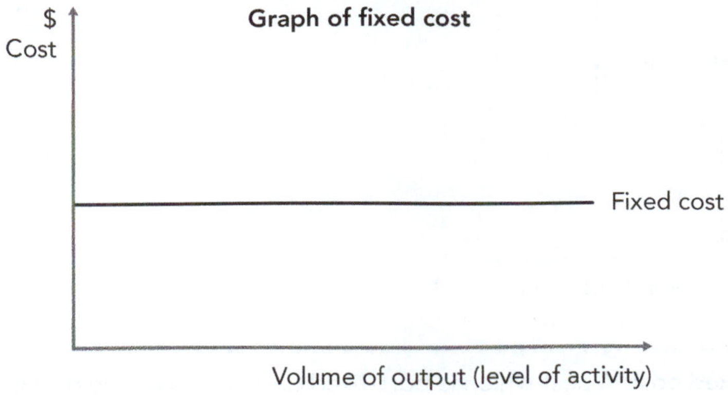

KEY TERM

> **Fixed cost:** A 'cost incurred for an accounting period, that, within certain output or turnover limits, tends to be unaffected by fluctuations in the levels of activity (output or turnover)'.
>
> (CIMA Official Terminology, 2005)

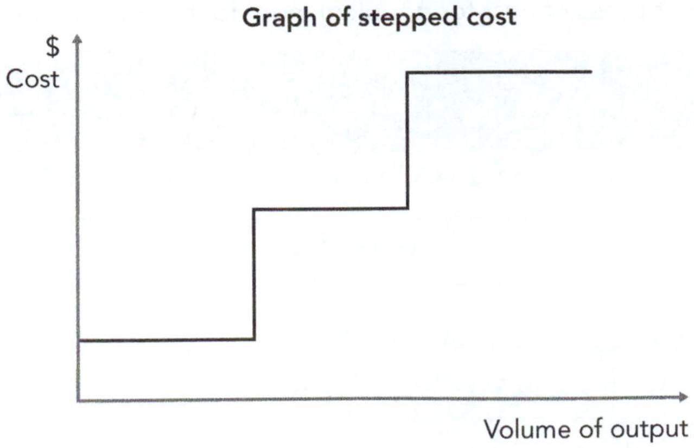

KEY TERM

> **Stepped cost:** A cost which is fixed in nature, but only within certain levels of activity. Depending on the time frame being considered, it may appear as fixed or variable.

Graph of variable cost

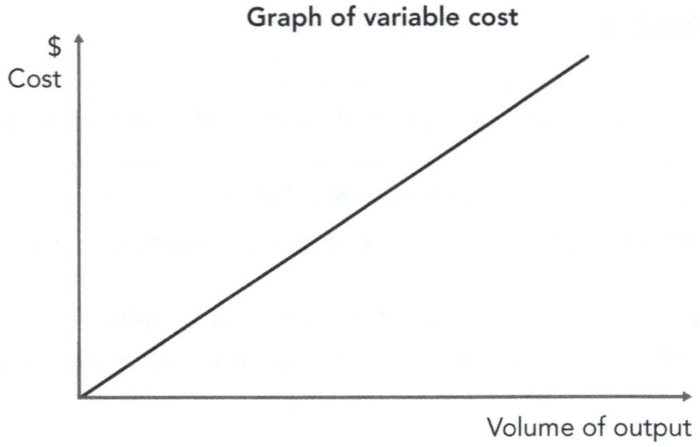

Variable cost: A cost which tends to vary directly with the volume of output. The variable cost **per unit** is the same amount for each unit produced, whereas **total** variable cost increases as volume of output increases.

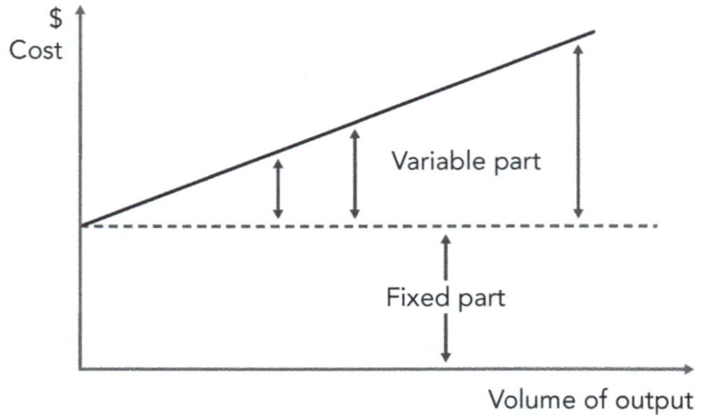

Semi-variable, semi-fixed or mixed cost: A cost which is part-fixed and part-variable and is therefore partly affected by a change in the level of activity. It is a cost that has both fixed and variable components.

Activity 1: Cost behaviour examples

Give two examples of each of the different types of cost for a typical manufacturing business.

Type of cost	Examples rates eg council tax.
Fixed	Rent Equipment depreciation (straight-line).
Stepped	salaries of staff. insurance.
Variable	units bought from suppliers. materials, labour costs.
Semi-variable	telephone, light + heat.

1.2 Non-linear variable costs

Although variable costs are usually assumed to be linear, there are situations where variable costs are **curvilinear**. Have a look at the following graphs.

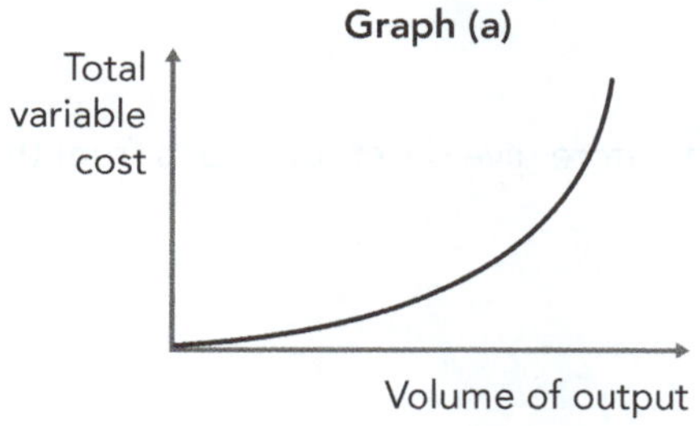

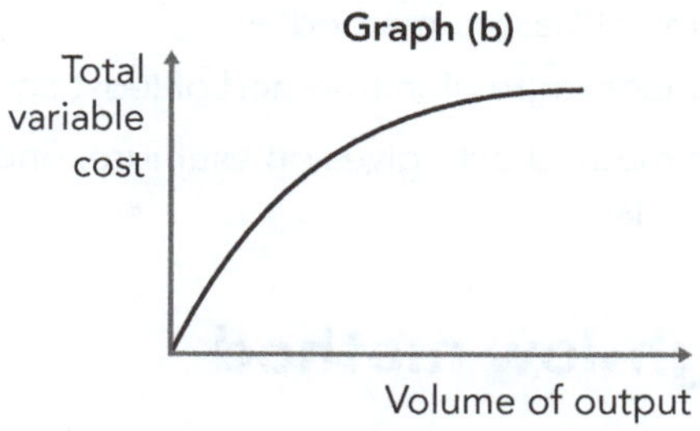

Graph (a) becomes steeper as levels of activity increase. Each additional unit of activity is adding more to total variable cost than the previous unit (for example, raw materials may become scarce and therefore more expensive at higher levels of output). Graph (b) becomes less steep as levels of activity increase. Each additional unit is adding less to total variable cost than the previous unit (an example of this may be bulk buying discounts reducing the cost of materials).

KEY TERM

Relevant range: Refers to the activity levels which an organisation has had experience of operating at in the past and for which cost information is available.

Within the relevant range, costs are often assumed to be either fixed, variable or semi-variable. This **'linear assumption'** is key to many of the costing techniques you will see in this paper.

KEY TERM

Linear assumption: States that total fixed costs remain constant, and variable costs are a constant amount per unit.

1.3 The importance of timescale

Whether a cost is classified as fixed or variable will depend on the timescale being considered. The longer the timescale, the greater the proportion of costs that can be considered as variable. For example, rent is fixed in the short run, but can be considered a stepped cost in the medium term, and even a variable cost in the long run.

2 Determining the fixed and variable elements of semi-variable costs

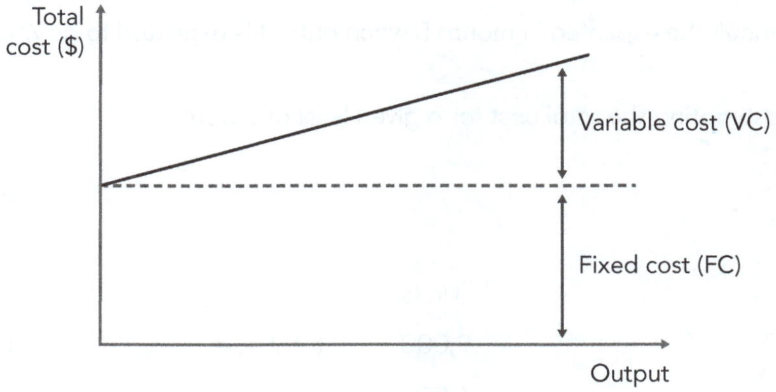

Total cost = Fixed cost + (VC/unit × Output)

2.1 Estimation methods

How can we estimate fixed and variable costs if we only know total cost?

- High-low method
- Line of best fit method
- Linear regression (method of least squares)

Each method only gives an estimate, and can therefore give differing results from the other methods.

3 High-low method

KEY TERM

> **High-low method:** Involves extrapolating (extending) a line drawn between the highest and lowest data items (activity levels).

This is a four-step method:

Step 1 Find highest and lowest activity levels

Step 2 Subtract low from high

Step 3 Use remainder to calculate VC (increase in costs/increase in activity)

Step 4 Substitute VC back into high or low total cost formula to calculate FC

Illustration 1: High-low method

The costs of operating the maintenance department of a computer manufacturer, Bread and Butter company, for the last four months have been as follows:

Month	Cost £	Production volume Units
1	110,000	7,000
2	115,000	8,000
3	111,000	7,700
4	97,000	6,000

Required

1 Calculate the costs that should be expected in month 5 when output is expected to be 7,500 units. Ignore inflation.

2 What is the equation for estimating the total cost for a given level of output?

Solution

1

	Units		$
High Output	8,000	total cost	115,000
Low Output	6,000	total cost	97,000
Variable cost of	2,000		18,000
Variable cost per unit	$18,000/ 2,000 = $9		

Substituting in either the high or low volume cost

	High		Low
	$		$
Total cost	115,000		97,000
Variable costs (8,000 × $9)	72,000	(6,000 × $9)	54,000
Fixed costs	43,000		43,000

Estimated maintenance costs when output is 7,500 units

	$
Fixed Costs	43,000
Variable costs (7,500 × $9)	67,500
Total costs	110,500

2 The equation is:

y = $43,000 + 9x

Where: x is the number of units and

y is the total cost.

Activity 2: High-low method

The total costs of a business for differing levels of output are as follows:

Month	*Output*	*Total costs*
	Units	$'000
January	500	70
February	200	30
March	800	90
April	1,000	110

Required

1 What are the fixed and variable elements of the total cost using the high-low method?

○ Y = $30,000 + $100x

○ Y = $10,000 + $110x

○ Y = $30,000 + $110x

● Y = $10,000 + $100x

2 What is the total cost if output is 400 units?

substitute

	high	low
total	110,000	30,000
variable =		2000

(10 x 1000) = 10,000

100,000

	High	Low	
output	1000	200	800
cost	110	30	80

= $10 per unit

Solution

4 Line of best fit (Scattergraph) method

KEY TERM

> **Scattergraph method :** An alternative way of estimating cost behaviour, by plotting observed data on a graph and using judgement to estimate a line of best fit through all the points on this graph.

A **scattergraph** with total cost on the vertical axis and output on the horizontal axis is prepared.

A line of best fit, which is a line of **judgement,** is drawn to pass through the middle of the points.

A scattergraph of the cost and output in Activity 2 is shown below.

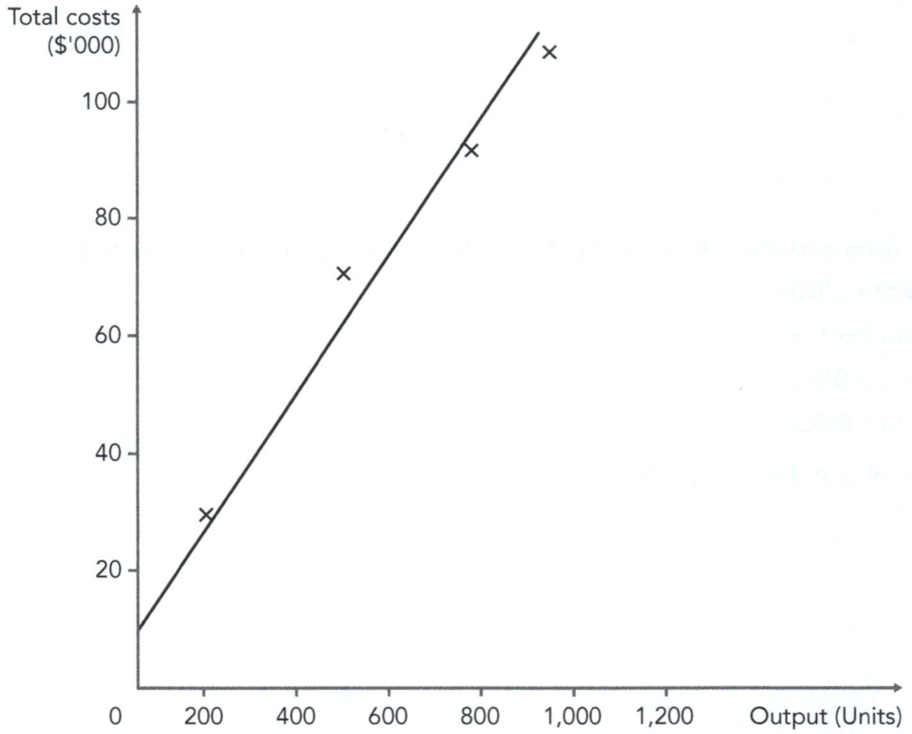

The point where the line cuts the vertical axis (approximately \$10,000) is the fixed cost.

If we take the value of one of the plotted points which lies **close** to the line and deduct the fixed cost from the total cost, we can calculate variable cost per unit.

Example:

Total cost for 1,000 units	=	\$110,000
Variable cost for 1,000 units	=	\$110,000 – \$10,000 = \$100,000
Variable cost per unit	=	\$100,000/1,000 = \$100 per unit

Note. As BA2 is examined by CBA you will not be required to draw a scattergraph; however, you could be required to answer objective test questions about how the technique works.

5 Regression analysis method

KEY TERM

Linear regression analysis (the least squares method): Finds the line of best fit using mathematical formulae and calculates the best estimates for a and b in the linear equation below.

Using all of the pairs of data available this method minimises the deviations between the line of best fit and each data point. This is also known as the 'method of least squares'.

The method can be used to find the relationship between any pairs of data, not just output and cost.

The basic linear relationship is defined mathematically as:

$y = a + bx$

eg Total cost = fixed cost + (variable cost per unit × output)

where

y is the dependent variable (eg costs)

x is the independent variable (eg output)

a is the intercept on the vertical axis (eg fixed costs)

b is the slope (gradient) of the line (eg variable cost per unit)

Formula provided

Formulae used are:

$$b = \frac{n\Sigma xy - \Sigma x \Sigma y}{n\Sigma x^2 - (\Sigma x)^2}$$

$$a = \bar{y} - b\bar{x}$$

n = number of pairs of data in the sample

$\bar{y}$ is the average (mean) of the y values $= \frac{\Sigma y}{n}$

$\bar{x}$ is the average (mean) of the x values $= \frac{\Sigma x}{n}$

Illustration 2: Least squares method

Suppose we have the following pairs of data about output and costs.

Month	Cost $'000	Production Volume '000 units
1	82	20
2	70	16
3	90	24
4	85	22
5	73	18

Required

Calculate an equation to determine the expected level of costs, for any given volume of output, using the least squares method.

Solution

Y = 28 + 2.6X

Working

X	Y	XY	X^2
20	82	1,640	400
16	70	1,120	256
24	90	2,160	576
22	85	1,870	484
18	73	1,314	324
$\sum X = 100$	$\sum Y = 400$	$\sum XY = 8{,}104$	$\sum X^2 = 2{,}040$

n = 5 (There are five pairs of data for X and Y values)

$$b = \frac{n\sum XY - \sum X \sum Y}{n\sum X^2 - (\sum X)^2} = \frac{(5 \times 8{,}104) - (100 \times 400)}{(5 \times 2{,}040) - 100^2}$$

$$= \frac{40{,}520 - 40{,}000}{10{,}200 - 10{,}000} = \frac{520}{200} - 2.6$$

$$a = \bar{Y} - b\bar{X} = \frac{400}{5} - 2.6\left(\frac{100}{5}\right) = 28$$

Y = 28 + 2.6X

Where Y = total cost, in thousands

X = output, in thousands of units

Activity 3: Regression analysis

n = 5

x	y	xy	x^2
Units	$'000		78,400
280	46.5	13020	122,500
350	49.1	17185	40,000
200	36.7	7340	25,600
160	32.0	5120	57,600
240	44.5	10680	
1230	208.8	53,345	324,100

Required

1 Calculate the regression line.

2 Use the line to estimate costs for output of 240 units and 700 units.

Solution

y = 17.16 + 0.10 x

~~n 5 x (1230 x 208.8)~~

(5 x 53,345) − (1230 x 208.8)

266,725 − 277,704 = 10,979

(5 x 324,100) − (1230)² =

1620500 − 1512900 = 107,600

10,979 / 107,600 = 0.10 = b.

a = Ȳ − b X̄

41.76 − 0.1 (246) = 17.16.

2) 240 = 17.16 + (0.10 x 240) = 41.16

700 = 17.16 + (0.10 x 700) = 87.16.

5.1 Reliability of regression line (r = correlation coefficient)

The correlation coefficient, r, **indicates** the strength of the linear relationship between the two variables, x and y. The nearer r is to +1 or -1, the stronger the relationship. However, it does not **prove** a cause and effect relationship.

Formula to learn

$$r = \frac{(n\sum xy)-(\sum x\sum y)}{\sqrt{[(n\sum x^2-(\sum x)^2)][(n\sum y^2-(\sum y)^2)]}}$$

where r = correlation coefficient and must lie in the following range.

$-1 \leq r \leq +1$

5.1.1 Examples of correlation coefficients

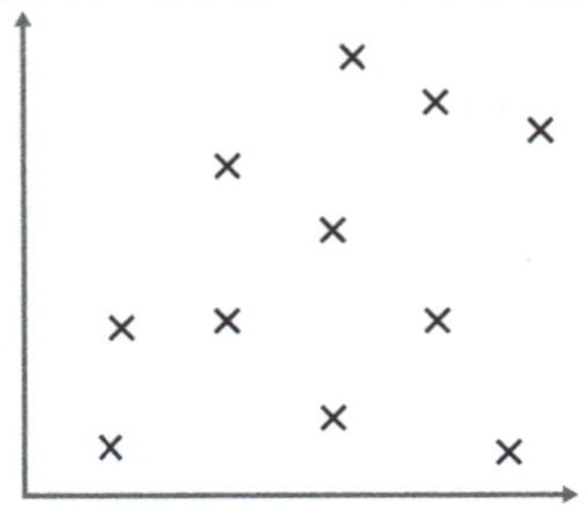

No correlation r = 0

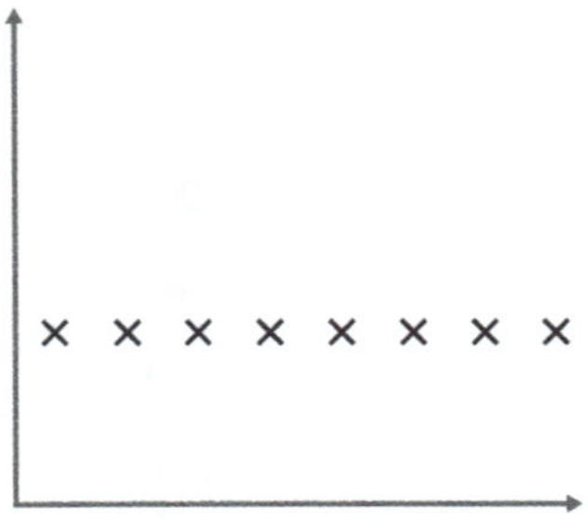

No correlation r = 0

Perfect negative correlation r = -1

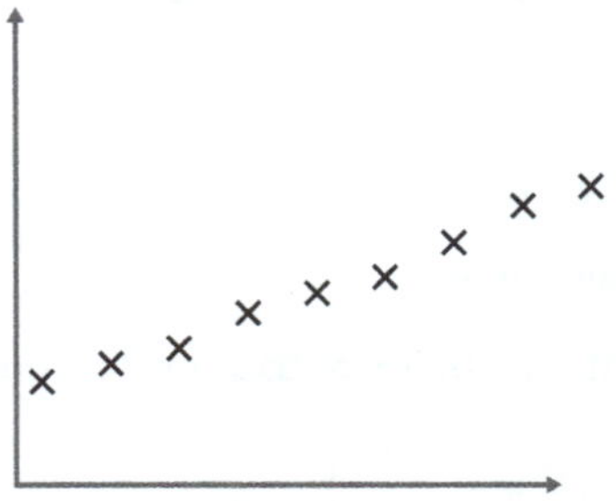

Perfect positive correlation r = +1

5.1.2 Coefficient of determination = r^2 = (correlation coefficient)^2

where

(a) The value must be between 0 and 1.

(b) The value indicates the proportion of change in y which would be explained by change in x.

(c) The value is only indicative. It still does not prove a cause and effect relationship.

For example, if $r^2 = 0.81$ then we say that 81% of the variation in y can be explained by variations in x.

5.1.3 Limitations of linear regression analysis

(a) Assumes linearity between x and y.

(b) The observations used may be untypical.

(c) Historic data is used and patterns may change in the future.

(d) Each observation should be independent from the others.

(e) Forecasting usually involves extrapolation outside the given range of observations, where working conditions and therefore cost patterns may change.

Chapter summary

Cost behaviour

Cost behaviour and output

Cost behaviour

- The way in which a cost changes as activity level (volume of output) changes

Types of cost behaviour

- Fixed cost
- Stepped cost
- Variable cost
- Mixed cost (semi-variable)

Non-linear variable costs

- Relevant range
- Stepped cost

The importance of timescale

- Explanation

Determining the fixed and variable elements of semi-variable costs

Determining the fixed and variable elements of semi-variable costs

- Total cost = Fixed cost + (VC/unit × Output)

Estimation methods

- Three estimation methods

High-low method

High-low method

- Involves extrapolating (extending) a line drawn between the highest and lowest data items (activity levels)

Line of best fit (Scattergraph) method

Line of best fit (Scattergraph) method

- Plotting observed data on a graph and using judgement to estimate a line of best fit through all the points on this graph

Regression analysis method

Regression analysis method

- Finds the line of best fit using mathematical formulae

Reliability of regression line (r = correlation coefficient)

- Formula

Examples of correlation coefficients

- Examples of correlation coefficients

Coefficient of determination = r^2 = (correlation coefficient)^2

- Example

Limitations of linear regression analysis

- Examples of limitations of linear regression analysis

Key terms

Cost behaviour: The way in which a cost changes as activity level (volume of output) changes.

Fixed cost: A 'cost incurred for an accounting period, that, within certain output or turnover limits, tends to be unaffected by fluctuations in the levels of activity (output or turnover)'.

(CIMA Official Terminology, 2005)

Stepped cost: A cost which is fixed in nature, but only within certain levels of activity. Depending on the time frame being considered, it may appear as fixed or variable.

Variable cost: A cost which tends to vary directly with the volume of output. The variable cost **per unit** is the same amount for each unit produced, whereas **total** variable cost increases as volume of output increases.

Semi-variable, semi-fixed or mixed cost: A cost which is part-fixed and part-variable and is therefore partly affected by a change in the level of activity. It is a cost that has both fixed and variable components.

Relevant range: Refers to the activity levels which an organisation has had experience of operating at in the past and for which cost information is available.

Linear assumption: States that total fixed costs remain constant, and variable costs are a constant amount per unit.

High-low method: Involves extrapolating (extending) a line drawn between the highest and lowest data items (activity levels).

Scattergraph method : An alternative way of estimating cost behaviour, by plotting observed data on a graph and using judgement to estimate a line of best fit through all the points on this graph.

Linear regression analysis (the least squares method): Finds the line of best fit using mathematical formulae and calculates the best estimates for a and b in the linear equation below.

Activity answers

Activity 1: Cost behaviour examples

Type of cost	Examples
Fixed	Rent (in the short term), straight line depreciation, insurance, salary of MD
Stepped	Rent (longer term where additional premises required), labour costs of salaried employees
Variable	Raw materials, direct labour, sales commissions
Semi-variable	Utility bills (standing charge plus charge for consumption), sales staff salary (if paid a salary plus commission per item sold)

Activity 2: High-low method

1 The correct answer is: Y = $10,000 + $100x

	Units	Costs $
Highest (April)	1,000	110,000
Lowest (February)	200	30,000
	800	80,000

$$\therefore \text{Variable cost per unit} = \frac{\$80,000}{800} = \$100$$

Fixed cost element:

Take highest output (1,000 units)

	$
Total cost	110,000
Less variable cost (1,000 × 100)	100,000
∴ Fixed cost element	10,000

Note. Alternatively, fixed cost element can be found by taking the lowest output (200 units).

	$
Total cost	30,000
Less variable cost (200 × 100)	20,000
∴ Fixed cost element	10,000

Answer: TOTAL COSTS, Y = $10,000 + $100 × (fourth option)

First, second and third options – confuse both fixed costs (as costs at lowest output) and unit cost (as costs at highest output divided by volume).

2 If x = 400

Using TC = FC + VC

TC = 10,000 + (100 × 400) = 50,000

Activity 3: Regression analysis

1

x	y	xy	x^2
Units	$'000		
280	46.5	13,020	78,400
350	49.1	17,185	122,500
200	36.7	7,340	40,000
160	32.0	5,120	25,600
240	44.5	10,680	57,600
1,230	208.8	53,345	324,100

$$b = \frac{(5 \times 53{,}345) - (1{,}230 \times 208.8)}{(5 \times 324{,}100) - (1{,}230)^2}$$

$$= \frac{9{,}901}{107{,}600} = 0.092$$

$$a = \frac{208.8}{5} - 0.092 \times \frac{1{,}230}{5}$$

$$= 19{,}128$$

so y = 19,128 + 0.092x (y in $'000, x in units)

y = $19,128 + $92x

2 Interpolation, when output is 240 units

Cost predicted = $19,128 + $92 × 240 = $41,208

Extrapolation, when output is 700 units

Cost predicted = $19,128 + $92 × 700 = $83,528

Test your learning

1 The basic principle of cost behaviour is that as the level of activity rises, costs will usually fall.

- ○ True
- ◉ False

2 Fill in the gaps for each of the graph titles below.

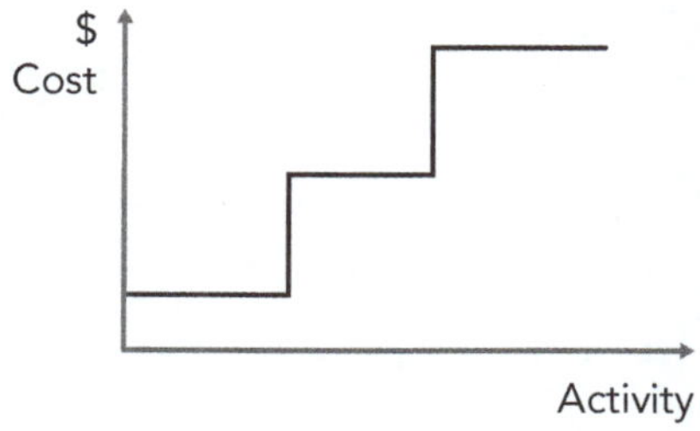

Graph of a [stepped] cost. Example: [salaries of employees] ✓

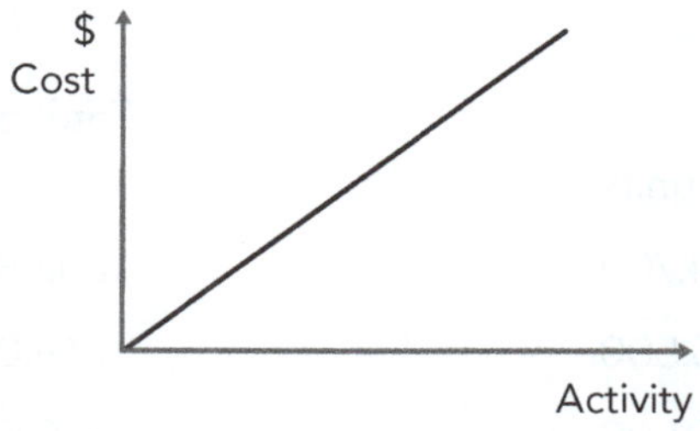

Graph of a [variable] cost. Example: [materials / supplies.] ✓

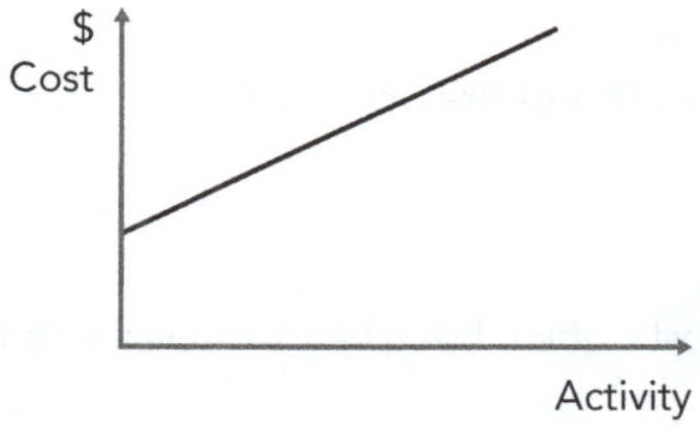

Graph of a [semi-fixed] cost. Example: [telephone bill] ✓ Heat + light.

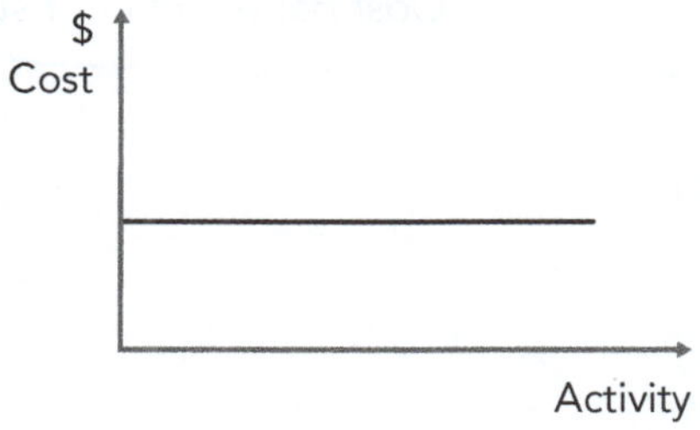

Graph of a [fixed] cost. Example: [rent] ✓

3 Costs are assumed to be either fixed, variable or semi-variable within the normal or relevant range of output.

- ○ True
- ○ False

4 The costs of operating the canteen at 'Eat a lot Company' for the past three months are as follows:

Month	*Cost*	*Employees*
	$	
1	72,500	1,250
2	75,000	1,300
3	68,750	1,175

Required

Variable cost (per employee month) = $ [ ]

Fixed cost per month = $ [ ]

5 Pen Co produced the following units at the following costs during October, November and December.

Month	Number of units	Total cost $
October	4,700	252,800
November	5,500	264,000
December	9,500	320,000

Required

The costs could be subdivided into variable costs of $14 per unit and fixed costs of:

$ [ ] per month.

6 The management accountant at G Co is analysing some costs which have been entered into the computer as 'miscellaneous staff expenses'.

No. of staff	*Cost per member of staff*
20	$5
100	$5
150	$5
250	$5

Required

What type of cost is the miscellaneous staff expense?

O Fixed

O Variable

O Semi-variable

O Non-linear

7

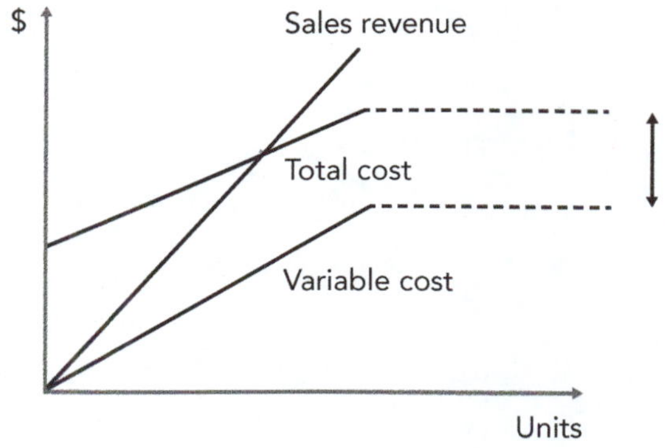

Required

7 In the above graph, what does the arrow represent?

- O Fixed cost
- O Contribution
- O Profit
- O Breakeven quantity in units

8 A cost which is unaffected in total by increases and decreases in the volume of output is called:

- O Stepped-fixed
- O Variable
- O Constant
- O Fixed

9 Which one of the following is an example of a mixed cost?

- O Factory rent
- O Salaries
- O Telephone bill
- O Straight line depreciation

10 A particular cost is classified as being semi-variable.

Required

What is the effect on the cost per unit if activity increases by 10%?

- O Decrease by 10%
- O Decrease by less than 10%
- O Increase by less than 10%
- O Remain constant

4 Absorption costing

Learning outcomes

Having studied this chapter you will be able to:
• Prepare overhead cost statements
• Calculate the full cost of products, services and activities

Chapter context

In this chapter we start to look at one of the key questions that management accountants have to answer: 'How much does it cost to produce each item of our product?' Absorption costing is one method used to answer this question, and we will look at another approach in the following chapter. Absorption costing takes all of the production costs (both fixed and variable) and attributes them to individual units of production. By definition, overheads are going to be the most difficult costs to deal with because they can't objectively be traced to an individual cost unit.

Syllabus context

This chapter is part of syllabus **Section B**, which looks at **'Costing'**.

This syllabus area has a weighting of **25%** and is covered by **Chapters 2 to 5**.

In the exam, you will be expected to demonstrate competence in the following areas:

- Overhead cost statements: allocation, apportionment and reciprocal servicing.
- The treatment of direct and indirect costs in ascertaining the full cost of a "cost object" e.g. a product, service, activity, customer.
- Overhead absorption rates.
- Under or over absorbed overheads.

Chapter overview

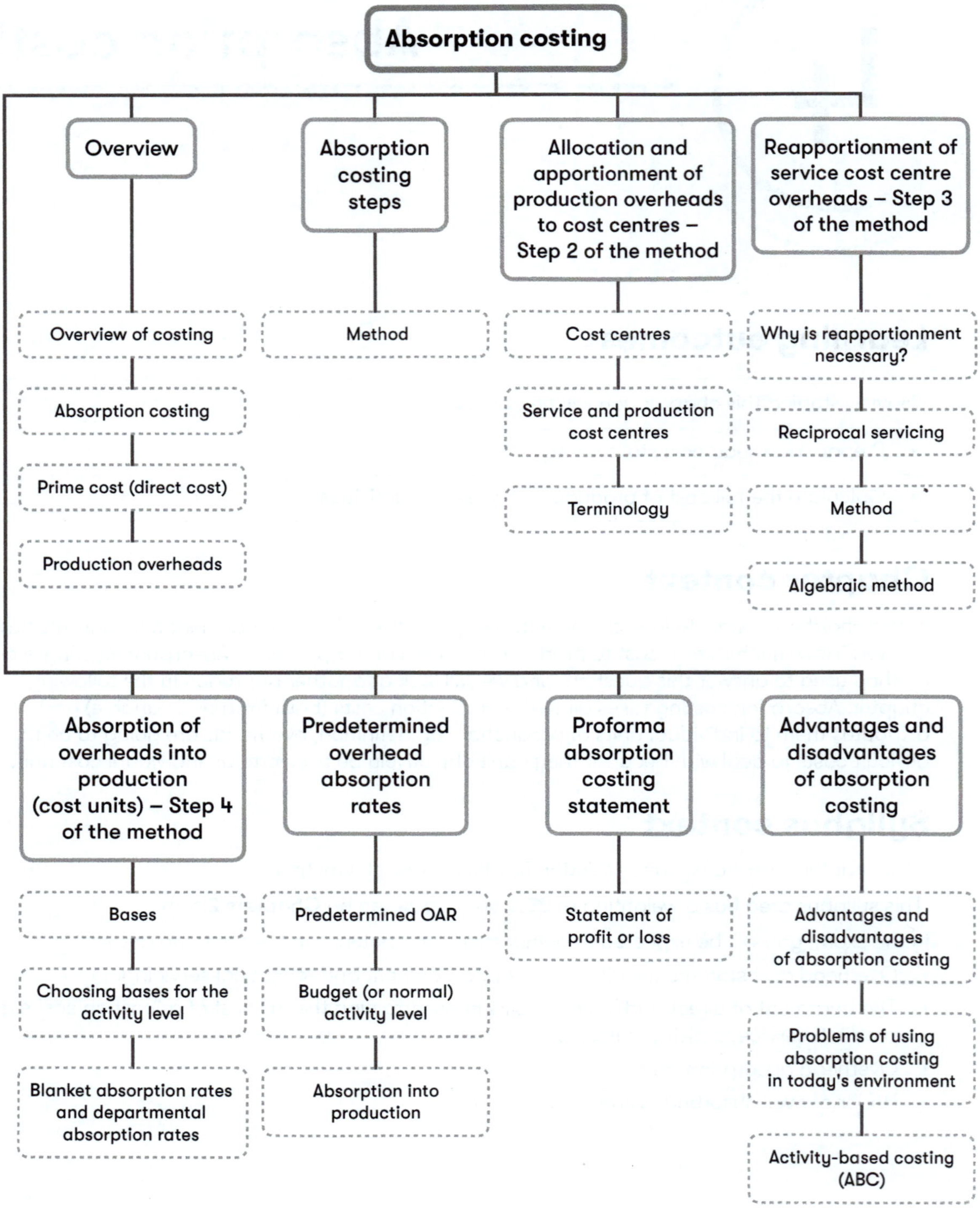

1 Overview

Businesses need to put a cost on goods/services they produce (ie cost units) for many reasons.

AIM → To find the cost of making one unit

WHY? → Pricing
Inventory valuation
Profitability analysis

HOW? → Absorption costing (this chapter)
or
Marginal costing (Chapter 5)

1.1 Absorption costing

KEY TERM

> **Absorption costing:** A product costing/inventory valuation method which includes **all production costs** in the valuation and is required by IAS 2 Inventories for external reporting purposes.

A cost card shows us the cost to make one unit.

	$/unit
Direct materials	X
Direct labour	X
Prime cost	**X**
Production overheads	X
Product cost	**X**

1.2 Prime cost (direct cost)

The direct costs of a cost unit are usually straightforward to ascertain since by definition they are identified with a cost unit.

Direct materials: x kg of material at $y per kg

Direct labour: a hrs of labour at $b per hour

This is Step (1) in the method for absorption costing below.

1.3 Production overheads

Since these are not identified with specific cost units, some method must be used to charge a share of the total production overhead to each cost unit.

Steps (2) to (4) in the method below represent the traditional absorption costing method by which we achieve this.

2 Absorption costing steps

2.1 Method

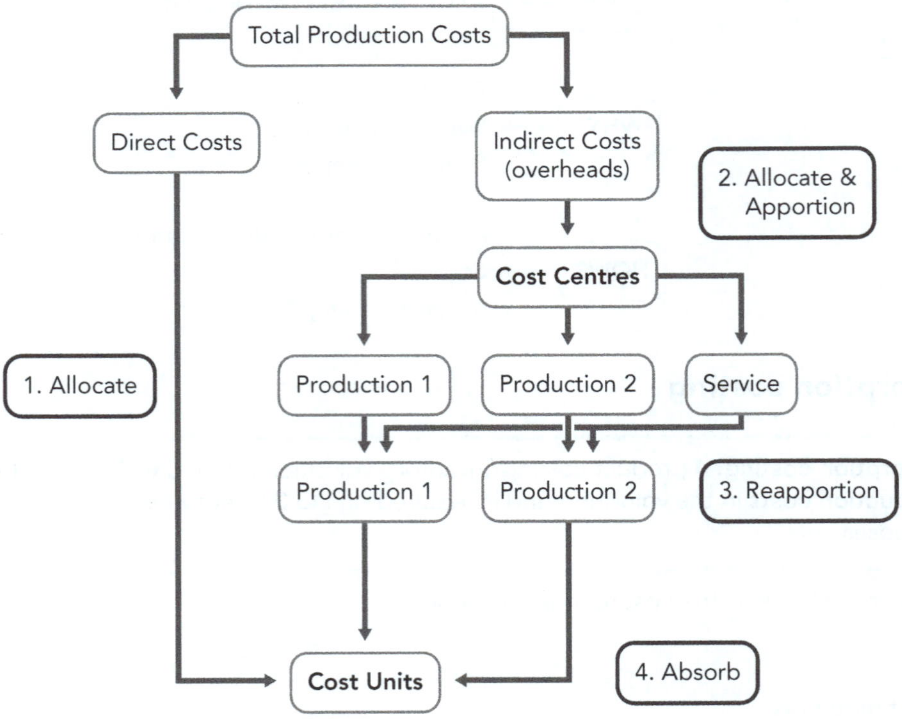

To get the full absorbed production cost there are four steps:

(1) **Allocate** direct costs to cost units

(2) **Allocate and apportion** production overheads to cost centres

(3) **Reapportion** overheads in **service cost centres** to **production cost centres**

(4) **Absorb** overheads into cost units

3 Allocation and apportionment of production overheads to cost centres – Step 2 of the method

The first stage in valuing the overhead cost of a cost unit is to allocate and apportion overheads between cost centres.

3.1 Cost centres

A cost centre is a location, function or item of equipment in respect of which costs may be ascertained and related to cost units for control purposes.

Each cost centre acts as a 'collecting place' for certain costs before they are analysed further.

Notes.

1 Cost centres may be set up in any way the business thinks appropriate.

2 Usually, only manufacturing costs are considered and hence we will focus on factory cost centres.

3.2 Service and production cost centres

KEY TERM

Production cost centres: Factory cost centres through which cost units actually flow.
Service cost centres: Support/service the production cost centres.

Activity 1: Production or service

Split the following between two types of cost centres:

assembly, canteen, maintenance, packing, stores, finishing

Production cost centres	Service cost centres
assembly	canteen
packing	maintenance.
finishing.	stores

3.3 Terminology

KEY TERM

Allocation: When whole cost items are charged to a cost centre.

Apportionment: When cost items are divided between several cost centres.

Example 1: Overhead allocation

Consider the following costs of a company:

	$
Wages of the supervisor of department A - Allocate to A	200
Wages of the supervisor of department B - Allocate to B	150
Indirect materials consumed in department A - Allocate to A	50
Rent of the premises shared by departments A and B	300

NEED TO APPORTION COST

The cost accounting system might include three cost centres.

Cost centre:	101	Department A
	102	Department B
	201	Rent

Overhead costs would be allocated directly to each cost centre, ie $200 + $50 to cost centre 101, $150 to cost centre 102 and $300 to cost centre 201. The rent of the factory will be subsequently shared between the two production departments but, for the purpose of day to day cost recording in this particular system, the rent will first of all be charged in full to a separate cost centre.

Apportioning general overheads

Overhead apportionment follows on from overhead allocation. The first stage of overhead apportionment is to identify all overhead costs as production department, production service department, administration, or selling and distribution overhead. This means that the costs for heat and light, rent and rates, the canteen and so on (that is, costs which have been allocated to general overhead cost centres) must be shared out between the other cost centres.

Bases of apportionment

Overhead costs should be shared out on a fair basis. You will appreciate that because of the complexity of items of cost it is rarely possible to use only one method of apportioning costs to the various departments of an organisation. The bases of apportionment for the most usual cases are given below.

Overhead to which the basis applies	Basis
Rent, rates, heating and light, repairs and depreciation of buildings	Floor area occupied by each cost centre
Depreciation, insurance of equipment	Cost or book value of equipment
Personnel office, canteen, welfare, wages and cost offices, first aid	Number of employees, or labour hours worked in each cost centre
Heating, lighting (see above)	Volume of space occupied by each cost centre

Example 2: Overhead apportionment

Continuing the previous example, rent for the period was $300. The following data has been identified about departments A and B:

NOT RELEVANT

Department	A	B
Number of staff	50	30
Floor space occupied	1000 m^2	250 m^2

The most appropriate basis for apportioning rent is floor space. Therefore after apportioning on this basis, Department A will be allocated (1,000/1,250 × $300) = $240 of the rent cost, and Department B will be allocated the remaining $60 (250/1,250 × $300).

Activity 2: Overhead allocation and apportionment

Step 2 of method

Mars Co has the following overheads in the year ended 31 December 20X5:

Overhead:	$
Rent and rates - apportion - floor space.	90,000
Insurance of machinery and equipment - apportion - NBV machinery.	40,000
Stores costs (wages and salaries) - stock room - allocate.	75,000
Heating costs - apportion - floor space.	57,000
	262,000

1) would be to allocate or apportion.

Required

Allocate and apportion overhead costs to mixing dept, stirring dept, stores and canteen using the following information:

	Mixing	*Stirring*	*Stores*	*Canteen*	*Total*
Floor space (square ft)	9,000	3,000	1,000	2,000	15,000
NBV of machinery and equipment	2,000	1,000	600	400	4,000

Solution

	Mixing	**Stirring**	**Stores**	**Canteen**	**Total**
Stores cost			75,000		75,000
Rent & rates					
Floor space / total	54,000	18,000	6000	12,000	90,000
Insurance					
NBV / total	20,000	10,000	6000	4000	40,000
Heating					
Floor space /	34,200	11400	3800	7600	57,000
total	108200	39400	90,800	23600	262,000

4 Reapportionment of service cost centre overheads – Step 3 of the method

KEY TERM

Reapportionment: The process of transferring all service cost centre overheads to the production cost centres.

4.1 Why is reapportionment necessary?

All service cost centre overheads must be transferred to the production centres so that all production overheads for the period are shared between the production cost centres alone – as it is through these cost centres that cost units flow.

4.2 Reciprocal servicing

The reapportionment becomes a little more complicated where:

- There is more than one service cost centre; and
- The service centres do work for one another (reciprocal servicing).

4.3 Method

To reapportion service cost centre overheads to production cost centres and to recognise all inter-service department work, an approach known as the **repeated distribution** method can be used. This method involves starting with the service cost centre with the largest allocated overheads, apportioning those between **all** the other cost centres (including the other service cost centres); repeating this process with the other service cost centre (again, spreading its overheads across **all** other cost centres) and repeating until the numbers are very small, at which point the distribution is rounded. No overheads may be left in any service cost centre.

Example: Repeated distribution method

A company has two production and two service departments (stores and maintenance). The following information about activity in the recent costing period is available.

	Production departments		Stores department	Maintenance department
	A	B		
Overhead costs	$10,030	$8,970	$10,000	$8,000
Cost of material requisitions	$30,000	$50,000	–	$20,000
Maintenance hours needed	8,000	1,000	1,000	–

Recognition is made of the fact that the stores and maintenance department do work for each other. Service department costs are apportioned as follows.

	Dept A	Dept B	Stores	Maintenance
Stores (100%)	30%	50%	–	20%
Maintenance (100%)	80%	10%	10%	–

The reapportionment of service department costs in this situation can be done using the **repeated distribution method of apportionment.**

	Production dept A	Production dept B	Stores	Maintenance
	$	$	$	$
Overhead costs	10,030	8,970	10,000	8,000
First stores appointment (see Note 1)	3,000	5,000	(10,000)	2,000
			0	10,000
First maintenance appointment	8,000	1,000	1,000	(10,000)
			1,000	0
Second stores appointment	300	500	(1,000)	200
Second maintenance appointment	160	20	20	(200)

	Production dept A	Production dept B	Stores	Maintenance
	$	$	$	$
Third stores appointment	6	10	(20)	4
Third maintenance appointment (see Note 2)	4	–	–	(4)
	21,500	15,500	0	0

30% 50% 20%

37,000 = total overheads related to department

Notes.

1 The first apportionment is done from the service department with the higher costs (in this case, stores).

2 When the repeated distributions bring service department costs down to small numbers (here $4) the final apportionment to production departments is an approximate rounding.

4.4 Algebraic method

An alternative to repeated distribution is to use the **algebraic method,** which uses simultaneous equations to solve the problem. This will be illustrated in the example below.

Activity 3: Service cost reapportionment (repeated distribution)

Step 3 of the method

	Production depts		*Service centres*	
	Mixing	*Stirring*	*Stores*	*Canteen*
	$	$	$	$
Allocated and apportioned overheads				
From Activity 2	108,200	39,400	90,800	23,600
Estimated work done by the service centres for other departments				
Stores	50%	30%	–	20%
Canteen	45%	40%	15%	–

Required

Using the repeated distribution method, after the apportionment of the service departments to the production departments, what will the total overhead costs for the production departments be?

Solution

	Mixing	Stirring
Overheads		

		Mixing			Stirring
		$			$

		Production depts		Service centres	
		Mixing	Stirring	Stores	Canteen
Overheads		108,200	39,400	90,800	23,600
Reapportion					
Stores	50:30:20	45,400	27,240	(90,800)	18 160
			27240	0	41760
Reapportion					
Canteen	45:40:15	18792	16704	6264	(41760)
				6264	0
Reapportion					
Stores	50:30:20	3132	1879.2	(6264)	1252.8
				0	1252.8
Reapportion					
Canteen	45:40:15	563.76	501.12	187.92	(1252.8)
				187.92	0
Reapportion					
Stores	50:30:20	94	56	(188)	38
				0	38
Reapportion					
Canteen	45:40:15	17	15	6	(38)
				6	0
Reapportion					
Stores	50:30:20	3	2	(6)	1
				0	1
Reapportion					
Canteen	45:40:15	0.45	0.4	0.15	(1)
		176,202.45	85,797	0.15	0

Example: Algebraic method

Using the figures in Activity 3, and the algebraic method, the total overhead costs for the production departments would be found as follows:

	Mixing	Stirring
Overheads	$ ____	$ ____

Whenever you are using equations you must define each variable.

Let C = total overheads for the canteen

S = total overheads for the stores department

Remember that total overheads for the canteen consist of general overheads apportioned, allocated overheads and the share of stores overheads (20%).

Similarly, total overheads for stores will be the total of general overheads apportioned, allocated overheads and the 15% share of canteen overheads.

C = 0.2S + $23,600 (1)

S = 0.15C + $90,800 (2)

We now solve the equations.

5C = S + $118,000 (3), which can be rearranged as

S = 5C – $118,000 (4)

Subtract (2) from (4):

0 = 4.85C – $208,800

Rearrange to find C:

C = $208,800/4.85 = $43,052

Substitute to find S:

S = (0.15 × $43,052) + $90,800 = $97,258

These overheads can now be apportioned to the production departments using the proportions above.

	Production depts.		Service centres	
	Mixing	Stirring	Stores	Canteen
	$	$	$	$
from Activity 2	108,200	39,400	90,800	23,600
Apportion stores (50:30:20)	48,629	29,177	(97,258)	19,452
Apportion canteen (45:40:15)	19,373	17,221	6,458	(43,052)
Apportioned overheads	**176,202**	**85,798**	0	0

You will notice that the total overheads for the mixing and stirring production departments are the same regardless of the method used (any difference is due to rounding).

Activity 4: Reapportionment practice

ABC Co has a production department in Block H of the building and another in Block F. There are also two service departments, namely the canteen and the maintenance department. Fixed overheads are incurred as follows:

Department	*Overheads*
	$'000
H Block	400
F Block	700
Canteen	550
Maintenance	800

The canteen provides food for H Block (40%), F Block (40%) and the maintenance department (20%). Maintenance does work for H Block and F Block in the ratio 2:3.

Required

What would be the total fixed overhead of H Block if all service department overheads are allocated to production departments?

- O $546,000
- O $364,000
- O $984,000
- O $1,466,000

Solution

5 Absorption of overheads into production (cost units) – Step 4 of the method

5.1 Bases

All of the production overhead costs have now been apportioned to the production cost centres. We now need to charge these to the cost units passing through the production cost centres. This is termed **absorption.** We are going to absorb an element of total production overhead into each cost unit.

KEY TERM

OAR (overhead absorption rate):

$$= \frac{\text{Production overhead}}{\text{Activity level}}$$

5.2 Choosing bases for the activity level

Ideally, the basis chosen should be the one which most accurately reflects the way in which the overheads are in fact being incurred, and realistically reflects the characteristics of a given cost centre.

For example:

Basis

(a) Per unit (appropriate if all units of production are identical or very similar)

(b) Per labour hour (appropriate for labour-intensive cost centres)

(c) Per machine hour (where production is controlled or dictated by machines)

(d) % of direct labour cost (where labour of differing grades is being utilised in production)

(e) % of direct materials cost (if materials are a significant proportion of total costs)

(f) % of prime cost

5.3 Blanket absorption rates and departmental absorption rates

The use of **separate departmental absorption rates** instead of **blanket (or single factory) absorption rates** will produce more realistic product costs.

KEY TERM

> **Blanket or single factory overhead absorption rate:** An absorption rate **used throughout a factory** and for all jobs and units of output irrespective of the department in which they were produced.

Such a rate is not appropriate, however, if there are a number of departments and units of output do not spend an equal amount of time in each department.

It is argued that if a single factory overhead absorption rate is used, some products will receive a higher overhead charge than they ought 'fairly' to bear, whereas other products will be under charged. By using a separate absorption rate for each department, charging of overheads will be equitable and the full cost of production of items will be more representative of the cost of the efforts and resources put into making them.

Activity 5: Calculating absorption rates

Mars Co has now reapportioned the service centre costs to its two production departments resulting in total overheads of $176,203 and $85,797 for the mixing and stirring departments respectively (as calculated in Activity 3).

The mixing department is labour-intensive and the stirring department is machine-intensive.

During the year, the following data has been collected on the work done to produce the company's range of products.

	Mixing	*Stirring*
Direct labour hours	20,000	5,000
Direct machine hours	2,000	60,000
Number of units	10,000	10,000

Required

1

The overhead absorption rate for the mixing department was $ ______ per ______

2 The overhead absorption rate for the stirring department was $ ______ per ______

3 Mars Co has one particular product, the 'Venus', for which you obtain the following information.

Direct materials per unit	$15
Direct labour hours	
– Mixing	2 hours
– Stirring	0.5 hours
Direct machine hours	
– Mixing	NOT REQUIRED ← 0.2 hours
– Stirring	6 hours

Labour is paid $10 per hour.

Required

What is the total cost of this product?

- O $40
- O $58.30
- O $66.20 *
- O $77.33

cost card

Solution

stirring based on machine hrs

Direct material		$15
Direct labour		
– mixing	(2 × 10)	$20
– stirring	(0.5 × 10)	$5
PRIME COST		$40
overheads		
– mixing	(2 × 8.81)	$17.62
– stirring	(1.43 × 6)	$8.58

6 Predetermined overhead absorption rates

Businesses need to cost their production throughout the year, not at the end of an accounting period. Therefore, they predetermine or estimate their absorption rates for the year.

Formula to learn

$$\text{Predetermined OAR} = \frac{\text{Budgeted overhead}}{\text{Budgeted activity level}}$$

Note. Activity level refers to production activity not sales.

6.1 Budget (or normal) activity level

IAS 2 (paragraph 13) states that the activity level used for absorption of overheads should always be the budgeted (normal) activity, ie the expected long-term average. This is to stop fluctuations in OARs due to fluctuations in activity.

6.2 Absorption into production

Businesses will record overheads regularly **during the year.**

Formula to learn

Overhead Absorbed = Actual Activity × Predetermined OAR

At the end of the year actual overheads will be known.

Formula to learn

Under-/(over)-absorption = Actual Overhead less Overhead Absorbed

KEY TERM

Under-absorption: If overheads absorbed are less than actual overheads.

Over-absorption: If overheads absorbed are greater than actual overheads.

Overheads absorbed may differ from actual overhead costs incurred for either or both of the following two reasons:

(a) Actual expenditure was more or less than budget.

(b) Actual units produced (ie volume) were more or less than budget.

Exam focus point

You can always work out whether overheads are under- or over-absorbed by using the following rule.

- If **Actual** overhead incurred – **Absorbed** overhead = **NEGATIVE** (N), then overheads are **over-absorbed** (O) (NO).
- If **Actual** overhead incurred – **Absorbed** overhead = **POSITIVE** (P), then overheads are **under-absorbed** (U) (PU).

So, remember the **NOPU** rule when you go into your assessment and you won't have any trouble in deciding whether overheads are under- or over-absorbed!

Activity 6: Predetermined overhead absorption rates

Gurney Halleck Co had the following budgeted and actual figures for units of production and overheads.

	Budget	*Actual*
Units of production	20,000	24,000
Overheads	$100,000	$117,000

Required

Complete the following calculations.

Predetermined absorption rate	=	100,000 / 20,000 = 5
Overhead absorbed for period	=	Activity level x pre OAR 24,000 x 5 = 120,000

Under-/over-absorption	=	117,000 − 120,000 −3000 = over-absorbed.

7 Proforma absorption costing statement

7.1 Statement of profit or loss

	$	$
Sales		X
Less: Cost of sales		
Opening inventory (@ full cost)	X	
Production costs:		
Variable costs - materials	X	
- labour	X	
- variable overheads	X	
Fixed overhead **absorbed**	X	
Less: Closing inventory (@ full cost)	(X)	
Production cost of sales	X	
Adjustment for over-/under- absorbed overhead	X	
Total cost of sales		(X)
Gross profit sales - COS		X
Less sales and distribution costs		(X)
Net profit		X

actual overhead cost.

add in more expense if UNDER absorbed. or take out some cost - OVER ABSORBED.

Gross − = Net

Notes.

1. Inventory is valued at full production cost.
2. The method of costing by which 'actual production costs' include a figure based on a predetermined estimate is called **normal costing**.

Activity 7: Absorption costing practice

Selling price $25. / per unit.

Cost card per unit:

	$
Direct materials	7
Direct wages	8
Variable production overheads	5
Fixed production overheads	0.90

	$
	20.90

There is a variable selling cost per unit of $0.50.

	Year 1	*Year 2*
	Units	Units
Normal/Budgeted production	12,000	12,000
Actual production	14,000	11,500
Actual sales	13,000	12,500
Actual fixed production overheads	$11,000	$11,000
Actual fixed selling costs	$5,000	$5,000

There is no opening inventory. All variable costs were as budgeted, for the two years.

Required

1

The total budgeted fixed production overhead was $ [ ]

2

The overheads absorbed in Year 1 were $ [ ]

3

The net profit in Year 1 was $ [ ]

(Use the statement of profit and loss account below.)

4

The overheads in Year 2 were [ ] absorbed by $ [ ]

5

The net profit in Year 2 was $ [ ]

Solution

	Year 1	*Year 1*	*Year 2*	*Year 2*
	$	$	$	$
Sales				
[ ]				
[ ]				
Less: Cost of Sales:				
Opening inventory				
[ ]				
Production costs				
Variable costs				

		Year 1	Year 1	Year 2	Year 2
		$	$	$	$
– materials					
	7 x 14,000	98,000			
– wages (labour)					
	(8 x 14,000)	112,000			
– variable overheads					
	5 x 14,000	70,000			
– fixed overheads (absorbed)					
	0.9 x 14,000	12,600			
Less closing inventory					
	(1000 x 20.90)	(20 900)			
– Adj for under/(over) absorption					
	(11,000 – 12,600)	(1600)			(261,900)
Gross profit		(270,100)	54,900		
Less selling costs					
– variable selling cost					
	(13,000 x 0.5)	(6500)			
– fixed selling cost		(5000)			
Net Profit			43,400		

8 Advantages and disadvantages of absorption costing

Advantages	Disadvantages
Inventory valuation complies with IAS 2.	Unit cost includes costs which are not relevant for marginal decision making.
Fixed costs must be covered in the long run.	The nature of cost behaviour is obscured.
Production cannot be divorced from fixed costs since without them production could not occur.	The method of absorption is to some extent arbitrary.
	Profit can be manipulated by increasing production even if sales do not change.

8.1 Problems of using absorption costing in today's environment

Overhead absorption rates might be 200% or 300% of unit labour costs. Unit **costs** are **distorted** and so cost information is **misleading**.

Overheads are **not controlled** because they are hidden within unit production costs rather than being shown as individual totals.

Products bear an arbitrary share of overheads which **do not reflect the benefits** they receive.

Absorption costing **assumes** all products **consume all resources** in **proportion** to their **production volumes.**

(a) It tends to **allocate too great a proportion** of overheads to **high volumeproducts** (which cause relatively little diversity and hence use fewer support services).

(b) It tends to **allocate too small a proportion** of overheads to **low volume products** (which cause greater diversity and therefore use more support services).

Activity-based costing (ABC) attempts to overcome these problems.

8.2 Activity-based costing (ABC)

ABC is an alternative approach to absorption costing. It involves identification of the factors which cause the costs of an organisation's major activities. These factors are called 'cost drivers'.

KEY TERM

> **Activity-based costing (ABC):** An 'approach to the costing and monitoring of activities which involves tracing resource consumption and costing final outputs. Resources are assigned to activities, and activities to cost objects based on consumption estimates. The latter utilise cost drivers to attach activity costs to outputs'.
>
> (CIMA Official Terminology, 2005)

Detailed knowledge of ABC is not in your syllabus; however, the major ideas behind ABC are as follows.

Activities cause costs.	Activities include ordering and despatching.
↓	
The costs of an activity are caused or driven by factors known as **cost drivers**.	The cost of the ordering activity might be driven by the number of orders placed; the cost of the despatching activity, by the number of despatches made.
↓	
Costs associated with each activity are collected into **cost pools**. The costs of an activity are assigned to products on the basis of the number of the activity's cost driver products generated.	If product A requires 5 orders to be placed, and product B 15 orders, ¼ (ie 5/(5 + 15)) of the ordering cost will be assigned to product A and ¾ (ie 15/(5 + 15)) to product B.

Chapter summary

Absorption costing

Overview

Overview of costing

- Aim – to find the cost of making one unit
- Why – pricing, inventory valuation and profitability analysis
- How – absorption costing and marginal costing

Absorption costing

- A costing/inventory valuation method which includes all production costs in the valuation and is required by IAS 2 Inventories for external reporting purposes

Prime cost (direct cost)

- The direct costs of a cost unit

Production overheads

- Not identified with specific cost units, some method must be used to charge a share of the total production overhead to each cost unit

Absorption costing steps

Method

- Allocate direct costs to cost units
- Allocate and apportion production overheads to cost centres
- Reapportion overheads in service cost centres to production cost centres
- Absorb overheads into cost units

Allocation and apportionment of production overheads to cost centres – Step 2 of the method

Cost centres

- A location, function or item of equipment in respect of which costs may be ascertained and related to cost units for control purposes

Service and production cost centres

- Production cost centres – factory cost centres through which cost units actually flow
- Service cost centres – support/service the production cost centres

Terminology

- Allocation – when whole cost items are charged to a cost centre
- Apportionment – when cost items are divided between several cost centres

Reapportionment of service cost centre overheads – Step 3 of the method

Why is reapportionment necessary?

- Reapportionment – the process of transferring all service cost centre overheads to the production cost centres

Reciprocal servicing

- Complications

Method

- Repeated distribution method

Algebraic method

- Algebraic method

Absorption of overheads into production (cost units) – Step 4 of the method

Bases
- OAR (overhead absorption rate)

Choosing bases for the activity level
- Choosing bases

Blanket absorption rates and departmental absorption rates
- Blanket or single factory overhead absorption rate

Predetermined overhead absorption rates

Predetermined OAR
- Predetermined OAR formula

Budget (or normal) activity level
- IAS 2

Absorption into production
- Overhead Absorbed = Actual Activity × Predetermined OAR
- Under-/(over)-absorption = Actual Overhead less Overhead Absorbed
- Under-absorption
- Over-absorption

Proforma absorption costing statement

Statement of profit or loss
- Proforma

Advantages and disadvantages of absorption costing

Advantages and disadvantages of absorption costing
- Advantages
- Disadvantages

Problems of using absorption costing in today's environment
- Problems in modern businesses

Activity-based costing (ABC)
- Involves identification of the factors which cause the costs of an organisation's major activities
- Major ideas behind ABC

Key terms

Absorption costing: A product costing/inventory valuation method which includes **all production costs** in the valuation and is required by IAS 2 Inventories for external reporting purposes.

Production cost centres: Factory cost centres through which cost units actually flow.

Service cost centres: Support/service the production cost centres.

Allocation: When whole cost items are charged to a cost centre.

Apportionment: When cost items are divided between several cost centres.

Reapportionment: The process of transferring all service cost centre overheads to the production cost centres.

OAR (overhead absorption rate):

$$= \frac{\text{Production overhead}}{\text{Activity level}}$$

Blanket or single factory overhead absorption rate: An absorption rate **used throughout a factory** and for all jobs and units of output irrespective of the department in which they were produced.

Under-absorption: If overheads absorbed are less than actual overheads.

Over-absorption: If overheads absorbed are greater than actual overheads.

Activity-based costing (ABC): An 'approach to the costing and monitoring of activities which involves tracing resource consumption and costing final outputs. Resources are assigned to activities, and activities to cost objects based on consumption estimates. The latter utilise cost drivers to attach activity costs to outputs'.

(CIMA Official Terminology, 2005)

Activity answers

Activity 1: Production or service

Production cost centres	Service cost centres
Packing	Maintenance
Assembly	Canteen
Finishing	Stores

Activity 2: Overhead allocation and apportionment

	Mixing	Stirring	Stores	Canteen	Total
Stores cost	-	-	75,000	-	75,000
Rent & rates					
(9:3:1:2)	54,000	18,000	6,000	12,000	90,000
Insurance					
(2:1:0.6:0.4)	20,000	10,000	6,000	4,000	40,000
Heating					
(9:3:1:2)	34,000	11,400	3,800	7,600	57,000
	108,200	39,400	90,800	23,600	262,000

Activity 3: Service cost reapportionment (repeated distribution)

	Mixing	Stirring
Overheads	$ 176,203	$ 85,797

	Production depts		*Service centres*	
	Mixing	*Stirring*	*Stores*	*Canteen*
Overheads	108,200	39,400	90,800	23,600
Reapportion				
Stores (50:30:20)	45,400	27,240	(90,800)	18,160
			–	41,760
Reapportion				
Canteen (45:40:15)	18,792	16,704	6,264	(41,760)

	Production depts		*Service centres*	
	Mixing	*Stirring*	*Stores*	*Canteen*
			6,264	–
Reapportion				
Stores (50:30:20)	3,132	1,879	(6,264)	1,253
			–	1,253
Reapportion				
Canteen (45:40:15)	564	501	188	(1,253)
			188	–
Reapportion				
Stores (50:30:20)	94	56	(188)	38
			–	38
Reapportion				
Canteen (45:40:15)	17	15	6	(38)
			6	–
Reapportion				
Stores (50:30:20)	3	2	(6)	1
			–	1
Reapportion				
Canteen (45:40:15)	1	–	–	(1)
	176,203	85,797	–	–

Activity 4: Reapportionment practice

The correct answer is: $984,000

	H Block	*F Block*	*Canteen*	*Maintenance*
	$'000	$'000	$'000	$'000
Overheads	400	700	550	800
Canteen (2:2:1)	220	220	(550)	110
	620	920	–	910
Maintenance (2:3)	364	546		(910)
	984	1,466	–	–

Activity 5: Calculating absorption rates

1 The overhead absorption rate for the mixing department was $ [8.81] per [labour hour.]

Mixing OAR	$= \frac{176,203}{20,000}$ = $8.81 per labour hour

2

Stirring OAR	$= \dfrac{85{,}797}{60{,}000}$ = \$1.43 per machine hour

3 The correct answer is: \$66.20

Direct materials per unit

Direct labour per unit (total labour hours × £10 per hour)

Mixing overhead (**mixing labour** hours × OAR per hour)

Stirring overhead (**stirring machine** hours × OAR per hour)

Total production cost

Cost card for a Venus

	\$/unit
Direct material	15
Direct labour	
Mixing (2 hrs @ \$10/hr)	20
Stirring (0.5 hrs @ \$10/hr)	5
Prime cost	40
Overheads	
Mixing (2 hrs @ \$8.81)	17.62
Stirring (6 hrs @ \$1.43)	8.58
Product cost	66.20

Activity 6: Predetermined overhead absorption rates

$$\text{Predetermined overhead absorption rate} = \frac{\$100{,}000}{20{,}000\text{ units}} = \$5/\text{unit}$$

Overheads absorbed = 24,000 (actual units produced) × \$5/unit = \$120,000

Under-/over-absorption = 117,000 – 120,000 = \$3,000 over-absorbed

Activity 7: Absorption costing practice

1 The total budgeted fixed production overhead was \$ 10,800

OAR = \$0.90

$$\text{OAR} = \frac{\text{Budgeted fixed production overheads}}{\text{Normal activity}}$$

$$\therefore \$0.90 = \frac{\text{Budgeted fixed production overheads}}{12{,}000}$$

Budgeted fixed production overheads = 12,000 × \$0.90 = \$10,800

2 The overheads absorbed in Year 1 were \$ 12,600

14,000 units × $0.90 = $12,600

3 The net profit in Year 1 was $ [43,400]

(Use the statement of profit and loss account below.)

(see below)

4 The overheads in Year 2 were [under] absorbed by $ [650]

Under $650 ($11,000 – (11,500 units × $0.90))

5 The net profit in Year 2 was $ [39,350]

	Year 1	*Year 1*	*Year 2*	*Year 2*
	$	$	$	$
Sales		325,000		
(13,000 × 25)				
(12,500 × 25)				312,500
Less: Cost of Sales:				
Opening inventory			20,900	
(1,000 × $20.90)				
Production costs				
Variable costs				
– materials				
(14,000 × $7)	98,000			
(11,500 × $7)			80,500	
– wages				
(14,000 × $8)	112,000			
(11,500 × $8)			92,000	
– variable overheads				
(14,000 × $5)	70,000			
(11,500 × $5)			57,500	
– fixed overheads				
(absorbed)				
(14,000 × $0.90)	12,600			
(11,500 × $0.90)			10,350	
	292,600		261,250	
Less closing inventory				
(1,000 × $20.90) (W2)	(20,900)		–	
	271,700		261,250	
– Adj for under/(over) absorption (W1)	(1,600)	(270,100)	650	(261,900)
Gross profit		54,900		50,600

	Year 1	Year 1	Year 2	Year 2
	$	$	$	$
Less selling costs				
– variable selling cost				
(13,000 × $0.50)		(6,500)		
(12,500 × $0.50)				(6,250)
– fixed selling cost		(5,000)		(5,000)
Net Profit		43,400		39,350

Workings

1 ***Under-/over-absorption***

Year 1:

under-/(over-) absorption	=	Actual expenditure – overhead absorbed
under-/(over-) absorption	=	11,000 – 12,600 = $1,600 over-absorbed

Year 2:

under-/(over-) absorption	=	11,000 – 10,350 = $650 under-absorbed

2 You may have made some mistakes with opening and closing inventory. The question states that there was no opening inventory in Year 1. Then 14,000 units were produced during Year 1 and only 13,000 units were sold. This means that there were 1,000 units left unsold at the end of Year 1 and this is the closing inventory for Year 1. The closing inventory for Year 1 becomes the opening inventory for Year 2.

	Year 1	Year 2
	Units	Units
+ Opening inventory	0	1,000
+ Production	14,000	11,500
– Sales	13,000	12,500
= Closing inventory	1,000	0

Test your learning

1 Allocation involves spreading overhead costs across cost centres.

- True
- False

cost unit or cost centres -

2 Match the following overheads with the most appropriate basis of apportionment.

Overhead	Basis of apportionment
Depreciation of equipment	Book value ▼ ✓
Heat and light costs	floor area ▼ ✓
Canteen	N.O employees ▼ ✓
Insurance of equipment	N.O units ▼ Book value

Pull down list

- Book value of equipment
- Floor area
- Number of employees
- Number of units

3 Which of the following departments are directly involved in production?

Department	Involved in production ✓
Finished goods warehouse	
Canteen	
Machining department	✓
Offices	
Assembly department	✓

4 In relation to calculating total absorption cost, label the following descriptions in the correct order as Steps 1–5.

Description	Step
Apportion fixed costs over departments	2 ✓
Establish the overhead absorption rate	5 4
Choose fair methods of apportionment	1 ✓
Apply the overhead absorption rate to products	4 5

Description	Step
Reapportion service departments costs	3

5 In order to recognise the work service departments do for each other, the [distribution] or [algebraic] methods of reapportioning service department overheads should be used.

6 A direct labour hour basis is most appropriate in which of the following environments?

- Machine-intensive
- Labour-intensive
- When all units produced are identical
- None of the above

7 Over-absorption occurs when absorbed overheads are greater than actual overheads.

- True
- False

8 Choose the correct words from those highlighted.

Traditional costing systems tend to allocate (1) ▼ a proportion of overheads to high volume products and (2) ▼ a proportion of overheads to low volume products.

Pull down list 1

- Too great
- Too small

Pull down list 2

- Too great
- Too small

9 The following statements concern methods of absorbing fixed production overheads into units of production. Are they true or false?

(a) It is generally accepted that a time-based method should be used wherever possible (for example labour rate hours or machine rate hours).

- True
- False

(b) Direct materials price percentage is not usually considered to be a suitable method because there is no reason why a higher material cost should lead to a cost unit incurring more production overhead cost.

- True
- False

10 H Co bases its overhead absorption rate on labour hours. The following information is available for 20X9.

Budgeted overheads	$600,000
Actual overheads	$660,000
Budgeted labour hours	120,000
Actual labour hours	110,000

Required

Calculate the over- or under-absorption of overheads for 20X9.

- ○ $60,000 over-absorbed
- ○ $60,000 under-absorbed ✓
- ○ $110,000 over-absorbed
- ● $110,000 under-absorbed

(1) predetermined OAR = budgeted overheads / Activity level

(2) absorbtion = predetermined OAR × activity level

(3) under/over = Actual overheads less absorbtion overheads

(1) $\frac{600,000}{120,000} = 5$

(2) 5 × 110,000 = 550,000

660,000 − 550,000 = 110,000

positive = under-absorbed.

5 Marginal costing and pricing decisions

Learning outcomes

Having studied this chapter you will be able to:

- Calculate the marginal cost of products, services and activities
- Reconcile the differences between profits calculated using absorption costing and those calculated using marginal costing
- Apply cost information in pricing decisions

Chapter context

This first part of the chapter covers marginal costing which is a more straightforward alternative to absorption costing. The aim is the same, to find the cost of one unit of production, but marginal costing doesn't try to include any fixed costs within the unit cost; instead these are simply treated as a cost in the period in which they are incurred (a period cost).

Whether we use marginal or absorption costing, one of the benefits of knowing the cost of our products is that it can help in setting selling prices. The remainder of the chapter therefore looks at how prices can be set based on cost.

Syllabus context

This chapter is part of syllabus **Section B**, which looks at **'Costing'**.

This syllabus area has a weighting of **25%** and is covered by **Chapters 2 to 5**.

In the exam, you will be expected to demonstrate competence in the following areas:

- The treatment of direct and indirect costs in ascertaining the marginal cost of a 'cost object' eg a product, service, activity, customer.
- The difference between marginal and absorption profits.
- Marginal cost pricing and full-cost pricing to achieve specified targets (return on sales, return on investment, mark-up and margins).

Chapter overview

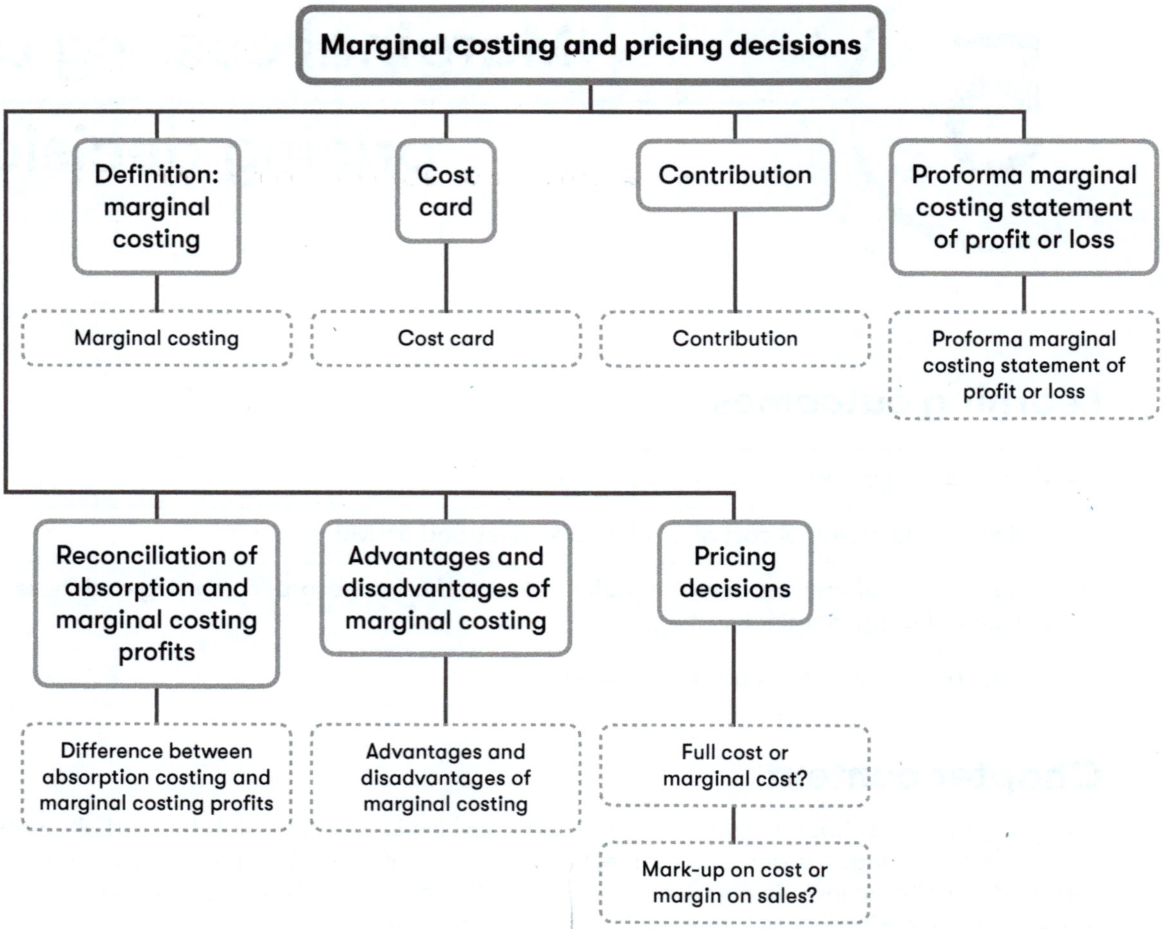

1 Definition: marginal costing

KEY TERM

Marginal costing: The variable cost of a product or a service. It is the cost which would be avoided if the unit was not produced or provided.

Marginal costing is an alternative method of costing to absorption costing. In marginal costing, only variable costs are charged as a cost of sale and a **contribution** is calculated. Closing inventories of work in progress or finished goods are valued at marginal (variable) production cost. Fixed costs are treated as a period cost, and are charged in full against profit in the accounting period in which they are incurred.

2 Cost card

Look at the difference between the marginal cost card and the absorption cost card.

	$/unit	
Direct materials	X	
Direct labour	X	
Variable overhead	X	
Marginal cost	**X**	→ Used to value inventory under **marginal** costing

	$/unit	
Direct materials	X	
Direct labour	X	
Variable overhead	X	
Fixed overhead	X	
Absorption cost	**X**	→ Used to value inventory under **absorption** costing

3 Contribution

KEY TERM

Contribution: Selling price less **all** variable costs.

	$	$
Selling price		X
Less: Variable production costs	X	
Variable non-production costs	X	
		(X)
Contribution		**X**

Any **fixed costs** are deducted in **total** from contribution to give net profit.

The term 'contribution' is really short for 'contribution towards covering fixed overheads and making a profit'.

Illustration 1: Marginal costing

Water Co makes a product, the Splash, which has a variable production cost of $6 per unit and a sales price of $10 per unit. At the beginning of September 20X0 there were no opening inventories. Production during the month was 20,000 units. Fixed costs for the month were $45,000 (production, administration, sales and distribution). There were no variable marketing costs.

Required

Calculate, at each of the following sales levels, the total contribution and total profit for September 20X0 and the contribution per unit and the profit/loss per unit, using marginal costing principles.

(1) 10,000 Splashes

(2) 15,000 Splashes

Solution

The first stage in the profit calculation must be to identify the variable costs, and then the contribution. Fixed costs are deducted from the total contribution to derive the profit. All closing inventories are valued at marginal production cost ($6 per unit).

	10,000 Splashes		15,000 Splashes	
	$	$	$	$
Sales (at $10)		100,000		150,000
Opening inventory	0			
Variable production cost	120,000		120,000	
	120,000		120,000	
Less value of closing inventory (at marginal cost)	60,000		30,000	
Variable cost of sales		60,000		90,000
Contribution		40,000		60,000
Less fixed costs		45,000		45,000
Profit/(loss)		(5,000)		15,000
Profit/(loss) per unit		$(0.50)		$1
Contribution per unit		$4		$4

4 Proforma marginal costing statement of profit or loss

		$	$
Sales			X
Less: Cost of sales			
Opening inventory (@ marginal cost)		X	
Production costs:			
Variable cost	– Materials	X	
	– Labour	X	
	– Variable overheads	X	
		X	
Less closing inventory (@ marginal cost)		(X)	
			(X)

	$	$
Less variable selling, distribution and administration costs		(X)
Contribution		X
Less fixed costs (production, selling, administration)		(X)
Profit		X

Note. Inventory is valued at marginal production cost only.

Activity 1: Marginal costing statement of profit or loss

(Used for absorption costing earlier.)

Selling price $25.

	$
Direct materials	7
Direct wages	8
Variable production overheads	5
	20

There is a variable selling cost/unit at $0.50.

	Year 1	*Year 2*
	Units	Units
Normal/budgeted production	12,000	12,000
Actual production	14,000	11,500
Actual sales	13,000	12,500
Actual fixed production overheads	$11,000	$11,000
Actual fixed selling costs	$5,000	$5,000

There is no opening inventory. All variable costs were as budgeted for the two years.

Required

Complete the statement of profit or loss below using marginal costing principles.

Solution

Statement of profit or loss

		Year 1		*Year 2*
	$	$	$	$
Sales		325,000		
25 x 13,000				
25 x 12,500				312,500
Less: COS				
Opening inventory				
(1000 x 20)			20,000	

		Year 1		Year 2
	$	$	$	$
Production costs				
– variable				
20 x 14,000	280,000			
20 x 11,500			230,000	
	280,000		250,000	
Less closing inventory				
1000 x 20	(20,000)			
		260,000		(250,000)
		65,000		62,500
Less variable non-production costs		(6500)		6250
0.5 x 13,000				
0.5 x 12,500				
Contribution		58,500		56250
Less: Fixed costs				
– Production	11,000		11,000	
– Selling	5,000		5,000	
		(16,000)		(16,000)
Net profit		42,500		40,250

5 Reconciliation of absorption and marginal costing profits

Here are the profits we calculated for the activity above and the absorption costing activity in the earlier chapter.

	Year 1	*Year 2*	*Total*
	$	$	$
Profit under absorption costing	43,400	39,350	82,750
Profit under marginal costing	42,500	40,250	82,750
Differences	900	(900)	–

(a) The difference arises from different inventory valuations (absorption costing inventory valued at $20.90 per unit and marginal costing inventory valued at $20 per unit).

(b) If inventory levels increase, absorption costing will report a higher profit than marginal costing.

Opening inventory at the start of Year 1 was 0 units. At the end of Year 1, it was 1,000 units. Inventory therefore increased during the year. Absorption costing therefore shows a higher profit for Year 1 than marginal costing.

(c) If inventory levels decrease, absorption costing will report the lower profit.

Opening inventory at the start of Year 2 was 1,000 units. At the end of Year 2, it was 0 units. Inventory therefore decreased during the year. Absorption costing therefore shows a lower profit for Year 2 than marginal costing.

(d) The difference in reported profit is equal to the change in **inventory volume** multiplied by the fixed production overhead rate per unit.

Year 1 difference: 1,000 units × \$0.90 = \$900

Year 2 difference: (1,000) units × \$0.90 = (\$900)

(e) In the long run, the total reported profit will be the same whether marginal or absorption costing is used.

Activity 2: Absorption v marginal costing

Suppose that a company makes and sells a single product. At the beginning of period 1, there are no opening inventories of the product, for which the variable production cost is \$4 and the sales price is \$6 per unit. Fixed costs are \$2,000 per period, of which \$1,500 are fixed production costs.

\$500 fixed selling costs

	Period 1	*Period 2*
Sales	1,200 units	1,800 units
Production	1,500 units	1,500 units

Required

1 Assuming normal output is 1,500 units per period, the absorption costing profit in each period and in total would be:

(1) Period 1 \$ 700

(2) Period 2 \$ 1300

(3) Total \$ 2000

OAR = prodn overhead / activity = 1500 / 1500 = 1 per unit.

2 The marginal costing profit in each period and in total would be:

(1) Period 1 \$ 400

(2) Period 2 \$ 1600

(3) Total \$ 2000

same value.

Solution

marginal cost = selling price − variable

contribution = (selling p per unit − variable per unit) × units sold =

6 − 4 = 2 × 1200 = 2400

2400 − 2000 = 400 = profit

P2 = 2 × 1800 = 3600

3600 − 2000 = 1600

> ### Exam focus point
>
> An assessment question may, for example, give you a marginal costing profit figure and ask you to use inventory figures and the overhead absorption rate to calculate the absorption costing profit. Remember, if inventory levels increase, absorption costing will report a higher profit than marginal costing. If inventory levels decrease, absorption costing will report the lower profit.

Activity 3: Marginal to absorption profit

The following information is available for H Co.

20X9

Opening inventory	900 units
Closing inventory	300 units
Marginal costing profit	$100,000

Required

Using an overhead absorption rate of $20 per unit, calculate what the profit would be if absorption costing were used.

Solution

18,000

Absorption profit	
+ opening	(900 x 20) = 18,000
- closing	(20 x 300) = (6000)
Marginal costing profit	100,000

6 Advantages and disadvantages of marginal costing

Advantages	Disadvantages
Appropriate for decision making (any activity that generates a positive contribution should be viewed favourably, at least in the short	Does not comply with IAS 2 (revised).

Advantages	Disadvantages
run).	
Fixed costs are treated in accordance with their nature.	Costs must be analysed into fixed and variable parts.
Profit depends on sales, not production activity levels.	Fixed costs cannot be ignored in the long run.

7 Pricing decisions

There are two considerations when deciding on a selling price for a product or service:

(a) Should the price be based on the full cost or just the marginal cost?

(b) Should the price be determined by a **'mark-up'** on cost or a **'margin'** on the selling price?

7.1 Full cost or marginal cost?

7.1.1 Full cost plus pricing

In full cost plus pricing, the full cost may be a fully absorbed production cost only, or it may include some absorbed non-production costs like administration or selling and distribution.

An amount will be added to this full cost base to represent the profit per unit a company wants to receive.

Advantage of full cost plus	Disadvantage of full cost plus
Should ensure that fixed costs are covered (if working at normal capacity)	Does not take into account market and demand conditions (ie lower prices offered by rival firms)

7.1.2 Marginal cost plus pricing

In marginal cost plus pricing, an amount for profit is added to the marginal cost only.

Advantages of marginal cost plus	Disadvantages of marginal cost plus
Simple and easy method to use	Pricing decisions cannot ignore fixed costs altogether – they must be covered in the long run to generate sustainable profits
Draws management attention to contribution, and creates a better awareness of concepts such as breakeven analysis	Still does not fully take into account market and demand conditions

7.2 Mark-up on cost or margin on sales?

The amount to be included in the selling price to represent profit per unit can be determined in one of two ways. It is very important to understand the mathematical difference between them. A good way to ensure you take the correct approach is to think in terms of percentages.

7.2.1 Mark-up on cost

KEY TERM

Mark-up: A percentage of cost, added to the cost to reach the selling price of a product or service. It is also known as a **return on costs**.

This method is traditionally used by retail companies, which will buy in products from wholesalers and then add on a 'retail mark-up', say 40%, to the wholesale price to determine a selling price in their store.

The mathematical approach for this is as follows:

(a) Consider the **cost base** to represent 100%

(b) Add to this the profit mark-up of 40% of the cost

(c) Calculate the selling price – ie 140% of the cost base

So, if the cost of a product is \$100, a selling price of \$140 will represent a mark-up of 40%.

7.2.2 Margin on sales

KEY TERM

> **Margin:** Profit expressed as a percentage of the selling price of a product. It is also known as a **return on sales.**

With this approach, the profit element is calculated with reference to the selling price, not the cost. Note the critical difference in the mathematical approach to calculate a selling price with a **sales margin** of 40%:

(a) Consider the **selling price** to represent 100%

(b) Realise that this will consist of the cost base (60%) and the profit margin (40%)

(c) Calculate the profit margin given the percentages in (2)

(d) Add this to the cost base to determine the selling price

So, if the cost of a product is \$100, and this represents 60% of the selling price, the sales margin will be (\$100/60 × 40) = \$66.67. The selling price will therefore be \$166.67.

Activity 4: Margins and mark-ups (1)

A company uses marginal cost plus pricing for its two products, Y and Z. The marginal cost of product Y is \$30/unit, and product Z is \$48/unit.

Required

Calculate the selling price for each in the following circumstances:

(1) To earn a return on costs (mark-up) of 25%

(2) To earn a return on sales (margin) of 40%

Solution

marn-up - 125 % selling price

Y = selling price = 125 %

cost plus = 100 %

margin = 25 %

Z = 60

30 = 100 %

Y = 37.5 = 38

Activity 5: Margins and mark-ups (2)

A selling price is determined by including a profit margin of 20% on sales.

Required

Calculate the percentage mark-up on costs needed to generate the same amount of profit.

mark-up

selling price =

Solution

---

cost = 80%
profit = 20%
selling price = 100%

translate to profit mark-up

80/20 = 25%.

profit to cost.

% mark-up =

$\frac{20\% \text{ margin}}{\text{cost} = 80\%}$ = 25%.

to cost.

2) margin = 40%.

selling price = 100%.
cost = 60%.
margin = 40%.

y = 30 = 60%.
y = 50

z = 48 = 60%.
100% = 80.

Chapter summary

Marginal costing and pricing decisions

Definition: marginal costing

Marginal costing

- The variable cost of a product or a service. It is the cost which would be avoided if the unit was not produced or provided

Cost card

Cost card

- Difference between the marginal cost card and the absorption cost card

Contribution

Contribution

- Contribution – selling price less all variable costs
- Contribution – fixed costs = profit

Proforma marginal costing statement of profit or loss

Proforma marginal costing statement of profit or loss

- Proforma

Reconciliation of absorption and marginal costing profits

Difference between absorption costing and marginal costing profits

- Inventory valuation

Advantages and disadvantages of marginal costing

Advantages and disadvantages of marginal costing

- Appropriate for decision making
- Fixed costs are treated in accordance with their nature
- Profit depends on sales, not production activity levels, but
- Does not comply with IAS 2 (revised)
- Costs must be analysed into fixed and variable parts
- Fixed costs cannot be ignored in the long run

Pricing decisions

Full cost or marginal cost?

- Full cost plus pricing
- Marginal cost plus pricing

Mark-up on cost or margin on sales?

- Mark-up on cost
- Margin on sales

Key terms

Marginal costing: The variable cost of a product or a service. It is the cost which would be avoided if the unit was not produced or provided.

Contribution: Selling price less **all** variable costs.

Mark-up: A percentage of cost, added to the cost to reach the selling price of a product or service. It is also known as a **return on costs**.

Margin: Profit expressed as a percentage of the selling price of a product. It is also known as a **return on sales.**

Activity answers

Activity 1: Marginal costing statement of profit or loss

Statement of profit or loss

		Year 1		Year 2
	$	$	$	$
Sales		325,000		
(13,000 × 25)				
(12,500 × 25)				312,500
Less: COS				
Opening inventory				
(1,000 × $20)	–		20,000	
Production costs				
– variable				
(14,000 × $20)	280,000			
(11,500 × $20)	–		230,000	
	280,000		250,000	
Less closing inventory				
(1,000 × $20)	(20,000)		–	
		(260,000)		(250,000)
		65,000		62,500
Less variable non-production costs		(6,500)		(6,250)
(13,000 × $0.50)				
(12,500 × $0.50)				
Contribution		58,500		56,250
Less: Fixed costs				
– Production	11,000		11,000	
– Selling	5,000		5,000	
		(16,000)		(16,000)
Net profit		42,500		40,250

Activity 2: Absorption v marginal costing

1

(1) Period 1 $ 700

(2) Period 2 $ 1,300

(3) Total $ 2,000

Working

The absorption rate for fixed production overhead is:

$$\frac{\$1{,}500}{1{,}500 \text{ units}} = \$1 \text{ per unit}$$

		Period 1		*Period 2*		*Total*
	$	$	$	$	$	$
Sales		7,200		10,800		18,000
Production costs						
Variable	6,000		6,000		12,000	
Fixed	1,500		1,500		3,000	
	7,500		7,500		15,000	
Add opening inventory b/f	–		1,500			
	7,500		9,000		15,000	
Less closing inventory c/f	(1,500)		–		–	
Production cost of sales	6,000		9,000		15,000	
(Under-)/over-absorbed overhead	–		–		–	
Total production costs		6,000		9,000		15,000
Gross profit		1,200		1,800		3,000
Other fixed costs		500		500		1,000
Net profit		700		1,300		2,000

2

(1) Period 1 $ 400

(2) Period 2 $ 1,600

(3) Total $ 2,000

Working

		Period 1		*Period 2*		*Total*
	$	$	$	$	$	$
Sales		7,200		10,800		18,000
Variable production cost	6,000		6,000		12,000	
Add opening inventory b/f	–		1,200		–	

		Period 1		Period 2		Total
	$	$	$	$	$	$
	6,000		7,200		12,000	
Less closing inventory c/f	(1,200)		–		–	
Variable production cost of sales		4,800		7,200		12,000
Contribution		2,400		3,600		6,000
Fixed costs		2,000		2,000		4,000
Profit		400		1,600		2,000

Alternative method

In period 1, inventory increased from 0 units to 300 units. This means that absorption profit will report a higher profit than marginal costing profit. The difference is 300 units × OAR of $1 = $300.

Profit under absorption costing = $700.

So profit under marginal costing = $700 – $300 = $400.

In period 2, inventory decreased from 300 units to 0 units. This means that absorption profit will report a lower profit than marginal costing profit. The difference is 300 units × OAR of $1 = $300.

Profit under absorption costing = $1,300.

So profit under marginal costing = $1,300 + $300 = $1,600.

Activity 3: Marginal to absorption profit

	Units	
Opening inventory	900	
Closing inventory	300	
Decrease	600	× $20 = $12,000 lower
Marginal profit	$100,000	
	$12,000	
Absorption profit	$88,000	

Activity 4: Margins and mark-ups (1)

(1)		X	Y
Cost	100%	$30	$48
Profit	25%	$7.50	$12
Price	125%	$37.50	$60

(2)		X	Y
Cost	60%	$30	$48
Profit	40%	$20	$32
Price	100%	$50	$80

Activity 5: Margins and mark-ups (2)

The cost structure under the sales margin of 20% is:

Cost	80%
Profit	20%

Price	100%

To translate this to a cost mark-up, need to relate profit to cost, ie 20/80 = 25%.

Test your learning

1 Fill in the blank:

Sales value – marginal cost of sales = ☐

2 Identify which of the following relate to either:

A = Absorption costing

M = Marginal costing

		A or M
(a)	Closing inventories valued at marginal production cost	☐
(b)	Closing inventories valued at full production cost	☐
(c)	Cost of sales include some fixed overhead incurred in previous period in opening inventory values	☐
(d)	Fixed costs are charged in full against profit for the period	☐

3 Which of the following are arguments in favour of marginal costing?

☐ It is simple to operate.

☐ There is no under- or over-absorption of overheads.

☐ Fixed costs are the same regardless of activity levels.

☐ The information from this costing method may be used for decision making.

4 ABC Co plans to sell 1,200 units of product B. A 12% return is required on the $1,000,000 annual investment in product B. A selling price of $500 per unit has been set.

Required

The full cost of product B is $ ☐

5 XYZ Co produces a component W. The standard cost card for component W is as follows:

		$
Production costs	Fixed	255.70
	Variable	483.50
Selling costs	Fixed	124.80
	Variable	75.60
	Profit	60.40
	Selling price	1,000.00

Required

(a) Under an absorption costing system, what would be the value per unit of inventory?

- O $255.70
- O $739.20

- O $483.20
- O $227.80

(b) Under a variable costing system, what would be the value per unit of inventory?

- O $483.50
- O $75.60
- O $136.00
- O $124.80

6 When comparing the profits reported under absorption costing and marginal costing during a period when the level of inventory increased:

- O Absorption costing profits will be higher and closing inventory valuations lower than those under marginal costing
- O Absorption costing profits will be higher and closing inventory valuations higher than those under marginal costing
- O Marginal costing profits will be higher and closing inventory valuations lower than those under absorption costing
- O Marginal costing profits will be higher and closing inventory valuations higher than those under absorption costing

7 What is a period cost in marginal costing?

8 Marginal costing and absorption costing are different techniques for assessing profit in a period. If there are changes in inventory during a period, marginal costing and absorption costing will report different profits.

Required

Which of the following statements are true?

(1) If inventory levels increase, marginal costing will report the higher profit.

(2) If inventory levels decrease, marginal costing will report the lower profit.

(3) If inventory levels decrease, marginal costing will report the higher profit.

(4) If the opening and closing inventory volumes are the same, marginal costing and absorption costing will report the same profit figure.

- O All of the above
- O (1), (2) and (4)
- O (1) and (4)
- O (3) and (4)

9 A product has the following costs:

	$/unit
Variable production costs	4.80
Total production costs	7.50
Total variable costs	5.90
Total costs	10.00

11,400 units of the product were manufactured in a period during which 11,200 units were sold.

Required

What is the profit difference using absorption costing rather than marginal costing?

- ○ The profit for the period is $540 lower.
- ○ The profit for the period is $540 higher.
- ○ The profit for the period is $820 lower.
- ○ The profit for the period is $820 higher.

10 A company currently uses absorption costing. The following information relates to Product X for Month 1:

Opening inventory	Nil
Production	900 units
Sales	800 units

Required

If the company had used marginal costing, which of the following combinations would be true?

	Profit	*Inventory valuation*
○	would be higher	would be higher
○	would be higher	would be lower
○	would be lower	would be higher
○	would be lower	would be lower

6 Breakeven analysis

Learning outcomes

Having studied this chapter you will be able to:
• Apply breakeven analysis

Chapter context

This chapter helps answer some important questions that any business will have:

- How much to we need to sell to break even?
- How much do we need to sell to earn a certain level of profit?

Syllabus context

This chapter is part of syllabus **Section D**, which looks at **'Decision Making'**.

This syllabus area has a weighting of **35%** and is covered by **Chapters 6 and 7 and 15 to 17**.

In the exam, you will be expected to demonstrate competence in the following areas:

- Breakeven charts, profit volume graphs, breakeven point, target profit, margin of safety.

Chapter overview

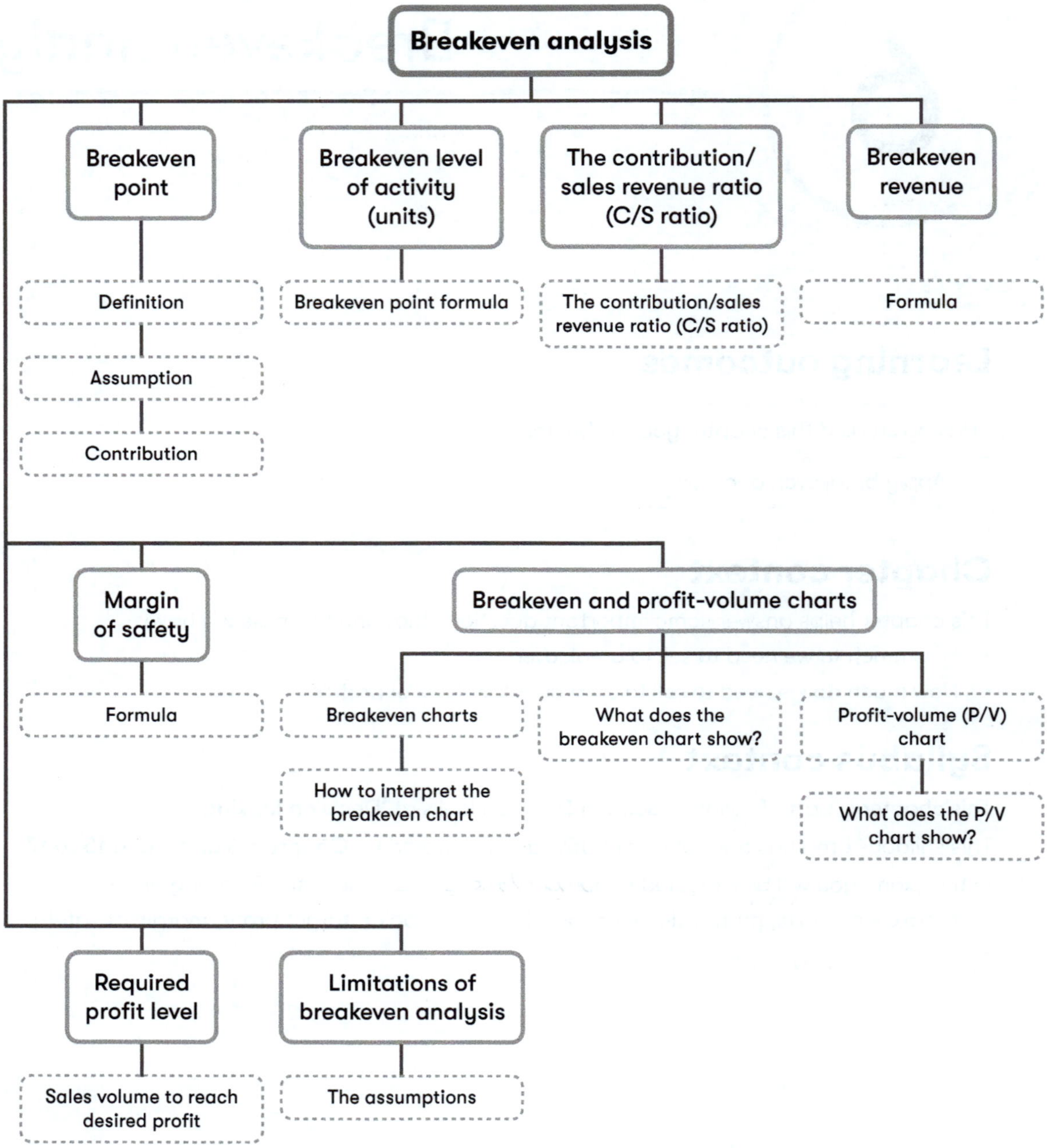

1 Breakeven point

1.1 Definition

KEY TERM

Breakeven point: The sales volume which will give the company a profit of $nil.

If sales exceed the breakeven point (BEP) the company will make a profit.

KEY TERM

Breakeven analysis: (calculations to determine the breakeven point) often referred to as **cost-volume-profit (CVP) analysis.** It analyses the relationships between activity levels, costs and profits.

1.2 Assumption

We will assume that selling price per unit and variable cost per unit and total fixed costs are all constant, that is, they do not change with varying output. This is a reasonable assumption for short-term decisions, although of course in the long term or for very high levels of output, this might not apply.

1.3 Contribution

Remember that **contribution** per unit = selling price less **all** variable costs per unit.

We will need this definition to set up the breakeven formula.

	$
Sales	15,000
Less VCs	(5,000)
Contribution	10,000 →
Fixed costs	(10,000) →
Profit	0

Must be **equal**

2 Breakeven level of activity (units)

2.1 Breakeven point formula

So we will break even when...

Total contribution = Fixed costs

ie Contribution per unit × number of units = Fixed costs

Formula to learn

$$\text{Breakdown level of activity (units)} = \frac{\text{Fixed costs}}{\text{Cont'n/unit}}$$

When calculating the BEP, always round the number of units up to the next whole unit.

Illustration 1: Breakeven point

Reardon Enterprises sells a single product with a selling price of $10 per unit. The variable costs of producing the product are $6 per unit and the fixed costs of the business are $200,000.

Required

What is the breakeven point in units?

Solution

$$\text{Breakeven point} = \frac{\$200{,}000}{\$10-6} = 50{,}000 \text{ units}$$

We can prove that this is the point where no profit or loss is made.

	$
Sales (50,000 × $10)	500,000
Variable costs (50,000 × $6)	300,000
Contribution	200,000
Fixed costs	(200,000)
Profit	–

Therefore the management of Reardon Enterprises will know that they must ensure that sales volumes exceed 50,000 units per year in order for the business to cover its total costs and make any profit.

Activity 1: Breakeven units

A business has a single product that it sells for $28. The variable costs of producing the product are $19 per unit and the fixed costs of the business are $360,000.

Required

What is the breakeven point in units?

Solution

$$\frac{360{,}000}{(28-19)} = \frac{360{,}000}{9} = 40{,}000 \text{ units}$$

✓

Activity 2: Breakeven point and breakeven revenue

A company has different output levels, and incurs different total production costs at each level, as follows.

6.5

Output	*Total costs*
Units	$
6,000	44,700
8,000	57,700

Required

1 If the selling price is $8/unit at all levels, what is the breakeven point?

2 What is the breakeven revenue?

Solution

3 The contribution/sales revenue ratio (C/S ratio)

An alternative method of finding the breakeven revenue is to use the C/S ratio.

KEY TERM

> **Contribution/sales revenue (C/S) ratio:** Calculated as contribution divided by sales, gives the amount of contribution earned per dollar of sales.
>
> It is also known as the **profit-volume (P/V) ratio.**

4 Breakeven revenue

> **Formula to learn**
>
> $$\text{Breakeven revenue (\$)} = \frac{\text{Fixed costs}}{\text{C/S ratio}}$$

Activity 3: C/S ratio

Using details from the breakeven revenue Activity 2 above, find the C/S ratio and breakeven revenue. 18.75%

8 - 6.5 = 1.5

C/S ratio = 0.1875

1.5 / 8 = 0.1875

Breakeven revenue = $ 30,400

Solution

Breakeven revenue =

BEP # x selling price per unit

or $\frac{\text{fixed costs}}{\text{C/S ratio}} = \frac{5700}{0.1875} = 30,400$

5 Margin of safety

As well as being interested in the BEP, management may be interested in the amount by which actual sales can fall below anticipated sales without a loss being made.

KEY TERM

Margin of safety: The measure of the amount by which sales must fall before we start making a loss.

A loss is made if sales volume is less than the BEP.

Formula to learn

Margin of safety (in units) = Budgeted sales volume - breakeven sales volume

or

$$\text{Margin of safety (as \%)} = \frac{\text{Budgeted sales volume} - \text{breakeven sales volume}}{\text{Budgeted sales volume}} \times 100$$

Activity 4: Margin of safety

Details are the same as the previous activity and with budgeted sales of 5,000 units.

Required

1

Margin of safety = 1200 units

2

Margin of safety = 24 %

Budgeted sales vol – breakeven point (breakeven sales vol)

Solution

$\frac{5000 - 3800}{5000}$

5000 – 3800 = 1200

BEP = $\frac{\text{fixed costs}}{\text{contribution per unit}}$ = 3800

6 Breakeven and profit-volume charts

6.1 Breakeven charts

A breakeven chart shows the profit or loss at different levels of sales.

It shows, in diagrammatic form, the relationship between sales volume or value, total revenue, and total costs. Breakeven occurs when total costs are equal to total revenue.

The horizontal axis is used for sales volume or value and the vertical axis for money (costs and revenue).

Three lines are plotted on the graph:

- Firstly the sales revenue line (which will pass through the origin, since when sales volume is nil, revenue is nil)
- Then the fixed costs line (which will be parallel to the horizontal axis)
- And finally the total costs line

Margin of safety = Budgeted vol – BEP = 70,000 – 50,000 = 20,000.

Illustration 2: Breakeven chart

The following information relates to Reardon Enterprises.

Selling price per unit	$10
Variable cost per unit	$6
Contribution per unit	$4
Fixed costs	$200,000
Breakeven point	50,000 units or $500,000
Budgeted sales	70,000 units

Breakeven point = $\frac{\text{fixed costs}}{\text{contribution per unit}}$

$\frac{200,000}{4}$ = 50,000.

Margin of safety = Budgeted sales – breakeven point

Solution

Breakeven chart

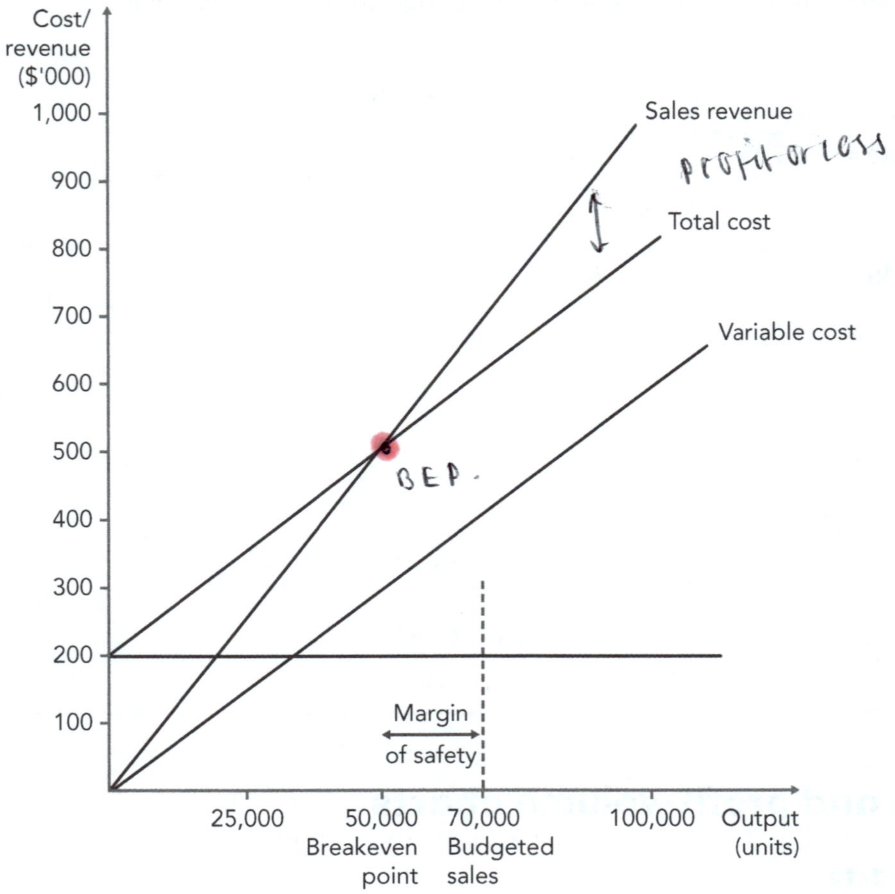

This chart shows variable costs, fixed costs, total costs and sales revenue at various different activity levels.

6.2 How to interpret the breakeven chart

- The fixed cost line is a horizontal line at $200,000.
- Variable costs start at the origin – if there are no sales then there are no variable costs. You can see, for example, variable costs at 100,000 units are $600,000.
- The total cost line is parallel to the variable cost line but starts at $200,000, the level of the fixed costs.
- Sales revenue again starts at the origin. You can see that the revenue is $1,000,000 if sales are 100,000 units.

6.3 What does the breakeven chart show?

- The BEP is the point where the sales revenue line crosses the total costs line.
- The margin of safety is the horizontal distance between budgeted sales of 70,000 units and breakeven sales of 50,000 units. - 20,000
- The amount of profit or loss at each activity level is the vertical distance between the sales revenue line and the total cost line.

6.4 Profit-volume (P/V) chart

Example: Profit-volume chart

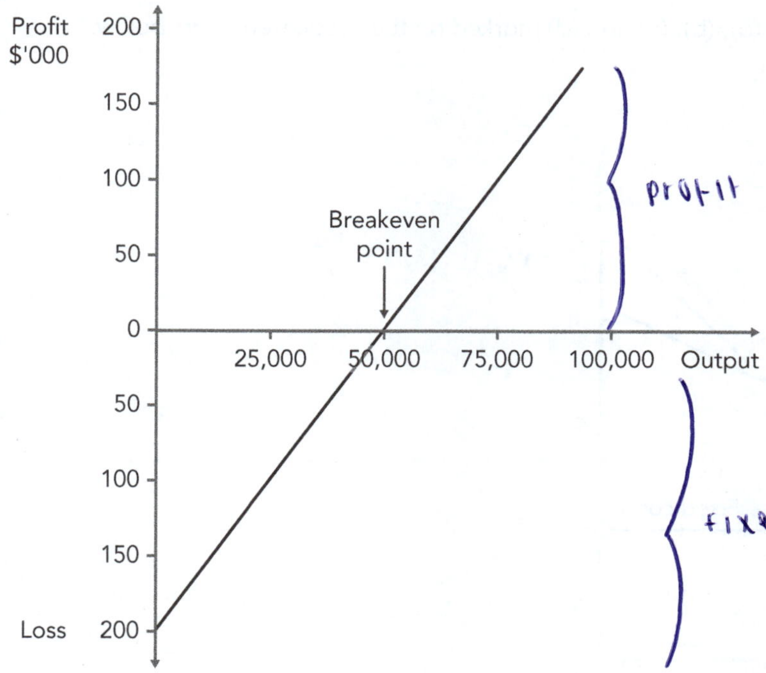

The P/V chart simply shows the level of profit or loss at any given level of activity.

6.5 How to interpret a P/V chart

- The loss when there are zero sales is equal to the fixed costs, $200,000.
- The profit at the 100,000 units activity level is $200,000.

6.6 What does the P/V chart show?

- The profit or loss at any level of activity can be read off the chart.
- The BEP is where the profit line crosses the horizontal axis – where profit is zero.
- The horizontal axis could alternatively have shown sales revenue rather than activity level.

Activity 5: Breakeven chart

Match the following labels to (a), (b), (c) and (d) marked on the breakeven chart below.

- Fixed costs
- Margin of safety
- Budgeted profit
- Budgeted variable costs

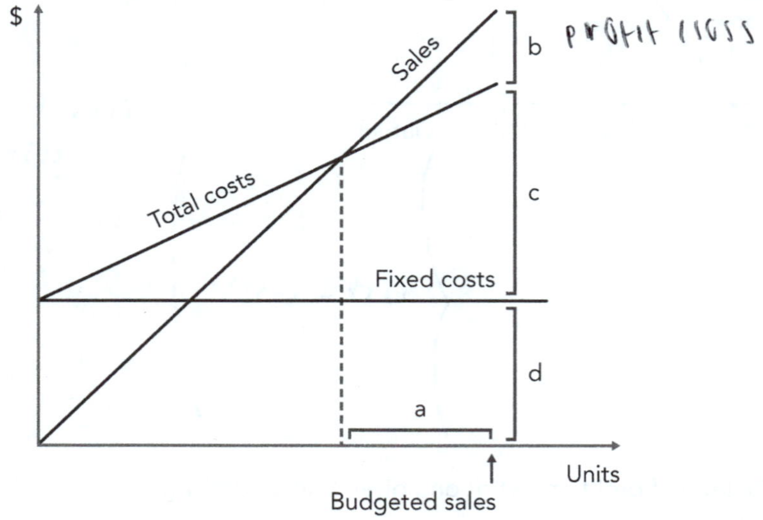

Solution

a) margin of safety

b) budgeted profit

c) budgeted variable costs.

d) fixed costs.

Activity 6: Profit-volume chart

G Co manufactures and sells a single product. The profit statement for May is as follows.

	$
Sales value (at $8 per unit)	80,000
Variable cost of sales (at $4.80 per unit)	48,000
Contribution	32,000
Fixed costs	15,000
Profit	17,000

The management accountant has used the data for May to draw the following profit volume graph.

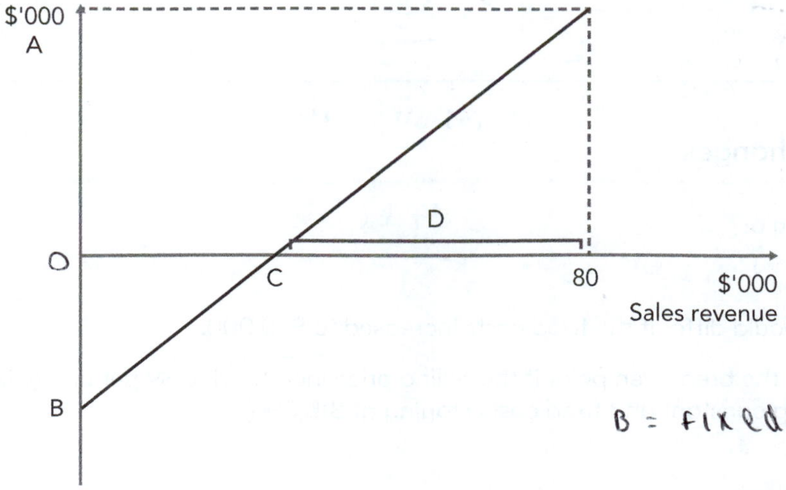

B = fixed cost

D = margin of safety.

Required

1 The monetary values indicated on the graph as A, B and C are:

A $ 17,000 ✓

B $ 15,000 ✓

C $ 37,500 ✓

2

The term used to describe the distance D on the graph is the Margin of safety.

3

112,500 units.

For the whole of the current year, G Co budgets to achieve a sales value of $900,000. Assuming that the unit variable costs and selling price achieved will be the same as that achieved during May, and that fixed costs for the year will be $180,000, the profit for the whole year will be $ 180,000.

contribution = selling price - variable.

4

360,000 = contribution - 180,000

The annual margin of safety for G Co's product is 53 ✗ % of budgeted sales.

50%.

80,000 - 37,500 / 80,000.

Solution

Breakeven point = fixed costs / contribution per unit.

15,000 / (8 - 4.8) = 15,000 / 3.2 = 4 687.5

BEP = 4687.5

Breakeven revenue = 4687.5 × selling price per unit.

4688.

37,500

Activity 7: Impact of changes

Using the data from Activity 6:

Required

1. Describe how the line would differ if the fixed costs increased to $20,000.
2. Describe the impact on the breakeven point if the selling price increased to $9 per unit (with variable costs remaining constant and fixed costs staying at $15,000).

Solution

7 Required profit level

The approach used to find an expression for the breakeven sales volumes can be extended to find the volume needed to attain a required profit level (or **target profit**).

Formula to learn

$$\text{Sales volume to reach required profit level} = \frac{\text{Fixed costs} + \text{required profit}}{\text{Contribution per unit}}$$

The required profit is like an additional fixed cost which must be covered before the company 'breaks even'.

Activity 8: Required profit level

Using the data from Activity 2:

Fixed costs = $5,700

Contribution per unit = $1.50/unit

Required

If we need to make a profit of $10,000 the sales units volume required is 10,467 units.

Solution

$$\frac{5700 + 10,000}{1.5} = \frac{15700}{1.5}$$

10,467

Activity 9: Manipulating the breakeven formula

BE units	25,000
Fixed costs	$75,000
Selling price	$11/unit

Required

Calculate the variable cost per unit. = $8 per unit

Solution

$$\frac{75,000}{(11 - x)} = 25,000$$

breakeven = fixed costs / contribution per unit

$11 - x = 3$

contribution = selling price - variable cost.

$x = 8$

8 Limitations of breakeven analysis

8.1 The assumptions

(a) All costs can be split into fixed and variable elements.

(b) Fixed costs are constant.

(c) Variable cost per unit is constant.

(d) Selling price is constant.

(e) Inventory levels are constant (sales volume = production volume).

Chapter summary

Breakeven analysis

- **Breakeven point**
  - Definition
    - The sales volume which will give the company a profit of $nil
  - Assumption
    - Selling price per unit and variable cost per unit and total fixed costs are all constant
  - Contribution
    - Breakeven point is where FC = contribution
- **Breakeven level of activity (units)**
  - Breakeven point formula
    - BE (units) = FC/ Contribution per unit
- **The contribution/ sales revenue ratio (C/S ratio)**
  - The contribution/sales revenue ratio (C/S ratio)
    - Contribution divided by sales, gives the amount of contribution earned per dollar of sales
- **Breakeven revenue**
  - Formula
    - BE (revenue) = FC/CS ratio
- **Margin of safety**
  - Formula
    - MoS = (Budgeted sales volume – Breakeven sales volume)/ Budgeted sales volume
- **Breakeven and profit-volume charts**
  - Breakeven charts
    - Sales revenue, total cost, variable cost, fixed cost, margin of safety
  - How to interpret the breakeven chart
    - Interpretation
  - What does the breakeven chart show?
    - What the chart shows
    - BEP is the point where the sales revenue line crosses the total costs line
    - The MoS is the horizontal distance between budgeted sales and breakeven sales
    - The amount of profit or loss at each activity level is the vertical distance between the sales revenue line and the total cost line
  - Profit-volume (P/V) chart
    - Profit
    - Loss
    - Output
    - BEP
  - What does the P/V chart show?
    - The profit or loss at any level of activity can be read off the chart
    - The BEP is where the profit line crosses the horizontal axis – where profit is zero
    - The horizontal axis could alternatively have shown sales revenue rather than activity level

Required profit level

Sales volume to reach desired profit

- SV = (Fixed costs + Required profit)/ Contribution per unit

Limitations of breakeven analysis

The assumptions

- All costs can be split into fixed and variable elements
- Fixed costs are constant
- Variable cost per unit is constant
- Selling price is constant
- Inventory levels are constant (sales volume = production volume)

Key terms

Breakeven point: The sales volume which will give the company a profit of $nil.

Breakeven analysis: (calculations to determine the breakeven point) often referred to as **cost-volume-profit (CVP) analysis.** It analyses the relationships between activity levels, costs and profits.

Contribution/sales revenue (C/S) ratio: Calculated as contribution divided by sales, gives the amount of contribution earned per dollar of sales.

It is also known as the **profit-volume (P/V) ratio.**

Margin of safety: The measure of the amount by which sales must fall before we start making a loss.

Activity answers

Activity 1: Breakeven units

$$\text{Breakeven point} = \frac{\$360{,}000}{\$28-\$19} = 40{,}000 \text{ units}$$

Activity 2: Breakeven point and breakeven revenue

1 Estimate cost behaviour via high-low technique

	Output	*Costs*
		$
High	8,000	57,700
Low	6,000	44,700
	2,000	13,000

$$\therefore \text{ VC/unit} = \frac{\$13{,}000}{2{,}000} = \$6.50$$

∴ Substituting in Low

$44,700 = FC + (6,000 × $6.50)

FC = $5,700

Total costs = 5,700 + ($6.50 × no. of units)

$$\text{BEP} = \frac{\text{Fixed costs}}{\text{Cont'n/unit}} = \frac{5{,}700}{8-6.50} = 3{,}800 \text{ units}$$

2 Breakeven revenue = 3,800 × $8 = $30,400

Activity 3: C/S ratio

C/S ratio = 0.1875

Breakeven revenue = $ 30,400

$$\text{C/S ratio} = \frac{\text{Contribution/unit}}{\text{Sales price}} = \frac{\$1.50}{\$8} = 0.1875$$

$$\text{Breakeven revenue} = \frac{\$5{,}700}{0.1875} = \$30{,}400$$

Activity 4: Margin of safety

1 Margin of safety = 1,200 units

Margin of safety = 5,000-3,800 = 1,200 units

2 Margin of safety = 24 %

$$\text{or } \frac{1,200}{5,000} \times 100 = 24\%$$

The sales volume must fall by 24% from budgeted level before a loss is made.

Activity 5: Breakeven chart

Margin of safety (a)

Budgeted profit (b)

Budgeted variable costs (c)

Fixed costs (d)

Activity 6: Profit-volume chart

1 A $ [17,000]

B $ [(-15,000)]

C $ [37,500]

Working

A: profit achieved from $80,000 sales revenue = $17,000

B: loss at zero sales revenue = fixed costs = ($15,000)

C: breakeven point = $37,500 sales revenue (see below)

C/S ratio = 32/80 = 40%

$$\text{Breakeven point} = \frac{\text{Fixed costs}}{\text{C/S ratio}} = \frac{\$15,000}{0.4} = \$37,500 \text{ sales revenue}$$

2 The term used to describe the distance D on the graph is the [margin of safety]

This is the difference between the sales revenue budgeted or achieved, and the revenue required to break even.

3 For the whole of the current year, G Co budgets to achieve a sales value of $900,000. Assuming that the unit variable costs and selling price achieved will be the same as that achieved during May, and that fixed costs for the year will be $180,000, the profit for the whole year will be $ [180,000] .

Working

Contribution achieved	=	sales revenue × C/S ratio	
	=	$900,000	× 0.4
	=	$360,000	
Fixed costs		$180,000	
∴ Profit for whole year		$180,000	

4 The annual margin of safety for G Co's product is [50] % of budgeted sales.

Working

$$\text{Annual breakeven point} = \frac{\text{Fixed costs}}{\text{C/S ratio}} = \frac{\$180{,}000}{0.4} = \$450{,}000 \text{ sales revenue}$$

Margin of safety = $900,000 - $450,000 = $450,000 sales revenue
= 50% of budgeted sales

Activity 7: Impact of changes

1 The line would start at -$20,000 and cross the x axis at $50,000 using

$$\text{BER} = \frac{\text{FC}}{\text{C/S ratio}} = \$\frac{20{,}000}{0.4} = \$50{,}000$$

2 If selling price is $9 per unit, contribution will become ($9 – $4.80) = $4.20 per unit.
The breakeven point (in units) will therefore be

$$\frac{\$15{,}000}{\$4.20} = 3{,}572 \text{ units}$$

The breakeven revenue will be

$$\$\frac{15{,}000}{0.467} = \$32{,}148\ (3{,}572 \times \$9)\ *$$

* Note that this figure is rounded; the breakeven point must always be rounded up to the next whole unit.

Activity 8: Required profit level

If we need to make a profit of $10,000 the sales units volume required is [10,467] units.

$$\text{Sales volume} = \frac{\text{Fixed costs + required profit}}{\text{Unit contribution}}$$

$$= \frac{\$5{,}700 + \$10{,}000}{\$1.50}$$

$$= 10{,}467 \text{ units}$$

Activity 9: Manipulating the breakeven formula

The variable cost is $8.

Working

$$\text{BEP} = \frac{\text{Fixed cost}}{\text{Contribution per unit}} = \$25{,}000 = \frac{\$75{,}000}{\$11 - \text{VC}}$$

So variable cost = $8

Test your learning

1 Use the following to make up four formulae which can be used to calculate the breakeven point.

Contribution per unit
Contribution per unit
Fixed costs
Fixed costs
Contribution required to break even
Contribution required to break even
C/S ratio
C/S ratio

(a) Breakeven point (sales units)

= ____________

or ________________

(b) Breakeven point (sales revenue)

= ____________

or ________________

2 The P/V ratio is a measure of how much profit is earned from each $1 of sales.

O True

O False

3 Profits are maximised at the breakeven point.

O True

O False

4 Fill in the blank:

At the breakeven point, total contribution = [ ] .

5 Fill in the blank:

The total contribution required for a target profit = [ ] .

6 Breakeven charts show approximate levels of profit or loss at different sales volume levels within a limited range.

Required

Which of the following are true?

(1) The sales line starts at the origin.

(2) The fixed costs line runs parallel to the vertical axis.

(3) Breakeven charts have a horizontal axis showing the sales/output (in value or units).

(4) Breakeven charts have a vertical axis showing $ for revenues and costs.

(5) The breakeven point is the intersection of the sales line and the fixed cost line.

- O (1) and (2)
- O (1) and (3)
- O (1), (3) and (4)
- O (1), (3), (4) and (5)

7 Fill in the blank:

On a breakeven chart, the distance between the breakeven point and the expected (or budgeted) sales, in units, indicates the [ ].

8 Thornbury produces a single product X and has a contribution to sales ratio of 35%. The annual fixed costs are $157,500.

Required

In order to break even, how many units of X will Thornbury need to make and sell?

- O 196,000
- O 450,000
- O 60,000
- O Cannot say without more information

9 The following information is available for product H.

Breakeven point	70,000 units
Contribution per unit	$4.50
Margin of safety	30%

Required

Calculate the budgeted profit.

- O $100,000
- O $135,000
- O $315,000
- O $765,000

10 Give five limitations of CVP analysis.

7 Limiting factor analysis

Learning outcomes

Having studied this chapter you will be able to:
• Demonstrate make or buy decisions
• Calculate the profit maximising sales mix after using limiting factor analysis

Chapter context

This chapter helps answer some important questions that any business will have:

- If we can't produce everything our customers want, which products should we give priority to?
- Should we make our products (and all their components) ourselves, or outsource the production?

Syllabus context

This chapter is part of syllabus **Section D**, which looks at **'Decision Making'**.

This syllabus area has a weighting of **35%** and is covered by **Chapters 6 and 7 and 15 to 17**.

In the exam, you will be expected to demonstrate competence in the following areas:

- Make or buy decisions.
- Limiting factor analysis for a multiproduct company that has one scarce resource.

Chapter overview

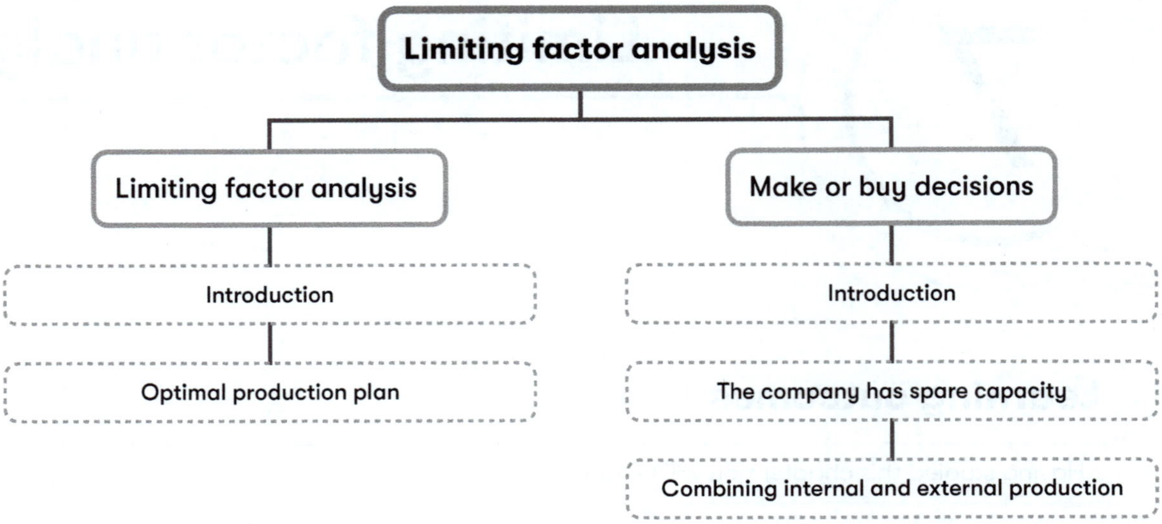

BPP

1 Limiting factor analysis

1.1 Introduction

One of the more common problems faced by management is a situation where there are not enough resources to meet the potential sales demand, and so a decision has to be made about what mix of products to produce, using what resources there are as effectively as possible.

The production and sales plans of a business may be limited by a **limiting factor/scarce resource.**

KEY TERM

> **Limiting factor:** Anything which limits the activity of an entity.
>
> **Scarce resource:** Any limiting factor other than sales demand.

There are a number of potential limiting factors.

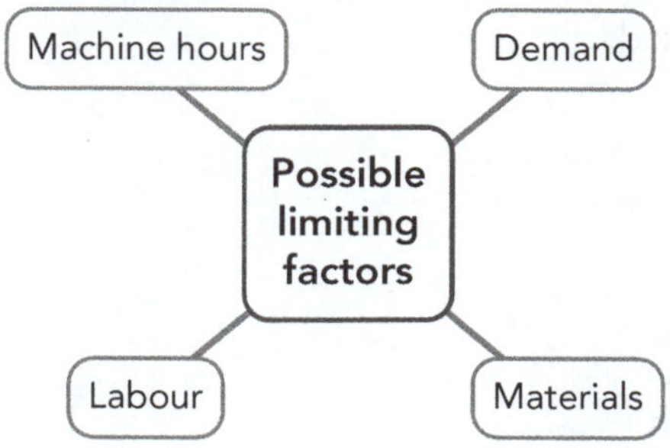

The plans of the business must be built around the limiting factor.

1.2 Optimal production plan

If the business makes more than one product, it will want to find the product mix which will maximise profit given the limiting factor.

KEY TERM

> **Optimal production plan:** The production budget that maximises contribution from the limiting factor.

The limiting factor decision therefore involves the determination of **the contribution earned by each different product from each unit of the limiting factor** or scarce resource.

Illustration 1: Optimal production plan

AB Co makes two products, the Ay and the Be. Unit variable costs are as follows.

	Ay	*Be*
	$	$
Direct materials	1	3
Direct labour ($3 per hour)	6	3
Variable overhead	1	1
	8	7

The sales price per unit is $14 per Ay and $11 per Be. During July 20X2 the available direct labour is limited to 8,000 hours. Sales demand in July is expected to be 3,000 units for Ays and 5,000 units for Bes.

Required

Determine the profit-maximising production mix, assuming that monthly fixed costs are $20,000, and that opening inventories of finished goods and work in progress are nil.

Solution

Step 1 Confirm that the limiting factor is something other than sales demand.

	Ays	*Bes*	*Total*
Labour hours per unit	2 hrs	1 hr	
Sales demand	3,000 units	5,000 units	
Labour hours needed	6,000 hrs	5,000 hrs	11,000 hrs
Labour hours available			8,000 hrs
Shortfall			3,000 hrs

Labour is the limiting factor on production.

Step 2 Identify the contribution earned by each product per unit of limiting factor, that is, per labour hour worked.

	Ays	*Bes*
	$	$
Sales price	14	11
Variable cost	8	7
Unit contribution	6	4
Labour hours per unit	2 hrs	1 hr
Contribution per labour hour (= unit of limiting factor)	$3	$4

Although Ays have a higher unit contribution than Bes, two Bes can be made in the time it takes to make one Ay. Because labour is in short supply it is more profitable to make Bes than Ays.

Step 3 Determine the **optimal production plan.** Sufficient Bes will be made to meet the full sales demand, and the remaining labour hours available will then be used to make Ays.

(a)

Product	*Demand*	*Hours required*	*Hours available*	*Priority of manufacture*
Bes	5,000	5,000	5,000	1st
Ays	3,000	6,000	3,000 (bal)	2nd
		11,000	8,000	

(b)

Product	*Units*	*Hours needed*	*Contribution per hour*	*Total*
			$	$
Bes	5,000	5,000	4	20,000
Ays	1,500	3,000	3	9,000
		8,000		29,000
Less fixed costs				20,000
Profit				9,000

Conclusion

(1) Unit contribution is **not** the correct way to decide priorities.

(2) Labour hours are the scarce resource, and therefore contribution **per labour hour** is the correct way to decide priorities.

(3) The Be earns $4 contribution per labour hour, and the Ay earns $3 contribution per labour hour. Bes therefore make more profitable use of the scarce resource, and should be manufactured first.

Activity 1: Limiting factors

Machine time available is 300 hours.

Labour time available is 200 hours.

	A	B	C
	$	$	$
Selling price	150	120	100
Variable costs	100	80	70
Fixed costs	20	20	20
	30	20	10
Machine time	5 hrs	2 hrs	1 hr
Labour time	2 hrs	1 hr	0.5 hrs
Demand	50	50	50

Required

1 What is the limiting factor? machine time

2 The contribution per limiting factor for

A is $ 10

B is $ 20

C is $ 30

3 The optimum number of units to be produced of

A is 30 units

B is 50 units

C is 50 units

Solution

2 Make or buy decisions

2.1 Introduction

We looked at **relevant costing** principles in Chapter 2. One particular decision where relevant costing principles need to be applied is whether a company should make a product itself or buy it in from an outside supplier. The approach taken will depend on whether the company has spare capacity available to manufacture all of its required production internally, or whether there are limiting factors.

2.2 The company has spare capacity

The relevant cost of making the product will include all variable costs and any directly attributable fixed costs (that would be avoided if production were to cease). This is compared to the cost of purchasing the product externally.

Activity 2: Simple make or buy decisions

One of the items that GA Co currently manufactures is component MRB which is then used in the production of a variety of its products. The machine on which MRB is produced has sufficient capacity to meet all of GA Co's requirements.

The cost card for component MRB is:

	$
Direct materials	6.50
Direct wages	2.75
Variable production overheads	3.00
Fixed production overheads	5.25
	17.50

The fixed production overheads represent the rent and rates on the factory and as such would not be avoided if the component was not manufactured.

Required

1 What is the relevant cost of making component MRB? (We covered relevant costing in an earlier chapter.)

2 Should GA Co accept a quote of $14.75 from an external supplier for component MRB?

Solution

2.3 Combining internal and external production

An organisation might **want to do more things than it has the resources for,** and so its alternatives would be as follows.

(a) Make the best use of the available resources and ignore the opportunities to buy help in from outside by subcontracting some of the work

(b) Combine internal resources with buying externally so as to produce (and sell) more and so increase profitability

We can maximise profit by minimising costs. Total costs will be minimised if those units bought have the lowest extra variable cost per unit of scarce resource saved by buying. Extra variable cost is the difference between the variable cost of in-house production and the cost of buying from the subcontractor.

Illustration 2: Make or buy decisions with scarce resources

MM manufactures three components, S, A and T, using the same machines for each. The budget for the next year calls for the production and assembly of 4,000 of each component. The variable production cost per unit of the final product is as follows.

Relevant cost to make our self.

	Machine hours	Variable cost
		$
1 unit of S	3	20
1 unit of A	2	36
1 unit of T	4	24
Assembly		20
		100

Only 24,000 hours of machine time will be available during the year, and a subcontractor has quoted the following unit prices for supplying components: S $29; A $40; T $34.

Required

Advise MM which products should be manufactured internally, and which subcontracted.

3 x 4 000 = 12,000
2 x 4000 = 8,000
4 x 4000 = 16,000
36,000 – Limiting factor machine time.

Solution

The organisation's budget calls for 36,000 hours of machine time, if all the components are to be produced in-house. Only 24,000 hours are available, and so there is a shortfall of 12,000 hours of machine time, which is therefore a limiting factor. The shortage can be overcome by subcontracting the equivalent of 12,000 machine hours of output to the subcontractor.

The assembly costs are not relevant costs because they are unaffected by the decision.

The decision rule is to **minimise the extra variable costs of subcontracting per unit of scarce resource saved** (that is, per machine hour saved).

	S	A	T
	$	$	$
Variable cost of making	20	36	24
Variable cost of buying	29	40	34
Extra variable cost of buying	9	4	10
Machine hours saved by buying	3 hrs	2 hrs	4 hrs
Extra variable cost of buying per hour saved	$3	$2	$2.50

This analysis shows that it is **cheaper to buy A than to buy T** and it is **most expensive to buy S.** The **priority for making** the components in-house will be in the **reverse order:** S, then T, then A. There are enough machine hours to make all 4,000 units of S (12,000 hours) and to produce 3,000 units of T (another 12,000 hours). 12,000 hours' production of T and A must be subcontracted.

The cost-minimising and so profit-maximising make and buy schedule is as follows.

Component		*Machine hours used/saved*	*Number of units*	*Unit variable cost*	*Total variable cost*
				$	$
Make:	S	12,000	4,000	20	80,000
	T	12,000	3,000	24	72,000
		24,000			152,000
Buy:	T	4,000	1,000	34	34,000
	A	8,000	4,000	40	160,000
		12,000			346,000

Total variable cost of components, excluding assembly costs = $346,000

Activity 3: Make or buy with scarce resources

TW manufactures two products, the D and the E, using the same material for each. Annual demand for the D is 9,000 units, while demand for the E is 12,000 units. The variable production cost per unit of the D is $10, that of the E $15. The D requires 3.5 kg of raw material per unit; the E requires 8 kg of raw material per unit. Supply of raw material will be limited to 87,500 kg during the year.

A subcontractor has quoted prices of $17 per unit for the D and $25 per unit for the E to supply the product. How many of each product should TW manufacture in order to maximise profits?

Required

Fill in the blanks in the sentence below.

TW should manufacture [9000 ✓] units of D and [7000 ✓] units of E.

Solution

1. what is the limiting factor
2. variable cost per unit
3. cost to buy
   difference
4. difference ÷ limiting factor
5. rank
6. optimal prodn plan

---

7. what should make + buy

(1)

	D	E
Demand	9000	12,000
variable cost	10	15
raw material	3.5 kg	8 kg

3.5 × 9000 = 31,500 kg
8 × 12,000 = 96,000 kg
127,500

limited 87,500

(2)

	D	E
	10	15
buy	17	25
	7	10

Chapter summary

Limiting factor analysis

Limiting factor analysis

Introduction

- Limiting factor – anything which limits the activity of an entity
- Insufficient resources to meet demand

Optimal production plan

- Optimal production plan – the production budget that maximises contribution from the limiting factor
- Product mix which will maximise profit given the limiting factor

Make or buy decisions

Introduction

- Should a company should make a product itself or buy it in from an outside supplier?

The company has spare capacity

- Relevant cost is all variable costs and any directly attributable fixed costs

Combining internal and external production

- Where an organisation wants to do more things than it has the resources for
- Make the best use of the available resources and ignore the opportunities to buy help in from outside by subcontracting some of the work
- Combine internal resources with buying externally so as to produce (and sell) more and so increase profitability

Key terms

Limiting factor: Anything which limits the activity of an entity.

Scarce resource: Any limiting factor other than sales demand.

Optimal production plan: The production budget that maximises contribution from the limiting factor.

D £

(3) 7 / 3.5 10 / 8

$ 2 $ 1.25

(4) (1) (2)

(5) optimal prodn plan.

make 9000 × 3.5 = 31,500

7000 × 8 = 56,000

units 87,500

(6) Buy 2000 × 8 = 16,000 ugs

(7) variable costs

9000 × 10 = 90,000

7000 × 15 = 105,000

195,000

5000 × 25 = 125,000

Activity answers

Activity 1: Limiting factors

1 Machine hours

Labour time required	=	(50 × 2 hrs) + (50 × 1 hr) + (50 × 0.5 hrs)
	=	175 hrs
Labour time available	=	200 hrs
Machine time required	=	(50 × 5 hrs) + (50 × 2 hrs) – (50 × 1 hr)
	=	400 hrs
Machine time available	=	300 hrs

2 A is $ [10]

B is $ [20]

C is $ [30]

3 A is [30] units

B is [50] units

C is [50] units

Working

	A	*B*	*C*
Contribution/unit	$50	$40	$30
÷ limiting resource	÷ 5 hrs	÷ 2 hrs	÷ 1 hr
Contribution/machine hour	$10	$20	$30
Rank	3rd	2nd	1st

Production schedule	*Hrs used*
(1) Produce maximum 50 of C	50
(2) Produce maximum 50 of B	100
(3) Produce A with remaining hours	
$\frac{150}{5} = 30$ units	150
	300

Activity 2: Simple make or buy decisions

1 The relevant cost of making component MRB is:

	$
Direct materials	6.50

	$
Direct wages	2.75
Variable production overheads	3.00
Fixed production overheads	–
	12.25

2 The relevant cost of buying component MRB is $14.75.

Therefore GA Co should continue to make component MRB.

Activity 3: Make or buy with scarce resources

TW should manufacture [9,000] units of D and [7,000] units of E.

	D	*E*
	$ per unit	$ per unit
Variable cost of making	10	15
Variable cost of buying	17	25
Extra variable cost of buying	7	10
Raw material saved by buying	3.5 kg	8 kg
Extra variable cost of buying per kg saved	$2	$1.25
Priority for internal manufacture	1st	2nd

Production plan	*Material used*
	kg
∴ Make D (9,000 × 3.5 kg)	31,500
E (7,000 × 8 kg)	56,000
Total materials consumed (maximum available)	87,500

The remaining 5,000 units of E should be purchased from the subcontractor.

Test your learning

1 When determining the optimum production plan using limiting factor analysis, what three steps are involved?

Step 1 find the limiting factor

Step 2 work out contribution

Step 3 contribution / limited factor

2 Choose the correct word from below.

When there is just one limiting factor, the product with the biggest ▼ contribution earning ability per unit of limiting factor should be produced first.

Pull down list

- Biggest
- Smallest

3 Which of the following is not an example of a limiting factor?

- ○ Sales demand
- ○ Materials
- ○ Machine time
- ● Profit

4 A milkshake bar has three different products; the Chocolate Extreme, the Toffee Deluxe and the Strawberry Sensation. Along with flavourings (which are not restricted), they each require the following resources:

	CE	TD	SS
Ice cream	100 g	150 g	200 g
Milk	500 ml	400 ml	250 ml
Staff time	10 minutes	15 minutes	20 minutes
Daily demand	100	200	75

Due to shortages, only 60 kg of ice cream, 140 litres of milk and 100 hours of staff time are available.

Required

What is the limiting factor?

- ○ Ice cream
- ● Milk
- ○ Staff time
- ○ Demand

5 If a Chocolate Extreme generates contribution of \$10 per unit, a Toffee Deluxe \$9 and a Strawberry Sensation \$6, what is the optimal production plan?

- [x] 100 CE, 200 TD and 40 SS
- [ ] 100 CE, 200 TD and 75 SS
- [x] 82 CE, 200 TD and 75 SS
- [ ] 100 CE, 178 TD and 75 SS

X

ice cream

CE = 100g x 100 = 10,000g

= 10kg

TD = 150g x 200 = 30,000g

30kg

60kg ice cream

SS = 200g x 75 = 15,000g

= 15kg.

55kg.

Milk

CE = 500ml x 100 = 50000 ml

50 litres

TD = 400 x 200 = 80 litres.

SS = 250 x 75 = 18.75 litres.

148.75 = Milk is limiting factor

staff time:

CE = 10 x 100 = 1000 minutes.

TD = 15 x 200 = 3000 mins

SS = 20 x 75 = 1500 mins

60,000 mins

5500

① limiting factor is milk

② contribution per limiting factor.

	CE	TD	SS
	10 / 50	9 / 80	6 / 18.75
X	$ 5	$ 8.8	$ 3.13

③ Rank. | ② | ① | ③

TD ~~max make~~

400 x [200] = 80 litres = 80,000 ml

CE 500 x [100] = 50 litres = 50,000

SS 250 x [40] = 10 litres = 10,000 ml

140 litres.

↓

140,000 ml

② contribution per limiting factor :

CE 10 / 50 = 20

TD = 9/40 x 100 = 22.5 ②

SS 6 / 25 = [24] ③ ①

75 = SS

TD = 200

CE = 82.

③ optimal plan.

SS = 250 x [75] = 18,750 ml

TD = 400 x [200] = 80,000 ml

CE = 500 x 82.5 = 41,250 ml

140,000 ml

8 Standard costing

Learning outcomes

Having studied this chapter you will be able to:
• Explain why planned standard costs, prices and volumes are useful

Chapter context

This brief chapter introduces the concept of standard costing: estimating the cost of a unit of what we produce in advance. This is useful for planning the resources an organisation requires, setting targets, and also evaluating actual performance. This role in evaluating performance will be investigated in detail in the following chapter.

Syllabus context

This chapter is part of syllabus **Section C**, which looks at **'Planning and Control'**.

This syllabus area has a weighting of **30%** and is covered by **Chapters 8 to 14**.

In the exam, you will be expected to demonstrate competence in the following areas:

- Principles of standard costing.

Chapter overview

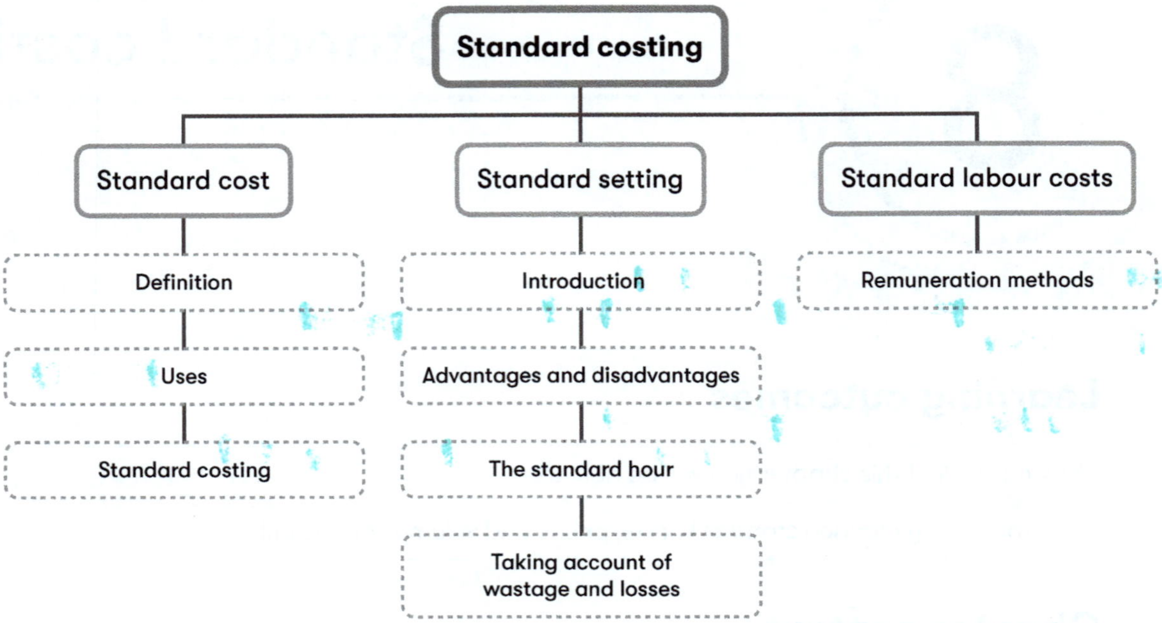

1 Standard cost

1.1 Definition

KEY TERM

Standard cost: An estimated unit cost, prepared in advance and calculated from management expectations of:

(a) Efficiency levels in the use of materials and labour;

(b) The expected price of materials, labour and expenses; and

(c) Budgeted overhead costs and activity levels.

1.2 Uses

It can be used in budgetary control (ie variance analysis – see Chapter 11) or as a means of valuing inventories and the cost of production.

Standard costing enables the principle of **management by exception** to be practised.

KEY TERM

Management by exception: The 'Practice of concentrating on activities that require attention and ignoring those which appear to be conforming to expectations. Typically standard cost variances or variances from budget are used to identify those activities that require attention'. (CIMA Official Terminology, 2005)

1.3 Standard costing

Standard costing may be used in a system of absorption costing or marginal costing. A **standard cost card** will usually be prepared for each product manufactured by the business.

Example: Standard cost card

STANDARD COST CARD – PRODUCT 1234

	$	$
Direct materials		
Material X: 3 kg at $4 per kg	12	
Material Y: 9 litres at $2 per litre	18	
		30
Direct labour		
Grade A: 6 hours at $7 per hour	42	
Grade B: 8 hours at $8 per hour	64	
		106
Standard direct cost		136
Variable production overhead: 14 hours at $0.50 per hour		7
Standard variable cost of production		143
Fixed production overhead: 14 hours at $4.50 per hour		63
Standard full production cost		206
Administration and marketing overhead		15

	$	$
Standard cost of sale		221
Standard profit		20
Standard sales price		241

Activity 1: Standard cost card preparation

B Company makes one product, the J. Two types of labour are involved in the preparation of a J, skilled and semi-skilled. Skilled labour is paid $10 per hour and semi-skilled $5 per hour. Twice as many skilled labour hours as semi-skilled labour hours are needed to produce a J, four semi-skilled labour hours being needed.

A J is made up of three different direct materials. Seven kilograms of direct material A, four litres of direct material B and three metres of direct material C are needed. Direct material A costs $1 per kilogram, direct material B $2 per litre and direct material C $3 per metre.

Variable production overheads are incurred at B Company at the rate of $2.50 per direct labour (skilled) hour.

A system of absorption costing is in operation at B Company. The basis of absorption is direct labour (skilled) hours. For the forthcoming accounting period, budgeted fixed production overheads are $250,000 and budgeted production of the J is 5,000 units.

Administration, selling and distribution overheads are added to products at the rate of $10 per unit.

A mark-up of 25% is made on the J.

Required

Using the above information complete the standard cost card below for the J.

STANDARD COST CARD – PRODUCT J

		$	$
Direct materials			
A	1 x 7	7	
B	4 x 2	8	
C	3 x 3	9	
			24
Direct Labour			
	skilled 10 x 8	80	
	semi skilled 5 x 4	20	
			100
Standard direct cost			124
Variable production overhead	8 x 2.5		20
Standard variable cost of production			144
Fixed production overhead	250,000/5000		50

	$	$
Standard full production cost		194
Administration, selling and distribution overhead		10
Standard cost of sale		204
Standard Profit		51
Standard sales price		255

Solution

selling price = 125%
cost = 100% 204
profit = 25%

2 Standard setting

2.1 Introduction

Standard setting can be challenging for management. Accurate information is required from various departments (for example, the purchasing department will provide information on current and expected material prices; human resources will confirm current rates of pay and pay rises agreed with trade unions). Inflation will also need to be considered and factored into the standard cost card. Management also need to decide how challenging the standard should be. There are four different types of performance standard that an organisation could aim for:

Bases

Expected/attainable standards
- Based on efficient, not perfect, operating conditions
- Should be practically possible
- Can motivate employees to improve level of performance

Ideal standards
- Perfect operating conditions
- No wastage, breakdowns or idle time
- Difficult to achieve
- Demotivating for staff

Current standards
- Based on current performance levels
- Include current inefficiencies
- Can lead to stagnation and underperformance

Basic standards
- Unaltered over long periods of time
- Become outdated quickly
- Least useful to evaluate strengths or weaknesses in production performance

2.2 Advantages and disadvantages

Advantages of setting standards	Disadvantages of setting standards
(a) Facilitates budgetary control	(a) Difficult to forecast accurately
(b) Leads to more accurate budgeting	(b) Time consuming
(c) Assists performance measurement	(c) Regular revision required
(d) Assists in target setting for staff	(d) Demotivating if wrong
(e) Assists in price setting	(e) Not suitable if output is not homogenous
(f) Simplifies bookkeeping	(f) Not focused on continuous improvement

2.3 The standard hour

KEY TERM

Standard hour: Can be used to overcome the problem of how to measure output when a number of dissimilar products are manufactured.

Example: Standard hour

S Co manufactures plates, mugs and eggcups. Production during the first two quarters of 20X5 was as follows.

	Quarter 1	*Quarter 2*
Plates	1,000	800
Mugs	1,200	1,500
Eggcups	800	900

The fact that 3,000 products were produced in Quarter 1 and 3,200 in Quarter 2 does not tell us anything about S Co's performance over the two periods because plates, mugs and eggcups are so different. The fact that the production mix has changed is not revealed by considering the total number of units produced. This is where the concept of the standard hour is useful.

The standard hour (or standard minute) is the **amount of work achievable, at standard efficiency levels, in an hour or minute.**

(a) The standard time allowed to produce one unit of each of S Co's products is as follows.

	Standard time
Plate	$^1/_2$ hour
Mug	$^1/_3$ hour
Eggcup	$^1/_4$ hour

(b) By measuring the standard hours of output in each quarter, a more useful output measure is obtained.

			Quarter 1		*Quarter 2*
Product	*Standard hours per unit*	*Production*	*Standard hours*	*Production*	*Standard hours*
Plate	$^1/_2$	1,000	500	800	400
Mug	$^1/_3$	1,200	400	1,500	500
Eggcup	$^1/_4$	800	200	900	225

Product	Standard hours per unit	Production	Quarter 1 Standard hours	Production	Quarter 2 Standard hours
			1,100		1,125

The output level in the two quarters was therefore very similar.

2.4 Taking account of wastage and losses

If, during processing, the quantity of material input to the process is likely to reduce (due to wastage or evaporation), the quantity input must be greater than the quantity in the finished product and a material standard must take account of this.

Suppose that the fresh raspberry juice content of a litre of Purple Pop is 100ml and that there is a 10% loss of raspberry juice during process due to evaporation. The standard material usage of raspberry juice per litre of Purple Pop will be:

$$100\text{ml} \times \frac{100\%}{(100-10)\%} = 100\text{ml} \times \frac{100\%}{90\%} = 111.11\text{ml}$$

3 Standard labour costs

3.1 Remuneration methods

(a) **Time-based systems.** These are based on the principle of paying an employee for the hours attended, regardless of the amount of work achieved (wages = hours worked × rate of pay per hour).

- (i) Overtime premium = **extra** rate per hour for hours over and above the basic hours.
- (ii) Quality of output is more important than quantity of output.
- (iii) There is no incentive for improvements in employee performance.

(b) **Piecework systems.**

KEY TERM

> **Piecework system:** A scheme where an employee is paid per unit of output.

Pay is calculated according to the output achieved (wages = units produced × rate of pay per unit).

(c) **Incentive/bonus schemes.** There are a variety of these schemes, all of which are designed to encourage workers to be more productive.

Activity 2: Remuneration systems

Match the descriptions of remuneration schemes to the graphs below.

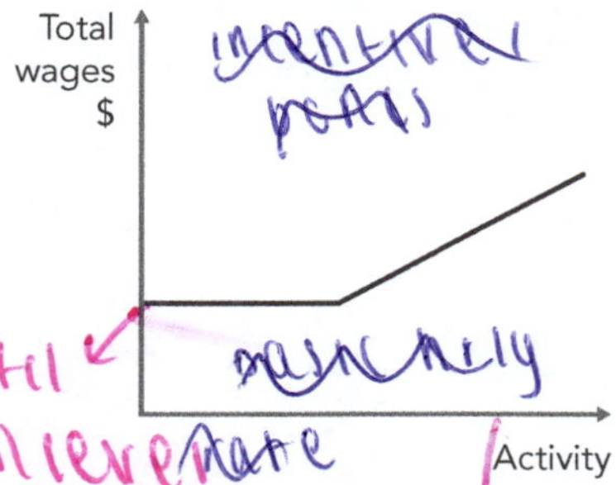

Graph A

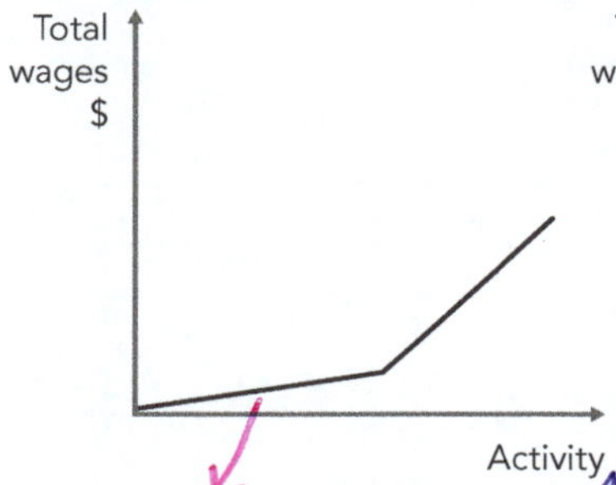

Graph B

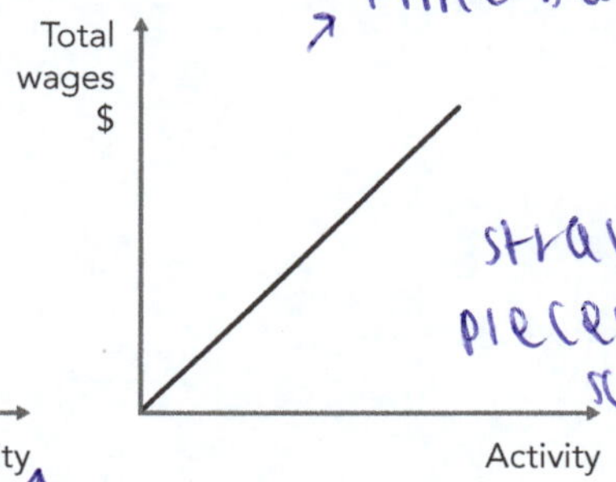

Graph C

Descriptions

(1) A basic hourly rate is paid for hours worked, with an overtime premium payable for hours worked in excess of 35 per week.

(2) A straight piecework scheme is operated.

(3) A straight piecework scheme is operated, with a minimum guaranteed weekly wage.

Solution

Chapter summary

Standard costing

Standard cost

Definition
- An estimated unit cost, prepared in advance and calculated from management expectations

Uses
- Management by exception

Standard costing
- Used in management and absorption costing

Standard setting

Introduction
- Expected/attainable and ideal standards
- Current and basic standards

Advantages and disadvantages
- Advantages and disadvantages

The standard hour
- Standard hour – used to overcome the problem of how to measure output when a number of dissimilar products are manufactured

Taking account of wastage and losses
- Wastage and losses

Standard labour costs

Remuneration methods
- Time-based systems
- Piecework systems

Key terms

Standard cost: An estimated unit cost, prepared in advance and calculated from management expectations of:

(a) Efficiency levels in the use of materials and labour;

(b) The expected price of materials, labour and expenses; and

(c) Budgeted overhead costs and activity levels.

Management by exception: The 'Practice of concentrating on activities that require attention and ignoring those which appear to be conforming to expectations. Typically standard cost variances or variances from budget are used to identify those activities that require attention'.

(CIMA Official Terminology, 2005)

Standard hour: Can be used to overcome the problem of how to measure output when a number of dissimilar products are manufactured.

Piecework system: A scheme where an employee is paid per unit of output.

Activity answers

Activity 1: Standard cost card preparation

STANDARD COST CARD – PRODUCT J

	$	$
Direct materials		
A 7k g × $1	7	
B 4 litres × $2	8	
C 3m × $3	9	
		24
Direct Labour		
Skilled: 8 × $10	80	
Semi-skilled: 4 × $5	20	
		100
Standard direct cost		124
Variable production overhead 8 × $2.50		20
Standard variable cost of production		144
Fixed production overhead 8 × $6.25 (W)		50
Standard full production cost		194
Administration, selling and distribution overhead		10
Standard cost of sale		204
Standard Profit 25% × 204		51
Standard sales price		255

Working

$$\text{Overhead absorption rate} = \frac{\$250{,}000}{5{,}000 \times 8} = \$6.25 \text{ per skilled labour hour}$$

Activity 2: Remuneration systems

(1) Graph B

(2) Graph C

(3) Graph A

Test your learning

1 Choose the correct words from those in the pull down lists below.

A standard cost is a (1) ▼ (2) ▼ cost.

Pull down list 1

- Historical
- Planned

Pull down list 2

- Total
- Unit

2 The only use of standard costing is to value inventory.

Required

○ True

○ False

3 A control technique which compares standard costs and revenues with actual results to obtain variances which are used to stimulate improved performance is known as:

○ Standard costing

○ Variance analysis

○ Budgetary control

○ Budgeting

4 Standard costs may only be used in absorption costing.

Required

○ True

○ False

5 Four types of performance standard are:

(1) [ ]

(2) [ ]

(3) [ ]

(4) [ ]

6 Fill in the blank:

The formula for standard material cost per unit = [ ]

7 List three problems in setting standards.

8 Which **three** of the following are advantages of standard costing?

☐ Standards are an aid to more accurate budgeting.

- [x] Cost consciousness is stimulated.
- [ ] Inflation can be dealt with easily.
- [x] The principle of management by exception can be operated.

3 problems

- Demotivating for staff.
- unrealistic
- Doesn't account for external factors
- Not completely accurate / reliable.

9 Flexible budgeting

Learning outcomes

Having studied this chapter you will be able to:
• Prepare a flexible budget
• Calculate budget variances

Chapter context

The chapter looks at the role of budgeting in planning and control. At the planning stage it can be useful to produce several budgets based on different levels of activity so that managers can understand the impact on the business of producing and selling more or less than the main target. In using budgets to control an organisation, it makes sense to make the comparison with the actual results as meaningful as possible by adjusting the budget to reflect the actual level of output.

Syllabus context

This chapter is part of syllabus **Section C**, which looks at **'Planning and Control'**.

This syllabus area has a weighting of **30%** and is covered by **Chapters 8 to 14**.

In the exam, you will be expected to demonstrate competence in the following areas:

- Fixed and flexible budgeting.
- Budget variances.

Chapter overview

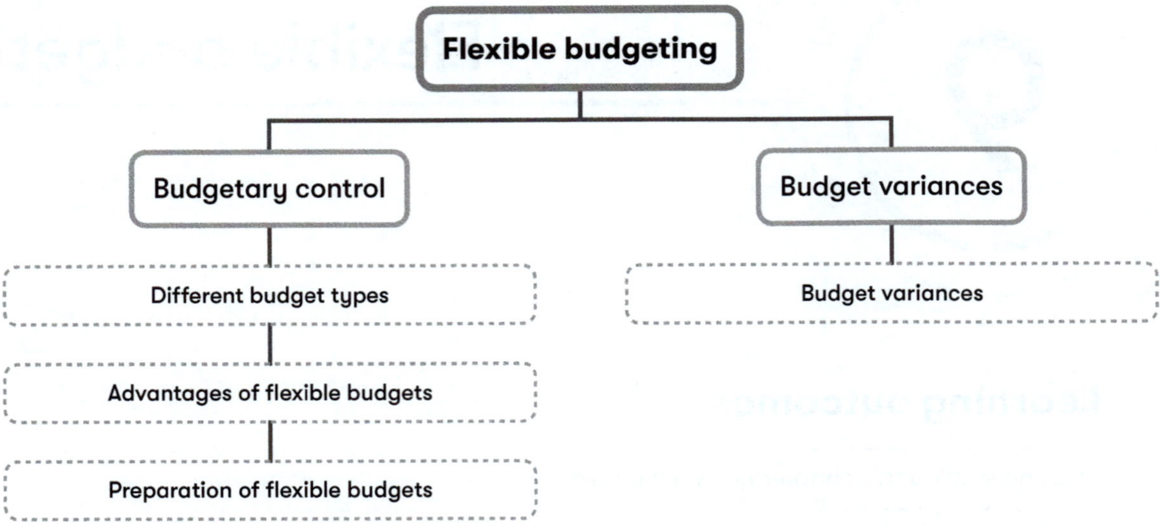

1 Budgetary control

1.1 Different budget types

Budgetary control is obtained by comparing actual results against budget. In order for that comparison to be meaningful, the budget needs to be amended or 'flexed' in line with the actual activity level.

KEY TERM

Fixed budget: The original budget set up for budgeted sales and production.

Flexible budget: A budget which is designed to change as volume of activity changes.

Flexed budget: Uses the original budget figures but for actual sales and production.

1.2 Advantages of flexible budgets

A **flexible budget** has two advantages.

(a) At the **planning** stage, it may be helpful to know what the effects would be if the actual outcome differs from the prediction. For example, a company may budget to sell 10,000 units of its product, but may prepare flexible budgets based on sales of, say, 8,000 and 12,000 units. This would enable **contingency plans** to be drawn up if necessary.

(b) At the end of each month or year, actual results may be compared with the relevant activity level in the flexible budget as a **control** procedure.

1.3 Preparation of flexible budgets

Step 1 The first step in the preparation of a flexible budget is the determination of cost behaviour patterns, which means deciding whether costs are fixed, variable or semi-variable.

- Fixed costs are easy to spot. They remain constant as activity levels change.
- For non-fixed costs, divide each cost figure by the related activity level. If the cost is a variable cost, the cost per unit will remain constant. If the cost is a semi-variable cost, the unit rate will reduce as activity levels increase.

Step 2 The second step in the preparation of a flexible budget is to calculate the **budget cost allowance** for each cost item.

KEY TERM

Budget cost allowance: The budgeted costs in the flexed budget for each cost item.

Budget cost allowance = budgeted fixed cost* + (number of units × variable cost per unit)**

* nil for variable cost

** nil for fixed cost

Semi-variable costs therefore need splitting into their fixed and variable components so that the budget cost allowance can be calculated.

Illustration 1: Preparing a flexible budget

Prepare a budget for 20X6 for the direct labour costs and overhead expenses of a production department flexed at the activity levels of 80%, 90% and 100%, using the information listed below.

(1) The direct labour hourly rate is expected to be $3.75.

(2) 100% activity represents 60,000 direct labour hours.

(3) Variable costs

Indirect labour	$0.75 per direct labour hour
Consumable supplies	$0.375 per direct labour hour

Canteen and other welfare services	6% of direct and indirect labour costs

(4) Semi variable costs are expected to relate to the direct labour hours in the same manner as for the last five years.

Year	*Direct labour hours*	*Semi-variable costs*
		$
20X1	64,000	20,800
20X2	59,000	19,800
20X3	53,000	18,600
20X4	49,000	17,800
20X5	40,000 (estimate)	16,000 (estimate)

(5) *Fixed costs*

	$
Depreciation	18,000
Maintenance	10,000
Insurance	4,000
Rates	15,000
Management salaries	25,000

(6) Inflation is to be ignored.

Solution

	80% level	*90% level*	*100% level*
	48,000 hrs	*54,000 hrs*	*60,000 hrs*
	$'000	$'000	$'000
Direct labour	180.00	202.50	225.0
Other variable costs			
Indirect labour	36.00	40.50	45.0
Consumable supplies	18.00	20.25	22.5
Canteen etc	12.96	14.58	16.2
Total variable costs ($5.145 per hour)	246.96	277.83	308.7
Semi-variable costs (W)	17.60	18.80	20.0
Fixed costs			
Depreciation	18.00	18.00	18.0
Maintenance	10.00	10.00	10.0
Insurance	4.00	4.00	4.0
Rates	15.00	15.00	15.0
Management salaries	25.00	25.00	25.0
Budgeted costs	336.56	368.63	400.7

Working

Using the high/low method:

	$
Total cost of 64,000 hours	20,800
Total cost of 40,000 hours	16,000
Variable cost of 24,000 hours	4,800
Variable cost per hour ($4,800/24,000)	$0.20

	$
Total cost of 64,000 hours	20,800
Variable cost of 64,000 hours (× $0.20)	12,800
Fixed costs	8,000

Semi variable costs are calculated as follows.

		$
60,000 hours	(60,000 × $0.20) + $8,000	20,000
54,000 hours	(54,000 × $0.20) + $8,000	18,800
48,000 hours	(48,000 × $0.20) + $8,000	17,600

Activity 1: Flexing a budget

Cosmic Co manufactures and sells a single product, X.

Cosmic's management uses a flexible budgeting system to control costs.

Output and sales (units)	2,000	2,750
Budget costs:	$	$
Direct material	4,000	5,500
Direct labour	10,000	12,250
Fixed production overheads	5,500	5,500
Selling and distribution overheads	1,000	1,375
Total expenditure	20,500	24,625

Production and sales of X amounted to 2,550 during 20Y7.

There are no opening or closing inventories for 20Y7. The total budgeted costs in the flexed budget for 20Y7 (known as the budget cost allowance) will be:

Required

1 Fill in the blank:

Direct material $ ______

2 Fill in the blank:

Direct labour (semi-variable cost) $ ______

3 Fill in the blank:

Fixed production overheads $ [ ]

4 Fill in the blank:

Selling and distribution overheads $ [ ]

Solution

---

2 Budget variances

KEY TERM

Budget variances: The differences between the flexible budget figures and the actual results. Control involves comparing a flexible budget (based on the actual activity level) with actual results.

The total variance between the original fixed budget and the actual results can be broken down into:

KEY TERM

Volume variance: Fixed budget v flexed budget. This quantifies the difference in costs/profits that is due to changes in the volume of output.

Expenditure variance: Flexed budget v actual results. This variance is meaningful for cost control. It is a measure of what managers should have achieved, given the production that took place, compared to what was actually achieved.

Favourable variance (F) : A variance where results were better than expected.

Adverse variance (A) : Results are worse than expected.

Activity 2: Budget variances

Dot Co issued its production budget based on a budget output of 2,000 units. The actual output for the period was 1,500 units.

	Budget	Actual
Output (units)	2,000	1,500
	$	$
Prime cost	50,000	31,000
Fixed overheads	130,000	132,000
Total cost	180,000	163,000

→ what should've happened

Flexed vs actual - 163,000

Required

1 What was the expenditure variance?

- O $17,000 favourable
- O $18,000 adverse
- O $4,500 favourable 4500
- O $4,500 adverse

~~37,500~~

37,500
130,000
167,500

167,500 -
163,000

2 What was the volume variance? → ~~actual~~

- O $12,500 favourable
- O $17,000 favourable
- O $4,500 favourable
- O $12,000 adverse

Fixed vs flexed. ✓

original vs what should've happened.

Solution

180,000 - 167,500

= 12,500

vol - fixed vs flexed

expenditure - flexed vs actual

Fixed - budgeted - original budget

→ moves budget.

Flexible ~~fixed~~ - based on volume; budget on activity

Flexed - based on actual prodn.

163,000 = actual

flexed = actual activity

1500

fixed = 180,000

Chapter summary

Flexible budgeting

Budgetary control

Different budget types
- Fixed budget
- Flexible budget
- Flexed budget

Advantages of flexible budgets
- A flexible budget has two advantages

Preparation of flexible budgets
- Determination of cost behaviour patterns
- Calculate the budget cost allowance for each cost item
- Budget cost allowance = budgeted fixed cost + (number of units × variable cost per unit)

Budget variances

Budget variances
- Volume variance
- Expenditure variance
- Favourable variance
- Adverse variance

Key terms

Fixed budget: The original budget set up for budgeted sales and production.

Flexible budget: A budget which is designed to change as volume of activity changes.

Flexed budget: Uses the original budget figures but for actual sales and production.

Budget cost allowance: The budgeted costs in the flexed budget for each cost item.

Budget variances: The differences between the flexible budget figures and the actual results. Control involves comparing a flexible budget (based on the actual activity level) with actual results.

Volume variance: Fixed budget v flexed budget. This quantifies the difference in costs/profits that is due to changes in the volume of output.

Expenditure variance: Flexed budget v actual results. This variance is meaningful for cost control. It is a measure of what managers should have achieved, given the production that took place, compared to what was actually achieved.

Favourable variance (F) : A variance where results were better than expected.

Adverse variance (A) : Results are worse than expected.

Activity answers

Activity 1: Flexing a budget

1 Direct material $ 5,100

Direct material is a variable cost of 4,000/2,000 = $2 per X.

Budget for 2,550 is = 2,550 X $2 = $5,100

2 Direct labour (semi-variable cost) $ 4,000

Direct labour is a semi-variable cost, therefore use the high-low method.

	Units of X	$
High	2,750	12,250
Low	2,000	10,000
Difference	750	2,250

Variable cost per unit = 2,250/750 = $3

Fixed cost: 12,250 = FC + (3)(2,750)

FC = $4,000

3 Fixed production overheads $ 5,500

Fixed cost = 5,500

4 Selling and distribution overheads $ 1,275

Selling and distribution is a variable cost of 1,000/2,000 = $0.50 per unit

Flexed budget for 2,550 units = 2,550 X $0.50 = $1,275.

Activity 2: Budget variances

1 The correct answer is: $4,500 favourable

Actual results		163,000
Flexible budgets		
Prime cost		
$\left(\frac{50,000}{2,000} \times 1,500 \text{ units}\right)$	37,500	
Fixed overheads	130,000	
		167,500
		4,500 F

2 The correct answer is: $12,500 favourable

Fixed budget	180,000
Flexible budget	167,500
	12,500 F

Test your learning

1 Fill in the blanks with the word 'fixed' or the word 'flexible'.

(1) At the planning stage, a [ ] budget can show what the effects would be if the actual outcome differs from the prediction.

(2) At the end of each period, actual results may be compared with the relevant activity level in the [ ] budget as a control procedure.

(3) Master budgets are [ ] budgets.

2 Flexible budgets are normally prepared on a marginal costing basis.

Required

- O True
- O False

3 Fill in the gaps.

Budget cost allowance = [ ] + ([ ] × [ ])

4 What are the disadvantages of using a fixed budget for budgetary control?

5 Distinguish between a fixed budget and a flexible budget.

6 What are the two main reasons for differences between a fixed budget profit and actual profit?

7 Fill in the gaps.

A flexible budget is a budget which, by recognising [ ], is designed to [ ] as the level of activity changes.

8 A flexible budget is:

- O A budget which by recognising different cost behaviour patterns is designed to change as the volume of activity changes
- O A budget for a defined period of time which includes planned revenues, expenses, assets, liabilities and cash flow
- O A budget which is prepared for a period of one year which is reviewed monthly, whereby each time actual results are reported, a further forecast period is added and the intermediate period forecasts are updated
- O A budget of semi-variable production costs only

9 Which of the following statements about a fixed budget is/are correct? A fixed budget is:

- ☐ A budget which ignores inflation
- ☐ A budget for fixed assets
- ☐ A budget which is most generally used for planning purposes
- ☐ A budget for a single level of activity
- ☐ A budget for fixed costs

10 Budget preparation

Learning outcomes

Having studied this chapter you will be able to:
• Explain why organisations prepare forecasts and plans
• Prepare functional budgets
• Explain budget statements
• Identify the impact of budgeted cash surpluses and shortfalls on business operations

Chapter context

Budgeting is a key tool in many organisations and is a term that you will no doubt have come across before. This chapter covers what a budget actually is, what it is used for, how the various types of budget are produced and how they fit together.

Syllabus context

This chapter is part of syllabus **Section C**, which looks at **'Planning and Control'**.

This syllabus area has a weighting of **30%** and is covered by **Chapters 8 to 14**.

In the exam, you will be expected to demonstrate competence in the following areas:

- Budgeting for planning and control.
- Functional budgets.
- Master budget, including statements of profit and loss, financial position and cash flow.
- The importance of cash budgets.

Chapter overview

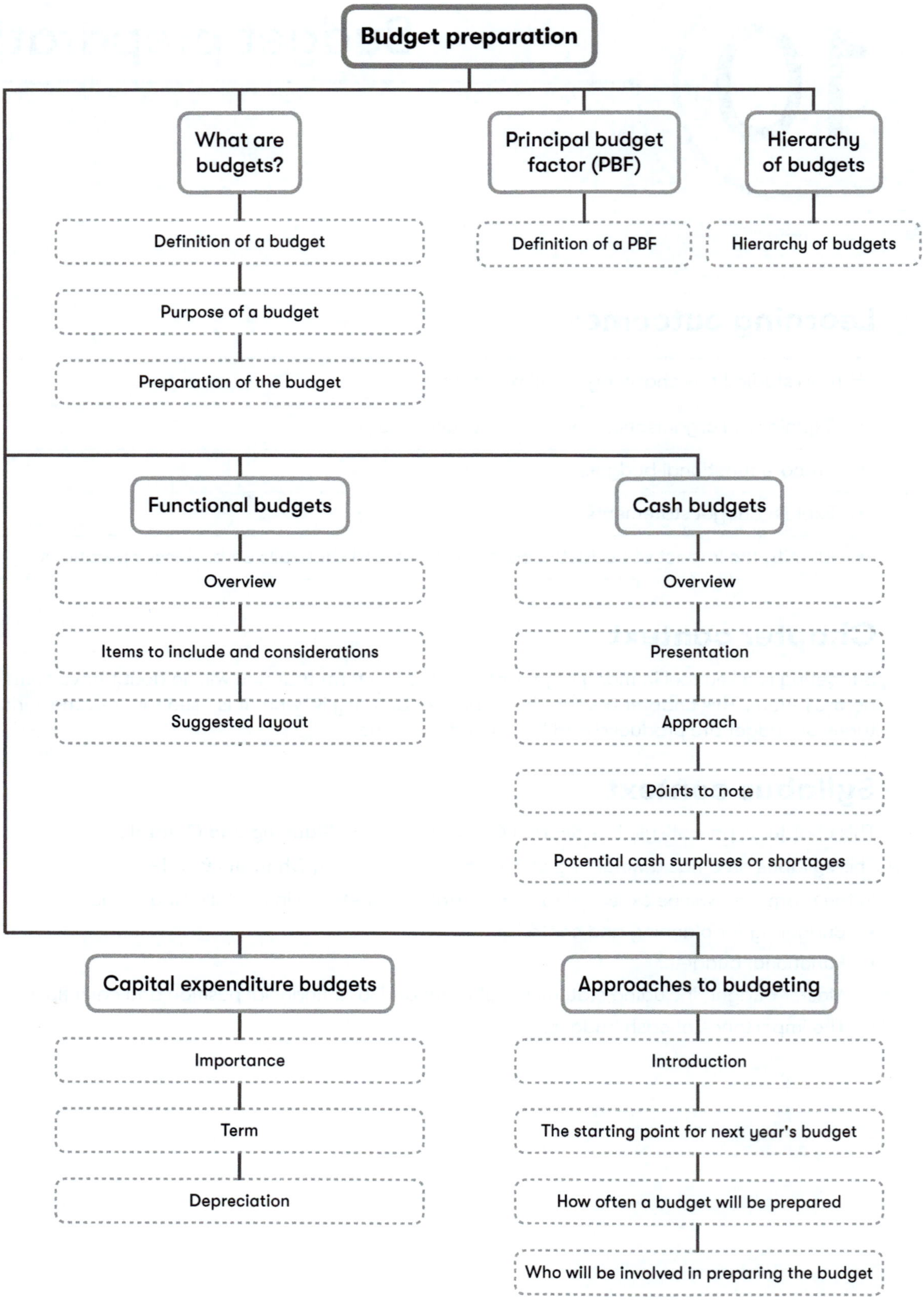

1 What are budgets?

Competent management should manage by objectives and this generalised aim is supported by a **plan of action** in the form of a **formalised budget**.

1.1 Definition of a budget

A **financial and/or quantitative** statement, prepared and **approved prior to a defined period** of time, of the **policy to be pursued** during that period for the purpose of **attaining a given objective.**

In essence it is a commitment to a **financial plan of action.**

1.2 Purpose of a budget

P – Planning (to achieve targets, identify problems)

R – Responsibility (managers made responsible for achieving targets)

I – Integration and co-ordination (of departments within the business)

M – Motivation (of employees to improve performance)

E – Evaluation and control (of performance by comparison of budget to actual results)

In summary, budgets help to ensure the smooth and efficient running of a business.

1.3 Preparation of the budget

This is normally co-ordinated by the **budget committee**, including representatives from every part of the organisation. The preparation of each **functional budget** (sales budget, production budget, direct labour budget and so on) should be the responsibility of the manager who will be carrying out that budget. Guidelines and information to aid budget preparation are contained in the **budget manual.** This will typically include the responsibilities of persons and the procedures, forms and records relating to the preparation and use of budgetary data.

KEY TERM

Budget committee: The co-ordinating body in the preparation and administration of budgets.

Budget manual: A detailed set of guidelines and information about the budget process.

Functional budget: A budget of income and/or expenditure applicable to a particular function of an organisation.

2 Principal budget factor (PBF)

The first task in the budgetary process is to identify the **principal budget factor (PBF).** This is also known as the **key budget factor** or **limiting budget factor**.

KEY TERM

Principal budget factor: The factor which limits the activities of an organisation (seen in Chapter 7).

Budgets should be constructed around the PBF:

- Identify the PBF eg raw materials availability (in kg). For most organisations this will be sales demand.
- Calculate the budget for the PBF.
- Work all the other budgets around it.

3 Hierarchy of budgets

KEY TERM

Master budget: Budgeted statement of profit or loss, budgeted statement of financial position and a cash budget.

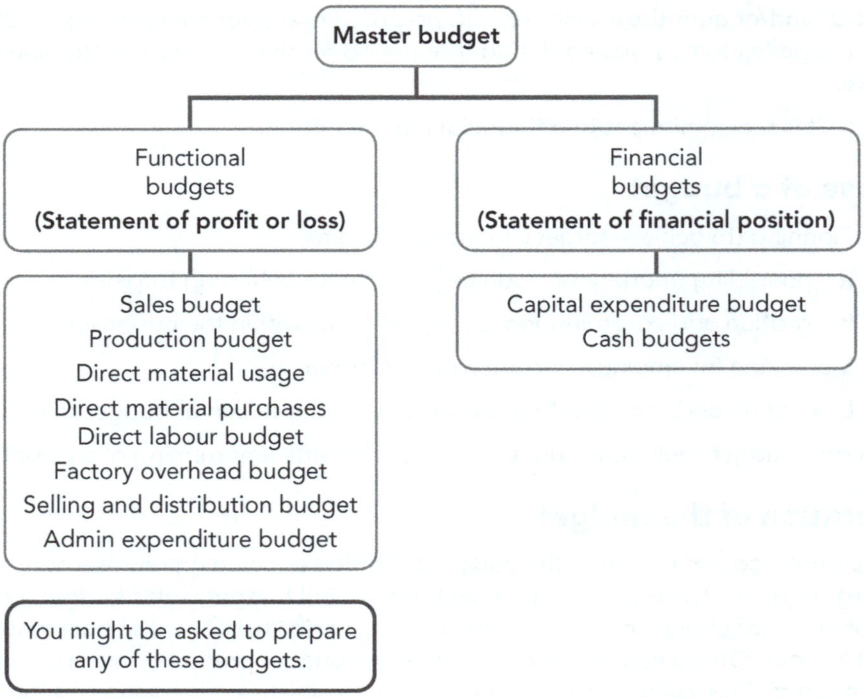

4 Functional budgets

4.1 Overview

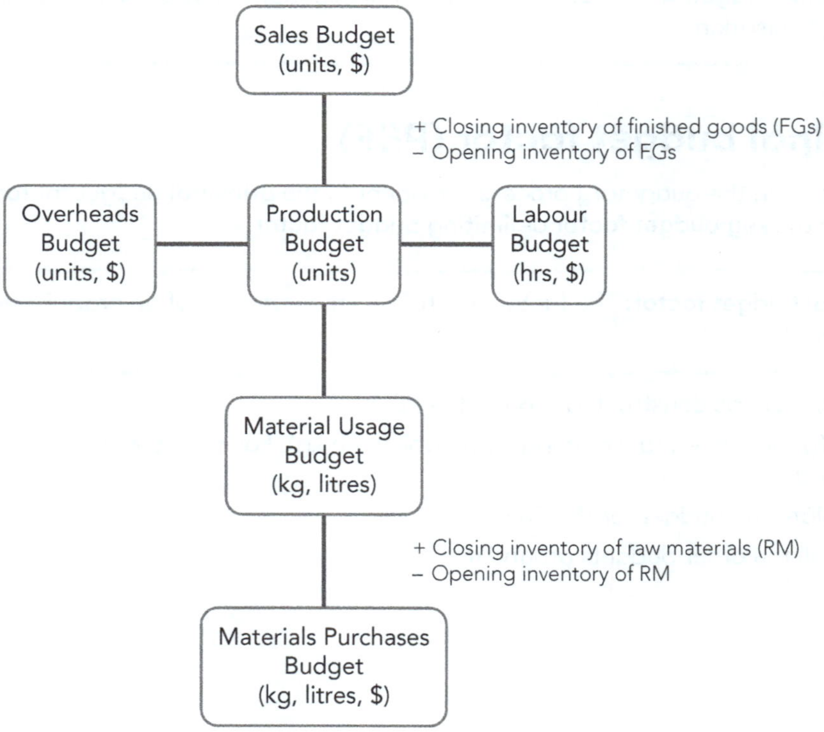

4.2 Items to include and considerations

(a) Sales budget – units and value

(b) Production budget – units

- Sales quantities
- Adjust by changes in finished goods inventory

(c) Resource requirements budgets

- Materials usage (scrap, waste)
- Labour hours (idle time)
- Machine hours (idle time)
- Other
- Apply costs to resources

(d) Overheads – fixed and variable

- Absorption costing, calculate fixed overhead absorption rate and full cost of units

(e) Materials purchases budgets ($)

- Materials usage quantities
- Adjust by changes in raw materials inventory
- Apply costs (any discounts?)

(f) Budgeted statement of profit or loss can be prepared from combining all the above

4.3 Suggested layout

The following is a suggested layout which ensures that all of the crucial elements of the budget are included.

(a) **Sales budget**

	A	*B*	*Total*
Quantities (units)	X	X	
Unit selling price	$Y	$Y	
Revenue	$Z	$Z	$Z

(b) **Production budget**

	A	*B*
	Units	Units
Sales	X	X
Closing inventory	X	X
	X	X
Opening inventory	(X)	(X)
Production	X	X

(c) **Material usage**

	Material P	*Material Q*
	kg	kg
A (@ Y kg*/unit)	X	X
B (@ Z kg*/unit)	X	X
Total usage	X	X

* Consider wastage

(d) **Material purchases**

	Material P	*Material Q*	*Total*
	kg	kg	
Usage	X	X	
Closing inventory of raw materials	X	X	
	X	X	
Opening inventory of raw materials	(X)	(X)	
Purchases	X	X	
Price/kg	$Y	$Y	
Total cost	$Z	$Z	$Z

(e) **Labour utilisation**

	Skilled	*Semi-skilled*	*Total*
	Hrs	Hrs	
A (@ Y hrs*/unit)	X	X	
B (@ Z hrs*/unit)	X	X	
	X	X	
Rate/hr	$Y	$Y	
Total cost	$Z	$Z	$Z

* Consider idle time

(f) **Statement of profit or loss**

	A	*B*	*Total*
	$	$	$
Revenue (from (1))	X	X	X
Less cost of sales	(X)	(X)	(X)
(sales unit × cost/unit*)			
Less selling and administrative costs	(X)	(X)	(X)
	X	X	X

* Assuming absorption costing

Exam focus point

You may get an assessment question which asks you to work out one budgeted figure from another. For example, you may be given the sales budget and asked to work out the production budget. Make sure that you learn this formula.

Units made = units sold + units in closing inventory – units in opening inventory.

The business must produce enough to cover its sales volume and to leave enough in closing inventory, but it gets a 'head start' from opening inventory. This is why opening inventory is deducted.

You can apply this principle to other areas of budgeting. For example:

Materials purchases = materials usage + closing inventory material – opening inventory material.

Activity 1: Material purchases budget

Suppose a company currently holds 100 units of inventory but it wishes to increase its inventory holding to 150 units during the next month. Sales are expected to be 850 units. Each unit requires 5 kg of material. Of units produced, 10% have to be discarded because they are defective. No inventories of raw materials are held.

↓ wastage.

Required

The material purchases for next month should be ________ kg

Solution

material purchases.

prod'n budget

↓

mats budget.

↓

mats purchase. + closing raw mats − opening raw mats.

5 Cash budgets

5.1 Overview

The level of cash held by a business is important. A cash budget shows how the balance will change over several months.

5.2 Presentation

XYZ Co: CASH BUDGET FOR THE THREE MONTHS ENDED 31 MARCH 2007

	Jan	Feb	Mar
Cash receipts			
Sales receipts	X	X	X
Loans, asset sales	–	X	X
	X	**X**	**X**
Cash payments			
Purchase payments	X	X	X
Wages	X	X	X
Overheads	X	X	X
Loan repayments		X	
Non-current assets	X	–	–
	X	**X**	**X**
Net cash flow	**X**	**(X)**	**X**
Opening balance	X	X	(X)
Closing balance	X	(X)	X

5.3 Approach

Fill in the easy figures first.

(a) Sundry receipts and payments: for example the purchase of non-current assets

(b) Wages and salaries: usually paid when due

(c) Sales receipts: total sales are given, you just have to check the payment pattern

(d) Payments to payables: these require more care

(e) The closing balance for one month becomes the opening balance for the next month

5.4 Points to note

Cash budgets consider the cash element of business transactions, whereas the statement of profit or loss records all transactions on an accruals basis regardless of when cash is received or paid. Therefore:

Transaction	Cash budget effect	SOPL effect
Purchase of non-current asset	Cash paid	Depreciation charged
Sell a non-current asset	Cash received	Profit or loss on sale
Sales made for cash and credit	Cash received	Accruals basis
Expenses paid	Cash paid	Accruals basis

Activity 2: Cash budget items

Tick the boxes to show which of the following should be included in a cash budget.

	Include	Do not include
Funds from the receipt of a bank loan	✓	
Revaluation of a non-current asset		✓
Receipt of dividends from outside the business	✓	
Depreciation of distribution vehicles		✓
Bad debts written off		✓
Share dividend paid	✓	

Illustration 1: Cash budget

Peter Blair has worked for some years as a sales representative, but has recently been made redundant. He intends to start up in business on his own account, using $15,000 which he currently has invested with a savings account. Peter also maintains a bank account showing a small credit balance, and he plans to approach his bank for the necessary additional finance. Peter asks you for advice and provides the following additional information.

(1) Arrangements have been made to purchase non-current assets costing $8,000. These will be paid for at the end of September and are expected to have a five-year life, at the end of which they will possess a nil residual value.

(2) Inventories costing $5,000 will be acquired on 28 September and subsequent monthly purchases will be at a level sufficient to replace forecast sales for the month.

(3) Forecast monthly sales are $3,000 for October, $6,000 for November and December, and $10,500 from January 20X4 onwards.

(4) Selling price is fixed at the cost of inventory plus 50%.

(5) Two months' credit will be allowed to customers but only one month's credit will be received from suppliers of inventory.

(6) Running expenses, including rent but excluding depreciation of non-current assets, are estimated at $1,600 per month.

(7) Blair intends to make monthly cash drawings of $1,000.

Required

Prepare a cash budget for the six months to 31 March 20X4.

Solution

The opening cash balance at 1 October will consist of Peter's initial $15,000 less the $8,000 expended on non-current assets purchased in September. In other words, the opening balance is $7,000. Cash receipts from credit customers arise two months after the relevant sales.

Payments to suppliers are a little more tricky. We are told that cost of sales is 100/150 × sales. Thus for October cost of sales is 100/150 × $3,000 = $2,000. These goods will be purchased in October but not paid for until November. Similar calculations can be made for later months. The initial inventory of $5,000 is purchased in September and consequently paid for in October.

Depreciation is not a cash flow and so is not included in a cash budget.

The cash budget can now be constructed.

CASH BUDGET FOR THE SIX MONTHS ENDING 31 MARCH 20X4

	Oct	*Nov*	*Dec*	*Jan*	*Feb*	*Mar*
	$	$	$	$	$	$
Payments						
Suppliers	5,000	2,000	4,000	4,000	7,000	7,000
Running expenses	1,600	1,600	1,600	1,600	1,600	1,600
Drawings	1,000	1,000	1,000	1,000	1,000	1,000
	7,600	4,600	6,600	6,600	9,600	9,600
Receipts						
Receivables	–	–	3,000	6,000	6,000	10,500
Surplus/(shortfall)	(7,600)	(4,600)	(3,600)	(600)	(3,600)	900
Opening balance	7,000	(600)	(5,200)	(8,800)	(9,400)	(13,000)
Closing balance	(600)	(5,200)	(8,800)	(9,400)	(13,000)	(12,100)

Activity 3: Customer receipts

Carol has forecast sales as follows:

December $10,000; January $10,000; February $12,000; March $15,000.

Sales are partly for cash and partly on credit, as follows.

- 40% for cash (no discount)
- 60% on credit

The cash sales receipts are received in the month of sale. A 5% discount is given to credit customers for payment within the current month and 25% of credit customers take up this option. All other cash is received in the month after the month of sale.

Required

Complete the following.

Solution

	January	February	March
	$	$	$
Sales	10,000	12,000	15,000
Cash sales			
40%	4000	4800	6000
Credit sales			
Pay in same month	1425	1710	2138
Pay in next month	4500	4500	5400
Cash receipts	9925	11,010	13,538

5.5 Potential cash surpluses or shortages

Cash budgets can give management an indication of any cash surpluses or shortages expected.

Management can then make decisions on financing any expected cash shortage or investing any cash surpluses. This will depend on whether the surplus or shortage is long term or short term.

Activity 4: Dealing with cash surplus or shortfall

Complete the following statements.

Required

1 Cash surpluses can be used to:

2 Cash shortfalls can be financed by:

Solution

6 Capital expenditure budgets

6.1 Importance

Because the monetary amounts involved in capital expenditure are often large, the capital expenditure budget is one of the principal statement of financial position subsidiary budgets.

6.2 Term

A capital expenditure budget should be prepared for the short-term budget period (eg 12 months) and the medium-term and long-term based on the organisation's requirements for land, buildings, plant, machinery, vehicles, fixtures and fittings and any other non-current assets.

6.3 Depreciation

Any depreciation on budgeted capital expenditure will need to be incorporated into the budgeted statement of profit or loss.

7 Approaches to budgeting

7.1 Introduction

There are a number of approaches to producing budgets that organisations can adopt. These approaches address a number of issues that are discussed below.

7.2 The starting point for next year's budget

KEY TERM

Incremental budgeting: An approach where the budget is based on the current year's budget (or results) adjusted for estimated growth, inflation, or expected cost savings.

Zero-based budgeting (ZBB): An alternative to incremental budgeting. It starts from the basic premise that next year's budget is zero; every process or item of expenditure, or intended activity, must be justified in its entirety before it can be included in the budget.

7.3 How often a budget will be prepared

KEY TERM

Periodic budgets: Prepared only once for each full budget period (usually one year) and used throughout that period.

Rolling budgets: Also called **continuous budgets**. Instead of preparing a periodic budget, budgets would be prepared, say, every 1, 2 or 3 months (4, 6, or even 12 budgets each year).

Each rolling budget would plan for the next twelve months so that the current budget is extended by an extra period as the current period ends. Cash budgets are usually prepared on a rolling basis.

7.4 Who will be involved in preparing the budget

KEY TERM

Participative budgeting: Participative (or bottom up) budgeting gives all budget holders the opportunity to participate in setting their own budgets.

Imposed budgeting: Imposed (or top down) budgeting involves budgets being set by senior managers without the involvement of the budget holders.

Activity 5: Budget approach comparison

Budge-it Removals Co is considering the approach that it should take to budgeting.

Required

To assist in its decision, list the advantages of each approach to budgeting when compared to its alternative:

(1) Incremental budgeting v ZBB

(2) Periodic v rolling budgets

(3) Participative v imposed budgeting

Solution

1) incremental → quick + less time consuming
not as accurate

zero-based → more accurate - justified.
↗ clear yr target.

2) periodic → less time consuming

rolling → more accurate based on current performance & up-to-date

3) participative - budget holder more aware of performance

imposed budgeting - quicker
- senior managers may be more skilled in imposing / predicting budgets.

Chapter summary

Budget preparation

What are budgets?

Definition of a budget
- A financial plan of action

Purpose of a budget
- Planning
- Responsibility
- Integration and co-ordination
- Motivation
- Evaluation and control

Preparation of the budget
- Budget committee
- Budget manual
- Functional budget

Principal budget factor (PBF)

Definition of a PBF
- The factor which limits the activities of an organisation

Hierarchy of budgets

Hierarchy of budgets
- Master budget
- Functional budgets
- Financial budgets

Functional budgets

Overview
- Sales budget
- Overheads budget
- Production budget
- Labour budget
- Material usage budget
- Material purchases budget

Items to include and considerations
- Sales budget – units and value
- Production budget – units
- Resource requirements budgets - usage, hours and costs of resources
- Overheads – fixed and variable
- Material purchases budget - purchases, adjusted for inventory
- Budgeted statement of profit or loss can be prepared from combining all the above

Suggested layout
- Proforma

Cash budgets

Overview
- The level of cash held by a business is important

Presentation
- Proforma

Approach
- Fill in the easy figures first
- Specific treatment for different elements

Points to note
- Transactions
- Effect on cash
- Effect on profit

Potential cash surpluses or shortages
- Dealing with a surplus
- Dealing with a deficit

Capital expenditure budgets

Importance
- Importance of a capital expenditure budget

Term
- Short-term
- Medium-term
- Long-term

Depreciation
- Depreciation to be included on budgeted statement of profit or loss

Approaches to budgeting

Introduction
- Different approaches are available

The starting point for next year's budget
- Incremental budgeting
- Zero-based budgeting (ZBB)

How often a budget will be prepared
- Periodic budgets
- Rolling (continuous) budgets

Who will be involved in preparing the budget
- Participative budgeting
- Imposed (top down) budgeting

Key terms

Budget committee: The co-ordinating body in the preparation and administration of budgets.

Budget manual: A detailed set of guidelines and information about the budget process.

Functional budget: A budget of income and/or expenditure applicable to a particular function of an organisation.

Principal budget factor: The factor which limits the activities of an organisation (seen in Chapter 7).

Master budget: Budgeted statement of profit or loss, budgeted statement of financial position and a cash budget.

Incremental budgeting: An approach where the budget is based on the current year's budget (or results) adjusted for estimated growth, inflation, or expected cost savings.

Zero-based budgeting (ZBB): An alternative to incremental budgeting. It starts from the basic premise that next year's budget is zero; every process or item of expenditure, or intended activity, must be justified in its entirety before it can be included in the budget.

Periodic budgets: Prepared only once for each full budget period (usually one year) and used throughout that period.

Rolling budgets: Also called **continuous budgets**. Instead of preparing a periodic budget, budgets would be prepared, say, every 1, 2 or 3 months (4, 6, or even 12 budgets each year).

Participative budgeting: Participative (or bottom up) budgeting gives all budget holders the opportunity to participate in setting their own budgets.

Imposed budgeting: Imposed (or top down) budgeting involves budgets being set by senior managers without the involvement of the budget holders.

Activity answers

Activity 1: Material purchases budget

The material purchases for next month should be | 5,000 | kg

Working

	Good
	Units
Sales	850
Closing inventory requirement	150
Less opening inventory	(100)
Production	900

To make 900 good units, need to produce 1,000 units.

1,000 units produced, 90% good = 900 good units

∴ 1,000 × 5 kg = 5,000 kg of materials are needed

No inventories of raw materials are held

∴ 5,000 kg need to be purchased

Activity 2: Cash budget items

Any item that is a **cash** flow will be included. Non-cash items are excluded from a cash budget.

	Include	Do not include
Funds from the receipt of a bank loan	✔	
Revaluation of a non-current asset		✔
Receipt of dividends from outside the business	✔	
Depreciation of distribution vehicles		✔
Bad debts written off		✔
Share dividend paid	✔	

No cash has been paid or received for the revaluation of the asset, depreciation of vehicles or the writing off of bad debts.

Activity 3: Customer receipts

	January	*February*	*March*
	$	$	$
Sales	10,000	12,000	15,000
Cash sales			
(Sales × 40%)	4,000	4,800	6,000
Credit sales			
Pay in same month	1,425	1,710	2,138

	January	February	March
	$	$	$
(Sales × 60% × 25% × 95%)			
Pay in next month	4,500	4,500	5,400
Cash receipts	9,925	11,010	13,538

'Pay in next month' entry = Previous month's sales × 60% × 75%

Activity 4: Dealing with cash surplus or shortfall

1 Pay suppliers early to obtain discount
  Pay suppliers early to obtain discount
  Attempt to increase sales by increasing receivables and inventory
  Make short- or long-term investments

2 Paying suppliers later
  Reducing credit terms to customers
  Arranging an overdraft or short-term loan for short-term shortages
  Arranging long-term loans or issue shares to finance long-term shortages

Activity 5: Budget approach comparison

Advantages of:

Incremental budgeting

- Easy, quick and cheap

Zero-based budgeting

- Necessitates close examination of organisation's operations
- Can identify and remove inefficient or obsolete operations
- Results in a more efficient allocation of resources

Periodic budgets

- Easy, quick and cheap
- Managers have a clear target for the year

Rolling budgets

- Forces managers to regularly reassess the budget
- Planning and control will be based on a more recent plan
- The budget always extends for some time into the future

Participative budgeting

- Budgets are based on more accurate information
- Budget holder's motivation is likely to be higher

Imposed budgeting

- Quicker
- Senior managers have a better overall view of organisational resources
- Senior managers may be more skilled in producing budgets
- Budget holders will not be able to submit budgets that are easy to achieve

(we refer to this as introducing 'budgetary slack')

Test your learning

1 Budgets have a number of purposes. Fill in the key words which are missing from the statements below.

(1) To ______ the activities of different departments towards a single plan

(2) To ______ targets to managers responsible for achieving them

(3) To establish a system of ______ by comparing budgeted and actual results

(4) To compel ______

2 Which of the following is unlikely to be contained within a budget manual?

- O Organisational structures
- O Objectives of the budgetary process
- O Selling overhead budget
- O Administrative details of budget preparation

3 The factor which limits the activities of an organisation is known as:

(1) The key budget factor

(2) The limiting budget factor

(3) The principal budget factor

(4) The main budget factor

- O (1), (2) and (4)
- O (1) and (3)
- O (2) and (3)
- O (1), (2) and (3)

4 If the principal budget factor is sales demand, in which order would the following budgets be prepared?

Materials usage	Materials purchase	Production	Sales	Cash

1st ______

2nd ______

3rd ______

4th ______

5th ______

5 Match the following cash positions with the appropriate management action.

Short-term surplus	Pay suppliers later
Long-term surplus	Replace/update non-current assets
Short-term shortfall	Issue share capital
Long-term shortfall	Increase credit terms to customers

6 Depreciation has an effect on net profit and is therefore included in a cash budget.

- True
- False

7 Which of the following are included in the master budget?

(1) Budgeted statement of profit or loss

(2) Budgeted statement of financial position

(3) Budgeted cash flow

(4) Functional budgets

- (1), (2) and (3)
- (2) and (3)
- (2), (3) and (4)
- (4) only

8 The following information is available for Biscuit Co.

	Jan	Feb
	$	$
Budgeted sales	60,000	80,000
Gross profit as a percentage of sales	40%	40%
Closing trade payables as a percentage of cost of sales	50%	50%
Opening inventory	nil	nil
Closing inventory	nil	nil

Note that all cost of sales are paid for on credit.

Required

How much money should be budgeted for supplier payments in February?

- $10,500
- $14,000
- $24,500
- $42,000

9 Jay Co produces a product called the Bee. There has been a surge in Bee sales as a result of an advertising campaign and so Jay Co is paying its staff overtime to build up the inventory levels.

Labour hours per unit	3
Basic wage rate per hour	$20
Overtime premium	25%
Normal number of labour hours per month	340,000 hours

Jay Co expects sales of 100,000 units in September and wants to have closing inventory at the end of September of 20,000 units. There will be no opening inventory on 1 September.

Required

Calculate the budgeted labour cost.

$ [7300000] ✓

10 Fill in the blanks.

When preparing a production budget, the quantity to be produced is equal to sales [less] opening inventory [plus] closing inventory.

overtime premium = 5 per hr

100,000

120,000 units

360,000 hrs 7,200,000

20,000 extra hrs. 7,300,000

20,000 x 5 =

11 Variance analysis

Learning outcomes

Having studied this chapter you will be able to:
• Calculate variances for materials, labour, variable overheads, sales prices and sales volumes
• Prepare a statement that reconciles budgeted profit with actual profit using marginal costing
• Explain why variances could have arisen and the inter-relationships between variances

Chapter context

This chapter looks at a system that organisations can use to analyse the reasons for differences between what they planned to happen (using budgets and standards) and what actually happened. This is important, because as management accountants we will be expected to be able to answer the question 'why didn't we make the return that we were expecting?'. In BA2 we will be focusing on contribution and will therefore not need to consider fixed costs.

Syllabus context

This chapter is part of syllabus **Section C**, which looks at **'Planning and Control'**.

This syllabus area has a weighting of **30%** and is covered by **Chapters 8 to 14**.

In the exam, you will be expected to demonstrate competence in the following areas:

- Standards for the selling price and variable costs of a product or service.
- Variances: materials (total, price and usage); labour (total, rate and efficiency); variable overhead (total, expenditure and efficiency); sales (sales price and sales volume contribution).
- The use of variances to reconcile the budgeted and actual profits that have been calculated using marginal costing.
- Interpretation of variances.

Chapter overview

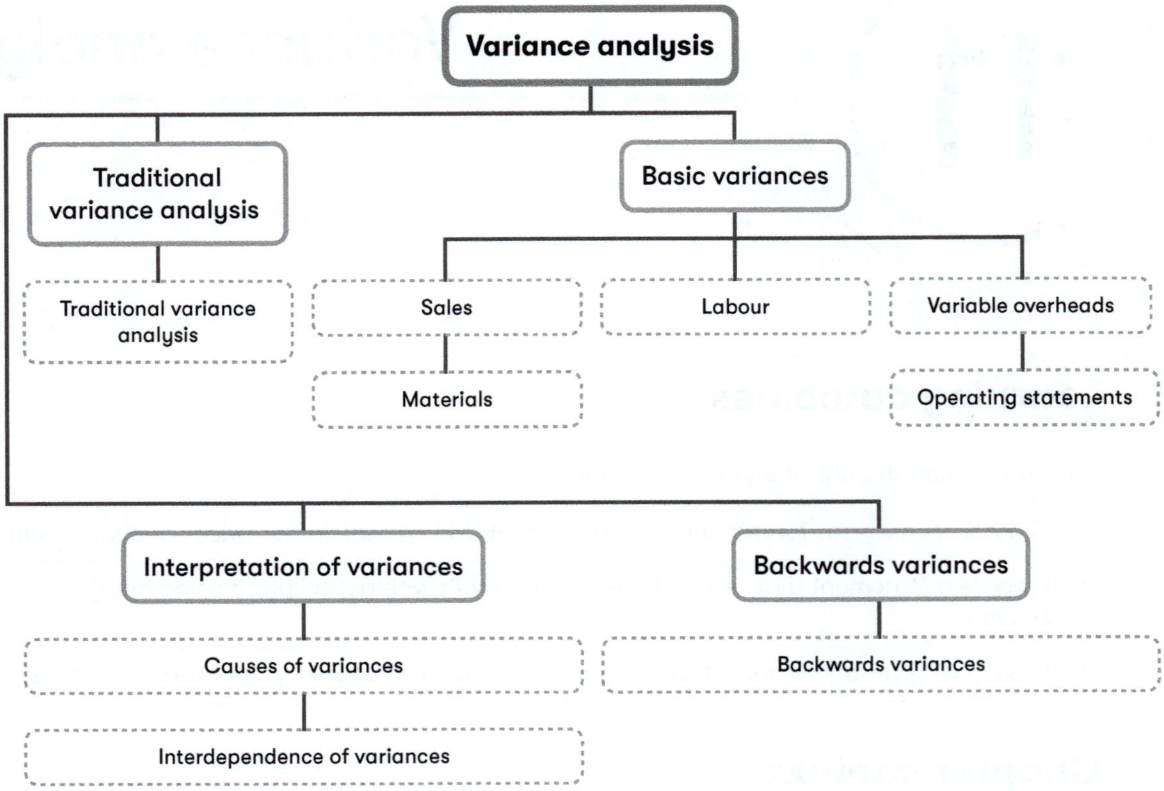

1 Traditional variance analysis

KEY TERM

Variances: Measure the difference between actual results and expected results. The process by which the total difference between standard and actual results is analysed is known as **variance analysis**.

Overview

	Original budget	*Flexed budget*		*Actual results*
Sales volume	X	X		X
	$	$		$
Sales revenue	X	X	Sales variance	X
Cost of sales:				
Materials	X	X	Material variance	X
Labour	X	X	Labour variance	X
Overheads	X	X	O'head variance	X
Profit	X	X		X
	Budgeted units × standard cost or selling price per unit	Actual units × standard cost or selling price per unit		Actual units × actual cost or selling price per unit

Variances can be either **favourable (F)** ie better than expected or **adverse (A)** ie worse.

2 Basic variances

2.1 Sales

Formula to learn

Price: based on **actual units sold** – what revenue was achieved? What revenue should have been achieved?

		$
'Should'	**Actual sales** should sell for (Act units × std $ per unit)	X
'Did'	Actual sales did sell for	(X)
		X

Volume: difference between budgeted and actual sales volume. Value at standard contribution per unit.

		Units
'Should'	**Budgeted sales**	X
'Did'	Actual sales	(X)
		X
	Difference valued at standard contribution	$X

2.2 Materials

Formula to learn

Total: based on **actual production** – what did it cost? What should it have cost?

		$
'Should'	**Actual units** should cost (Act units × std kg per unit × std $ per kg)	X
'Did'	Actual material used did cost	(X)
		X

Price: based on **actual purchases** – what did they cost? What should they have cost?

		$
'Should'	**Actual purchases** should cost (Act kg × std $ per kg)	X
'Did'	Actual purchases did cost	(X)
		X

Usage: based on **actual production** – what did it use? What should it have used? Difference valued at standard cost.

		Kg
'Should'	**Actual production** should use (Act units × std kg per unit)	X
'Did'	Actual production did use	(X)
		X
	Difference valued at standard cost	$X

2.3 Labour

Formula to learn

Total: based on **actual production** – what did it cost? What should it have cost?

		$
'Should'	**Actual units** should cost (Act units × std hrs per unit × std $ per hour)	X
'Did'	Actual labour used did cost	(X)
		X

Rate: based on **hours paid** – What did they cost? What should they have cost?

		$
'Should'	**Actual hours paid** should cost (Act hrs paid × std $ per hour)	X
'Did'	Actual hours paid did cost	(X)
		X

Idle time: difference between hours paid and worked. Value at std rate per hour.

		Hrs
'Should'	Hours paid for	X
'Did'	Hours worked	(X)
		X
	Difference valued at standard rate per hour	$X

Efficiency: based on **actual production** – how long did it take? How long should it have taken*? Difference valued at standard rate per hour.

'Should'	**Actual production** should take (Act units × std hrs per unit)	X
'Did'	Actual production did take (hours worked)	(X)
		X
	Difference valued at standard rate per hour	$X

* The standard time allowed for the actual production is sometimes referred to as **standard hours.**

2.4 Variable overheads

Formula to learn

Total: based on **actual production** – what did it cost? What should it have cost?

		$
'Should'	**Actual units** should cost	X
'Did'	Actual variable overheads did cost	(X)
		X

Expenditure: based on **actual hours worked** – what did they cost? What should they have cost?

		$
'Should'	**Actual hours paid** should cost (Act hrs paid × std OAR $ per hour)	X
'Did'	Actual hours paid did cost	(X)
		X

Efficiency: based on **actual production** – how long did it take? How long should it have taken? Difference valued at standard rate per hour.

		Hrs
'Should'	**Actual production** should take	X
'Did'	Actual production did take	(X)
		X
	Difference valued at standard variable overhead rate per hour	$X

KEY TERM

Price or rate variance: The difference between the actual and expected price paid for a unit of materials (price) or labour (rate).

Usage or efficiency variance: The difference between the actual and expected resources used in production.

Volume variance: The difference between actual and expected sales levels.

Illustration 1: Variance calculations

Sydney Co manufactures one product, and the entire product is sold as soon as it is produced. There are no opening or closing inventories and work in progress is negligible. The company operates a standard costing system and analysis of variances is made every month. The standard cost card for a product is as follows.

STANDARD COST CARD

		$
Direct materials	0.5 kilos at $4 per kilo	2.00
Direct wages	2 hours at $8.00 per hour	16.00
Variable overheads	2 hours at $0.30 per hour	0.60

Standard variable cost	18.60
Standard contribution	13.40
Standing selling price	32.00

Budgeted output for the month of June 20X7 was 5,100 units. Actual results for June 20X7 were as follows.

Production of 4,850 units was sold for $150,350.

Materials consumed in production amounted to 2,300 kg at a total cost of $9,800.

Labour hours paid for amounted to 8,500 hours at a cost of $67,800.

Actual operating hours amounted to 8,000 hours.

Variable overheads amounted to $2,600.

Required

Calculate all variances.

Solution

(a) Material price variance

	$
2,300 kg of material should cost ($4)	9,200
but did cost	9,800
Material price variance	600 (A)

(b) Material usage variance

4,850 units should use (0.5 kg)	2,425 kg
but did use	2,300 kg
Material usage variance in kg	125 kg (F)
standard price per kg	× $4
Material usage variance in $	$500 (F)

(c) Labour rate variance

	$
8,500 hours of labour should cost ($8)	68,000
but did cost	67,800
Labour rate variance	200 (F)

(d) Labour efficiency variance

4,850 units should take (× 2 hrs)	9,700 hrs
but did take (active hours)	8,000 hrs
Labour efficiency variance in hours	1,700 hrs (F)
× standard rate per hour	× $8
Labour efficiency variance in $	$13,600 (F)

(e) Idle time variance

Idle time variance 500 hours (A) × $8	$4,000 (A)

(f) Variable overhead expenditure variance

	$
8,000 hours incurring variable o/hd expenditure should cost (× $0.30)	2,400
but did cost	2,600
Variable overhead expenditure variance	200 (A)

(g) Variable overhead efficiency variance

Variable overhead efficiency variance in hours is the same as the labour efficiency variance:

1,700 hours (F) × $0.30 per hour	$510 (F)

(h) Sales price variance

	$
Revenue from 4,850 units should be (× $32)	155,200
but was	150,350
Sales price variance	4,850 (A)

(i) Sales volume contribution variance

Budgeted sales volume	5,100 units
Actual sales volume	4,850 units
Sales volume contribution variance in units	250 units (A)
× standard contribution per unit	× $13.40
Sales volume contribution variance	$3,350 (A)

Activity 1: Variance calculations

BUDGET		*Unit*	*Total*
		$	$
Sales	(8,000 units)	75	600,000
Production	(8,700 units)		
Materials	4 kg @ $4.50 per kg	18	156,600
Labour	5 hrs @ $5 per hr	25	217,500
Variable overheads	5 hrs @ $2 per hr	10	87,000

		53	461,100
Closing inventory	(700 units)		(37,100)
			424,000
Budgeted contribution			176,000

ACTUAL		$
Sales	(8,400 units)	613,200
Production	(8,900 units)	
Materials	34,928 kg (purchased and used)	160,985
Labour	45,400 hours (worked and paid)	224,515
Variable overheads		87,348
		472,848
Closing inventory	(500 units)	(26,500)
		446,348
Actual contribution		166,852

Required

1. What is the materials total variance?
2. What is the materials price variance?
3. What is the materials usage variance?
4. What is the labour total variance?
5. What is the labour rate variance?
6. What is the labour efficiency variance?
7. What is the variable overhead total variance?
8. What is the variable overhead expenditure variance?
9. What is the variable overhead efficiency variance?
10. What is the sales price variance?
11. What is the sales volume contribution variance?

Solution

2.5 Operating statements

KEY TERM

> **Operating statements:** Show how the combination of variances reconcile budgeted contribution and actual contribution.

So far, we have considered how variances are calculated without considering how they combine to reconcile the difference between budgeted contribution and actual contribution during a period. This reconciliation is usually presented as a report to senior management at the end of each control period. The report is called an operating statement or statement of variances.

(a) **Budgeted contribution** is adjusted by the **sales volume variance** to give the **budgeted contribution from actual sales.**

(b) The **sales price variance** is then included to give a figure representing the **actual sales revenue minus the standard variable cost of sales.**

(c) **Cost variances** are then taken into account to produce a figure for **actual contribution.**

Example: Operating statement

The operating statement using the data in Illustration 1 would be as follows:

SYDNEY CO – OPERATING STATEMENT JUNE 20X7

			$
Budgeted contribution ($13.40 × 5,100)			68,340
Sales volume variance			3,350 (A)
Budgeted contribution from actual sales			64,990
Sales price variance			4,850 (A)
Actual sales minus the standard variable cost of sales			60,140
Cost variances	(F)	(A)	
	$	$	
Material price		600	
Material usage	500		
Labour rate	200		
Labour efficiency	13,600		
Labour idle time		4,000	
Variable overhead expenditure		200	
Variable overhead efficiency	510	–	
	14,810	4,800	10,010 (F)
Actual contribution			70,150

Check	$	$
Sales		150,350
Materials	9,800	
Labour	67,800	
Variable overhead	2,600	
		80,200
Actual contribution		70,150

Activity 2: Operating statement

Using the data from Activity 1, complete the following reconciliation.

Solution

	$
Budgeted contribution	176,000.
Sales volume variance	

std contribution x units budgeted.

8000 x 22 = 176,000

		F	A	$
Sales price variance				(16,800) A
				168,000
Cost variances		**F**	**A**	
Materials	Price		3809	
	Usage	672		
Labour	Rate	2485		
	Efficiency		900	
Var O/H	Expenditure	3452		
	Efficiency		900	
		8961	10,109	1148 (A)
Actual contribution				166,852

3 Interpretation of variances

Care must be taken when interpreting variances, especially when they are being used to assess the performance of employees.

3.1 Causes of variances

(a) Excessive **controllable** expenditure, eg incorrect buying decisions

(b) Excessive **uncontrollable** expenditure, eg market price rise of raw materials, unexpected overtime working

(c) Inaccurate standard due to:

- Poor planning
- Unrealistic standard due to basis used (ideal standard) or incompetence

(d) Inaccurate measurement

The cause of the variance must be determined before appropriate action can be taken. Employees should only be judged on the factors which they have under their control.

Variance	Favourable	Adverse
(a) Material price	Unforeseen discounts received More care taken in purchasing Change in material standard	Price increase Careless purchasing Change in material standard
(b) Material usage	Material used of higher quality than standard More effective use made of material Errors in allocating material to jobs	Defective material Excessive waste Theft Stricter quality control Errors in allocating material to jobs
(c) Labour rate	Use of apprentices or other workers at a rate of pay lower	Wage rate increase Use of higher grade labour

BPP

Variance	Favourable	Adverse
	than standard	
(d) Idle time	If idle time is less than budgeted idle time	Machine breakdown Non-availability of material Illness or injury to worker
(e) Labour efficiency	Output produced more quickly than expected because of work motivation, better quality of equipment or materials, or better methods Errors in allocating time to jobs	Lost time in excess of standard allowed Output lower than standard set because of deliberate restriction, lack of training, or substandard material used Errors in allocating time to jobs
(f) Variable overhead expenditure	Change in types of overhead or their cost	Change in types of overhead or their cost
(g) Variable overhead efficiency	As for labour efficiency (if based on labour hours)	As for labour efficiency (if based on labour hours)

3.2 Interdependence of variances

Variances may affect each other, eg

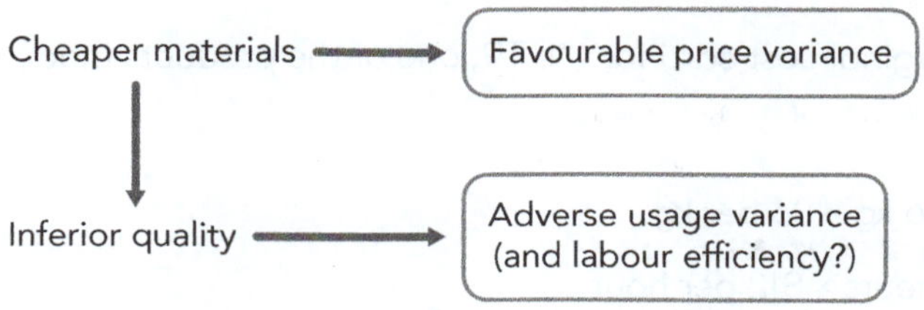

In order to interpret variances effectively any interdependence between variances must be identified. It is not always possible to look at individual variances in isolation.

When two variances are interdependent one will usually be adverse and the other favourable.

It is therefore important in analysing an unfavourable variance that the overall consequence should be considered in order to follow the appropriate control action.

Here are some common examples of interdependent variances:

- Materials price and usage (as above)
- Labour rate and efficiency (higher rates for experience and skill should result in favourable efficiency variances)
- Sales price and sales volume (reducing the price (adverse sales price variance) causes higher numbers of units to be sold (favourable sales volume variance))

Activity 3: Interdependence of variances

Hey Co has been let down by its supplier and has had to buy from an alternative source. The alternative materials are of better quality but are more expensive than the original supplier's.

Required

What effect is this change in supplier likely to have on the variances at the month end?

Materials price variance: Adverse ▼

Materials usage variance: favourable ▼

Pull down list

- Adverse
- Favourable

Solution

---

4 Backwards variances

Variances can be **manipulated** so as to derive actual data from standard cost details, or standard costs from actual results.

Illustration 2: Deriving actual data

The standard marginal cost card for the TR, one of the products made by P Co, is as follows.

	$
Direct material 16 kg × $6 per kg	96
Direct labour 6 hours × $12 per hour	72
	168

P Co reported the following variances in control period 13 in relation to the TR.

Direct material price: $18,840 favourable

Direct material usage: $480 adverse

Direct labour rate: $10,598 adverse

Direct labour efficiency: $8,478 favourable

Actual direct wages cost $171,320. P Co paid $5.50 for each kg of direct material. There were no opening or closing inventories of the material.

Required

Calculate the following.

1 Actual output

2 Actual hours worked

3 Average actual wage rate per hour

4 Actual number of kilograms purchased and used

Solution

1

$

Total direct wages cost	171,320
Adjust for variances:	
labour rate	(10,598)
labour efficiency	8,478
Standard direct wages cost	169,200

∴ Actual output = Total standard cost ÷ unit standard cost

= $169,200 ÷ $72

= 2,350 units

2

	$
Total direct wages cost	171,320.0
Less rate variance	(10,598.0)
Standard rate for actual hours	160,722.0
÷ standard rate per hour	÷ $12.0
Actual hours worked	13,393.5 hrs

3 Average actual wage rate per hour = actual wages/actual hours = $171,320/13,393.5 = $12.79 per hour.

4 Number of kg purchased and used = x

	$
x kg should have cost (× $6)	6.0x
but did cost (× $5.50)	5.5x
Direct material price variance	0.5x

∴ $0.5x = $18,840

∴ x = 37,680 kg

Activity 4: Backwards variance

Purchases of 6,850 kg of materials cost $21,920.

The materials price variance is $1,370(F).

Required

What is the standard price per kg?

23,290

$ 3.4 per kg ✓

Solution

Chapter summary

Variance analysis

Traditional variance analysis

Traditional variance analysis
- Variances
- Overview

Basic variances

Sales
- Price: what revenue was achieved? What revenue should have been achieved?
- Volume: the difference between budgeted and actual sales volume. Value at standard contribution per unit.

Materials
- Total: based on actual production – what did it cost? What should it have cost?
- Price: based on actual purchases – what did they cost? What should they have cost?
- Usage: based on actual production – what did it use? What should it have used? Difference valued at standard cost.

Labour
- Total: based on actual production – what did it cost? What should it have cost?
- Rate: based on hours paid – What did they cost? What should they have cost?
- Efficiency: based on actual production – how long did it take? How long should it have taken? Difference valued at standard rate per hour.

Variable overheads
- Total: based on actual production – what did it cost? What should it have cost?
- Expenditure: based on actual hours worked – what did they cost? What should they have cost?
- Efficiency: based on actual production – how long did it take? How long should it have taken? Difference valued at standard rate per hour.

Operating statements
- Show how the combination of variances reconcile budgeted contribution and actual contribution

Interpretation of variances

Causes of variances
- Controllable
- Uncontrollable
- Inaccurate standard
- Inaccurate measurement

Interdependence of variances
- Variances may affect each other

Backwards variances

Backwards variances
- Variances can be manipulated so as to derive actual data from standard cost details, or standard costs from actual results

Key terms

Variances: Measure the difference between actual results and expected results. The process by which the total difference between standard and actual results is analysed is known as **variance analysis**.

Price or rate variance: The difference between the actual and expected price paid for a unit of materials (price) or labour (rate).

Usage or efficiency variance: The difference between the actual and expected resources used in production.

Volume variance: The difference between actual and expected sales levels.

Operating statements: Show how the combination of variances reconcile budgeted contribution and actual contribution.

Activity answers

Activity 1: Variance calculations

1 $785 A

Materials

Total variance: based on production

	$
8,900 units should cost (@ $18 per unit)	160,200
8,900 units did cost	160,985
	785 A

2 $3,809 A

Price variance: based on purchases

	$
34,928 kg should cost (@ 4.50 per kg)	157,176
34,928 kg did cost	160,985
	3,809 A

3 $3,024 F

Usage variance: based on quantity used

8,900 units should use (@ 4 kg)	35,600 kg
8,900 units did use	34,928 kg
	672 kg F
Value at standard cost per kg ($4.50)	$3,024 F

4 **Labour**

$2,015 A

Total variance: based on actual production

	$
8,900 units should cost (@ $25)	222,500
8,900 units did cost	224,515
	2,015 A

5 $2,485 F

Rate variance: based on hours paid

	$
45,400 hours should cost (@ $5)	227,000
45,400 hours did cost	224,515
	2,485 F

6 $4,500 A

Efficiency variance: based on actual production and hours worked

8,900 units should take (@ 5 hours)	44,500 hrs
8,900 units did take	45,400 hrs
	900 hrs A
Valued at standard cost per hour ($5)	$4,500 A

7 **Variable overheads**

$1,652 F

Total variance: based on actual production

	$
8,900 units should cost (@ $10)	89,000
8,900 units did cost	87,348
	1,652 F

8 $3,452 F

Expenditure variance: based on actual labour hours

	$
45,400 hours should cost (@ $2)	90,800
45,400 hours did cost	87,348
	3,452 F

9 $1,800 A

Efficiency variance:

8,900 units should take (@ 5 hours)	44,500 hrs
8,900 units did take	45,400 hrs
	900 hrs A
Valued at standard rate per hour ($2)	$1,800 A

10 $16,800 A

Price variance: based on actual units sold

	$
8,400 units should sell for (@ $75)	630,000
8,400 units did sell for	613,200
	16,800 A

11 $8,800 F

Volume variance:

	Units
Budgeted sales	8,000

Actual sales	8,400
	400 F
Valued at standard contribution per unit ($75–$53)	$8,800 F

Activity 2: Operating statement

Operating statement for period (marginal costing)

				$
Budgeted contribution				176,000
Sales volume variance				8,800
Sales price variance				(16,800)
				168,000
Cost variances		**F**	**A**	
Materials	Price		3,809	
	Usage	3,024		
Labour	Rate	2,485		
	Efficiency		4,500	
Var O/H	Expenditure	3,452		
	Efficiency		1,800	
		8,961	10,109	(1,148)
Actual contribution				166,852

Activity 3: Interdependence of variances

Materials price variance: Adverse

Materials usage variance: Favourable

The materials are more expensive which will lead to an adverse price variance. However, they are better quality, which means that the material usage variance should be favourable.

Activity 4: Backwards variance

$3.40/kg

Working

If variance is 1,370 F

and actual cost is $21,920

Insert into format:

	$
6,850 kg should cost	?
6,850 kg did cost	21,920

1,370 F

∴ 6,850 should cost 21,920 + 1,370 = \$23,290

$$\frac{\$23,290}{6,850} = \$3.40/kg$$

Test your learning

1 Subdivide the following variances.

(1) Direct materials cost variance

(2) Direct labour cost variance

(3) Variable production overhead variance

2 Adverse material usage variances might occur for the following reasons.

(1) Defective material

(2) Excessive waste

(3) Theft

(4) Unforeseen discounts received

- O (1)
- O (1) and (2)
- O (1), (2) and (3)
- O (1), (2), (3) and (4)

3 Hat Co makes a product, Kap, which requires material budgeted at 50c per kg. During June, 6,200 kg were purchased for $3,224 and 6,000 kg were used. There was no opening inventory at the start of June. Inventory is valued at standard cost.

Required

(a) Calculate the material price variance for June.

- O $224
- O $124
- O $244
- O $144

(b) Is the variance favourable or adverse?

- O Favourable
- O Adverse

4 A regular report for management of actual cost and revenue, usually comparing actual with budget (and showing variances), is known as:

- O Bank statement
- O Variance statement
- O Budget statement
- O Operating statement

5 A favourable sales price variance can result from a combination of a lower than budgeted sales volume and a higher than standard selling price.

- O True
- O False

6 If two variances are interdependent, both must be either favourable or adverse.

- O True
- O False

7 Fill in the gaps using two of the following words.

The sales volume variance considers the difference between [▼] sales volume and [▼] sales volume.

Pull down list

- Actual
- Budgeted
- Confirmed
- Estimated
- Future
- Incremental
- Past
- Total

8 HF Co budgeted to produce 3,000 units of product K in June. The budgeted materials for product K were 1,500 kg at a cost of $3 per kg. The actual number of units produced was 2,200 and the material variances were as follows:

Direct material price variance	$825(A)
Direct material efficiency variance	$1,650(A)

Required

Calculate the actual direct material kg used.

- O 550 kg
- O 1,100 kg
- O 1,650 kg
- O 4,950 kg

9 Using the information in question 8, calculate the actual direct material cost for June.

- O $825
- O $4,125
- O $4,950
- O $5,775

12 Job and batch costing

Learning outcomes

Having studied this chapter you will be able to:
• Prepare appropriate accounts for job and batch costing

Chapter context

Job and batch costing are used where the work done by an organisation consists of separately identifiable items or groups of items (ie batches). As each cost unit is clearly identifiable, finding the cost per unit is relatively straightforward.

Syllabus context

This chapter is part of syllabus **Section C**, which looks at **'Planning and Control'**.

This syllabus area has a weighting of **30%** and is covered by **Chapters 8 to 14**.

In the exam, you will be expected to demonstrate competence in the following areas:

- Job and batch costing.

Chapter overview

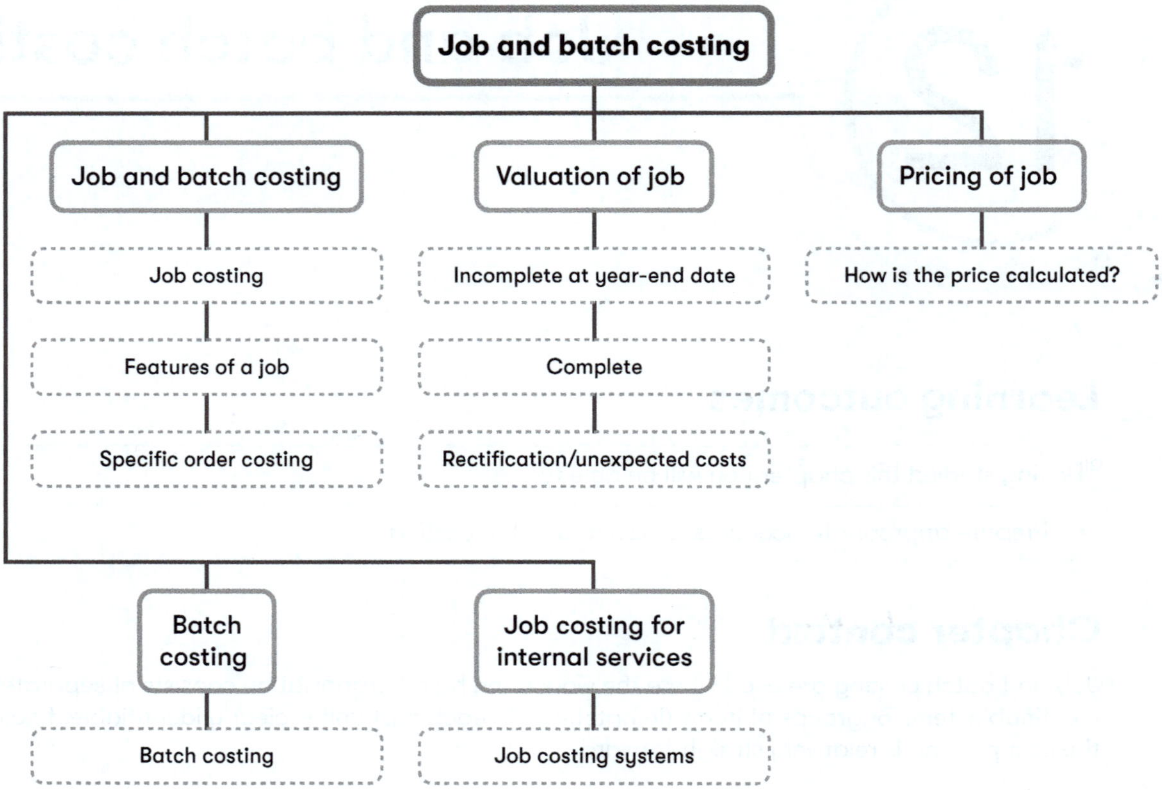

BPP

1 Job and batch costing

1.1 Job costing

KEY TERM

> **Job:** A cost unit which consists of a single order or contract.

1.2 Features of a job

(a) Work is undertaken according to customer specifications.

(b) Each order is of short duration.

(c) Each order is separately identifiable from all others, ie non-homogenous.

1.3 Specific order costing

Job costing is an example of specific order costing. A customer will approach the supplier and agree the exact specifications of the work to be done. The estimating department can then use this information to prepare an estimate of the costs of the job, onto which a profit margin will be added to produce a quotation. Once this is agreed, the work will be carried out at an appropriate time.

2 Valuation of job

2.1 Incomplete at year-end date

If the job is incomplete at the year-end date, it is valued at factory cost (if using absorption costing). Actual costs incurred are recorded on a **job cost card** (or **job account** in computerised systems).

KEY TERM

> **Job cost card:** A record of the actual costs incurred on a job (**job account** if computerised).

2.2 Complete

After completion the job is charged with administration, selling and distribution overheads so that the total cost of the job can be ascertained. When delivery is made to the customer, the costs become a cost of sale.

2.3 Rectification/unexpected costs

Rectification costs are costs incurred to correct substandard work.

(a) If these are unusual occurrences, charge directly to the job

(b) If these are a frequent occurrence, treat as part of production overhead and absorb across all jobs

A similar principle applies to **overtime premiums** (ie the extra amount paid per hour over the standard hourly rate of pay); if they are incurred at the specific request of the customer (for example to complete a job quickly), they are charged to that job, otherwise they become part of production overhead.

3 Pricing of job

3.1 How is the price calculated?

A desired profit is added to costs to determine a price. This may be calculated by using a mark-up percentage or a predetermined margin on sales.

Although this is a commonly used form of pricing, it is directly affected by the method used to determine cost. As you have seen, there are several methods of obtaining a cost per unit.

Illustration 1: Job costing

Twist and Tern Co is a company that carries out jobbing work. One of the jobs carried out in February was job 1357, to which the following information relates.

Direct material Y:	400 kilos were issued from stores at a cost of $5 per kilo.
Direct material Z:	800 kilos were issued from stores at a cost of $6 per kilo.
	60 kilos were returned.
Department P:	320 labour hours were worked, of which 100 hours were done in overtime.
Department Q:	200 labour hours were worked, of which 100 hours were done in overtime.

Overtime work is not normal in Department P, where basic pay is $8 per hour plus an overtime premium of $2 per hour. Overtime work was done in Department Q in February because of a request by the customer of another job to complete their job quickly. Basic pay in Department Q is $10 per hour and overtime premium is $3 per hour.

Overhead is absorbed at the rate of $3 per direct labour hour in both departments.

Required

1

The direct materials cost of job 1357 is $

2

The direct labour cost of job 1357 is $

3

The full production cost of job 1357 is $

Solution

1 The direct materials cost of job 1357 is $ 6,440

Working

	$
Direct material Y (400 kilos × $5)	2,000
Direct material Z (800 – 60 kilos × $6)	4,440
Total direct material cost	6,440

2 The direct labour cost of job 1357 is $ 4,560

Working

	$
Department P (320 hours × $8)	2,560
Department Q (200 hours × $10)	2,000
Total direct labour cost	4,560

In Department P, overtime premium will be charged to overhead. In Department Q, overtime premium will be charged to the job of the customer who asked for overtime to be worked.

3 The full production cost of job 1357 is $ 12,560

Working

	$
Direct material cost	6,440
Direct labour cost	4,560
Production overhead (520 hours × $3)	1,560
	12,560

Activity 1: Job costing

SB Co has been asked to quote for a job. The company aims to make a net profit of 30% on sales. The estimated cost for the job is as follows.

Direct materials	12 kg @ $10 per kg
Direct labour	7 hours @ $7 per hour

Variable production overheads are recovered at the rate of $4 per labour hour.

Fixed production overheads for the company are budgeted to be $106,000 each year and are recovered on the basis of labour hours. There are 10,600 budgeted labour hours each year.

Other costs in relation to selling, distribution and administration are recovered at the rate of $90 per job.

Required

To the nearest $, the company quote for the job should be $

Solution

	$
Direct materials	
Direct labour	
Variable overheads	
Fixed overheads	
Selling, distribution and administration costs	
Total costs	
Profit	
Sales price	

4 Batch costing

KEY TERM

> **Batch:** A cost unit which consists of a separate group of units.
>
> **Batch costing:** Similar to job costing in that each batch of similar articles is separately identifiable.

The **cost per unit** manufactured in a batch is the total batch cost divided by the number of units in the batch. Pricing and valuation principles are similar to those for job costing.

5 Job costing for internal services

Job costing systems may be used to **control the costs** of **internal service departments**, such as the maintenance department. A job costing system enables the cost of a specific job to be charged to a user department. Therefore, instead of apportioning the total costs of service departments, each job done is charged to the individual user department.

KEY TERM

> **Internal job costing:** Where the cost of a specific internal job is charged to a user department.

An **internal job costing system** for service departments will have the following advantages.

(a) **Realistic apportionment.** The service department costs are borne by those who incurred them.

(b) **Increased responsibility and awareness.** User departments appreciate the true cost of the facilities that they are using and can take decisions accordingly.

(c) **Control of service department costs.** It will be possible to measure the efficiency or inefficiency of the service department by recording the difference between the standard charges and the actual expenditure.

(d) **Budget information.** The purpose and cost of service department expenditure can be separately identified.

Chapter summary

Job and batch costing

- **Job and batch costing**
  - Job costing
    - Job – a cost unit which consists of a single order or contract
  - Features of a job
    - Three features of a job
  - Specific order costing
    - Specific order costing
- **Valuation of job**
  - Incomplete at year-end date
    - Job cost card
  - Complete
    - Total cost ascertained
  - Rectification/unexpected costs
    - Rectification costs are costs incurred to correct substandard work
    - Overtime premiums
- **Pricing of job**
  - How is the price calculated?
    - A desired profit is added to costs to determine a price
- **Batch costing**
  - Batch costing
    - Batch
    - Batch costing
    - Cost per unit
- **Job costing for internal services**
  - Job costing systems
    - Internal job costing
    - Internal job costing system for service departments

Key terms

Job: A cost unit which consists of a single order or contract.

Job cost card: A record of the actual costs incurred on a job (**job account** if computerised).

Batch: A cost unit which consists of a separate group of units.

Batch costing: Similar to job costing in that each batch of similar articles is separately identifiable.

Internal job costing: Where the cost of a specific internal job is charged to a user department.

Activity answers

Activity 1: Job costing

To the nearest $, the company quote for the job should be $ 10/hr

	$	
Direct materials (12 kg @ $10 per kg)	120	
Direct labour (7 hours @ $7 per hour)	49	
Variable overheads (7 hours @ $4 per hour)	28	
Fixed overheads (7 hours @ $10 per hour (W1)	70	
	267	
Selling, distribution and administration costs	90	
Total costs	357	70%
Profit	153	30%
Sales price	510	100%

(W1) OAR per hour = $106,000/10,600 hours = $10/hr

Test your learning

1 Which of the following are characteristics of job costing?

(1) Customer driven production

(2) Complete production possible within a single accounting period

(3) Homogeneous products

- O (1) and (2) only
- O (1) and (3) only
- O (2) and (3) only
- O (3) only

2 The cost of a job is $100,000.

Required

(a) If profit is 25% of the job cost, the price of the job = $ [ ]

(b) If there is a 25% margin, the price of the job = $ [ ]

3 Job costing would be most appropriate for which of the following businesses?

- O A pizza manufacturer
- O An architect designing a new school
- O A manufacturer of sugar
- O A manufacturer of screws

4 What is a batch?

5 How would you calculate the cost per unit of a completed batch?

6 A job cost estimate includes 630 productive labour hours. In addition, it is anticipated that idle time will be 10% of the total hours paid for the job. The wage rate is $12 per hour.

Required

What is the total estimated labour cost for the job?

- O $6,804
- O $7,560
- O $8,316
- O $8,400

7 A technical writer is to set up her own business. She anticipates working a 40-hour week and taking four weeks' holiday per year. General expenses of the business are expected to be $10,000 per year, and she has set herself a target of $40,000 a year salary.

Required

Assuming that only 90% of her time worked will be chargeable to customers, her charge for each hour of writing (to the nearest cent) should be $ [ ]

13 Performance measures and service costing

Learning outcomes

Having studied this chapter you will be able to:
• Explain the need for appropriate performance measures
• Calculate appropriate financial and non-financial performance measures in a variety of contexts
• Prepare reports in a range of organisations

Chapter context

Most of what we have covered so far has been based on manufacturing organisations. This chapter explores performance measures for these organisations, and then addresses what additional costing issues there are for organisations whose main activity isn't the provision of tangible goods, and appropriate performance measures for them.

Syllabus context

This chapter is part of syllabus **Section C**, which looks at **'Planning and Control'**.

This syllabus area has a weighting of **30%** and is covered by **Chapters 8 to 14**.

In the exam, you will be expected to demonstrate competence in the following areas:

- Characteristics of service industries.
- Responsibility accounting (authority, responsibility and controllability).
- The use of appropriate financial and non-financial performance measures in a variety of contexts (eg manufacturing and service sectors).
- Cost accounting statements for management information in manufacturing, service and not-for-profit organisations.

Chapter overview

Performance measures and service costing

- **Performance measurement**
  - Gross profit margin
  - Net profit margin
  - Return on capital employed (ROCE)
  - Asset turnover
  - Residual income
- **Service industry costing**
  - Service organisations
  - Characteristics of services
- **Charging customers for services**
  - Price determination
  - Determining the cost unit
- **Cost per unit**
  - Cost per unit
- **Composite cost units**
  - Composite cost units
- **Value for money** (not for profit orgs.)
  - Value for money
    - economy → efficiency → effectiveness
- **Non-financial performance indicators (NFPIs)**
  - Definition
  - Examples
  - Value of NFPIs
  - Problems with NFPIs
- **The balanced scorecard**
  - Introduction
  - Balanced scorecard perspectives and measures
  - Features

1 Performance measurement

One of the main roles of the management accountant is the evaluation of performance. To assist in this a number of financial performance measures can be calculated.

Performance measures for **profit centres** include:

1.1 Gross profit margin

The **gross profit margin** is calculated as

(gross profit ÷ sales) × 100%.

This measure calculates how efficiently a business is using its materials, labour and production overhead in the production process.

1.2 Net profit margin

The **net profit margin** is calculated as

(net profit ÷ sales) × 100%.

This measure indicates how well an organisation controls all its costs in the generation of income.

When looking at the performance of investment centres, which have control over the resources invested as well as income and expense decisions, the following measures can be used:

1.3 Return on capital employed (ROCE)

Return on capital employed (ROCE) (also called return on investment (ROI)) is calculated as

(net profit/capital employed) × 100%.

This shows how much profit has been generated in relation to the amount of resources invested.

In an assessment you may not be given the capital employed figure.

Capital employed = non-current assets + investments + currents assets – current liabilities

1.4 Asset turnover

Asset turnover is calculated as

sales ÷ capital employed.

This measures how efficiently assets are being used to generate income.

Note. Note that **ROCE = Net profit margin × Asset turnover**

Example: ROCE, asset turnover and net profit margin

A company has the following figures:

	$
Sales revenue	540,000
Net profit	50,000
Capital employed	300,000

Return on capital employed

$$= \frac{\$50,000}{\$300,000} \times 100 = 16.67\%$$

Asset turnover

$$= \frac{\$540,000}{\$300,000} = 1.8$$

Net profit margin

$$= \frac{\$50,000}{\$540,000} \times 100 = 9.26\%$$

Return on capital employed	= Asset turnover	×	Net profit margin
16.67%	= 1.8	×	9.26%

This is an important relationship as it means that any changes in return on capital employed can be accounted for by changes in the profitability measured by net profit margin and in the efficiency of the use of the net assets measured by asset turnover.

Activity 1: Ratio calculations

MPRUV plc's summarised results for the last two years are shown below.

	20X1	*20X2*
	$'000	$'000
Sales	40,000	50,000
Gross profit	11,000	15,000
Net profit	6,000	8,000
Capital employed	30,000	40,000

Required

Calculate the ratios shown in Section 1.1–1.4 for both 20X1 and 20X2.

Solution

	20X1	*20X2*
Gross profit margin	27.5%	30%
Net profit margin	15%	16%
ROCE	20%	20%
Asset turnover	133% 1.33	125% 1.25

1.5 Residual income

An alternative to the ROCE is **residual income.** This is calculated as net profit less a notional interest charge for invested capital.

Activity 2: Residual income

A division with capital employed of $400,000 currently earns a ROCE of 22%. It can make an additional investment of $50,000 for a five-year life with nil residual value. The average net profit from this investment would be $12,000. A notional interest charge amounting to 14% of the amount invested is to be charged to the division each year.

Required

The residual income of the division after the investment will be:

- $5,000
- $32,000
- $37,000
- $39,000

Solution

2 Service industry costing

2.1 Service organisations

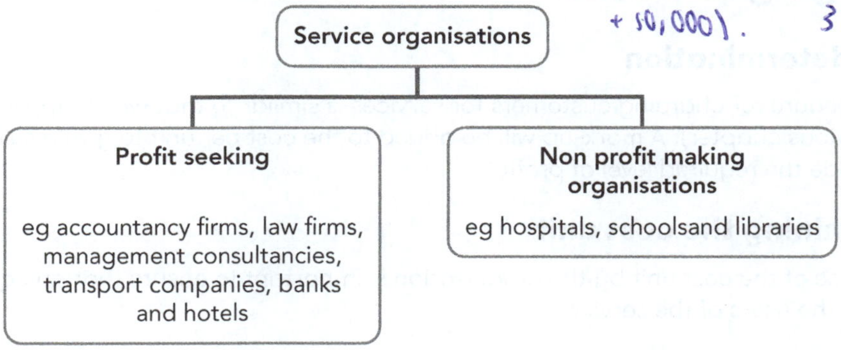

Service organisations do not make or sell tangible goods.

Service costing differs from product costing methods for a number of reasons.

(a) With many services, the cost of direct materials consumed will be relatively small compared to the labour, direct expenses and overheads cost. In product costing, the direct materials are often a greater proportion of the total cost.

(b) The output of most service organisations is difficult to define and hence a unit cost is difficult to calculate.

(c) The service industry includes such a wide range of organisations which provide such different services and have such different cost structures that costing will vary considerably from one to another.

2.2 Characteristics of services

KEY TERM

> **Simultaneity:** A service is consumed at the same time as it is produced.
>
> **Heterogeneity:** Services generally vary between customers more than goods.
>
> **Intangibility:** A service usually has no physical substance.
>
> **Perishability:** Something that cannot be stored or worked on over time.

> **Exam focus point**
>
> Make sure you learn the four specific characteristics of services. This will help you identify organisations that might use service costing.

Example: Characteristics of services

Consider the service of providing a haircut.

(a) A haircut is **intangible** in itself, and the performance of the service comprises many other intangible factors, like the music in the salon, the personality of the hairdresser, the quality of the coffee.

(b) The production and consumption of a haircut are **simultaneous,** and therefore it cannot be inspected for quality in advance, nor can it be returned if it is not what was required.

(c) Haircuts are **perishable;** that is, they cannot be stored. You cannot buy them in bulk, and the hairdresser cannot do them in advance and keep them stocked away in case of heavy demand. The incidence of work in progress in service organisations is less frequent than in other types of organisation.

(d) A haircut is **heterogeneous** and so the exact service received will vary each time: not only will two hairdressers cut hair differently, but a hairdresser will not consistently deliver the same standard of haircut.

---

3 Charging customers for services

3.1 Price determination

The procedure for charging customers for services is similar to that which applies in job costing (see previous chapter). A mark-up will be added to the cost per unit to give a selling price which will provide the required level of profit.

3.2 Determining the cost unit

The choice of the cost unit by the organisation is important to ensure that an equitable charge is made to the users of the service.

4 Cost per unit

$$\text{Cost per unit} = \frac{\text{Total costs for a period}}{\text{Number of service cost units in the period}}$$

↓

But what is a service cost unit? → Service companies often use composite cost units

5 Composite cost units

KEY TERM

> **Composite cost unit:** A cost unit that is used when a 'single' cost unit would not be appropriate (as more than one factor influences cost).

Organisations in the service industry often use **composite cost units** to analyse and monitor their costs, **particularly when a 'single' cost unit would not be appropriate.** As an example, an airline may base a charge for paying for excess baggage on:

(a) How far in km the baggage will be transported

(b) The weight of the baggage

Both of these will have an impact on the airline's fuel cost so it would be inappropriate to base the charge on km or weight alone.

An appropriate composite cost unit would therefore be $X per kg per km.

Activity 3: Composite cost units

Suggest composite cost units that could be used by companies operating in the following service industries:

Solution

Service	Cost unit
Road, rail and air transport services	per passenger per km; peak time? time of day; class of transport; How far going. destination.
Hotels amt of people	type of room; How long going for.
Education	per student per day
Hospitals	Amount of patients; treatments; per patient per day; per bed per night.

Activity 4: Using composite cost units

Carry Co operates a small fleet of delivery vehicles. Expected costs are as follows.

Loading	1 hour per tonne loaded
Loading costs: Labour (casual) Equipment depreciation Supervision	 $2 per hour $80 per week $80 per week
Drivers' wages (fixed)	$100 per man per week
Petrol	10c per kilometre
Repairs	5c per kilometre
Depreciation	$80 per week per vehicle
Supervision	$120 per week
Other general expenses (fixed)	$200 per week

There are two drivers and two vehicles in the fleet.

During a slack week, only six journeys were made.

Journey	Tonnes carried (one way)	One-way distance of journey Kilometres
1	5	100

Journey	Tonnes carried (one way)	One-way distance of journey Kilometres
2	8	20
3	2	60
4	4	50
5	6	200
6	5	300

Required

The expected average full cost per tonne-kilometre for the week is $ [ ]

Solution

6 Value for money

Many organisations are run on a not-for-profit basis. In this case the performance measures in the previous section are less valid. It is more important to assess whether the organisation is getting good **value for money** by measuring **economy, efficiency**, and **effectiveness**.

KEY TERM

Value for money: Getting the best possible combination of services from the least resources

Economy: Purchase of inputs of appropriate quality at minimum cost.

Efficiency: Use of these inputs to maximise output.

Effectiveness: Use of these inputs to achieve organisation's goals (quality, speed of response).

These are sometimes known as the 3Es.

Activity 5: Value for money measures

Birmington University is a public sector (state owned) higher education institution with 27,000 students, 500 staff and an annual budget of $243m.

not-for-profit

Required

Identify possible performance measures for Birmington University that would give an indication of its economy, efficiency and effectiveness.

Solution

Economy - how cost of input can be used to maximise resources.

cost per building.

Economy → cost per lecture Efficiency - process of getting most out of hrs.

Effectiveness - goals/output.

Efficiency → lecture per student. individual classes in lectures.

Effectiveness → overall grades/statistics about the university.

n.o employees in 1yr n.o dropouts.

7 Non-financial performance indicators (NFPIs)

7.1 Definition

KEY TERM

Non-financial performance indicators (NFPIs): Measures of performance based on non-financial information which operating departments use to monitor and control their activities.

7.2 Examples

Examples of NFPIs are summarised in the table below.

Area assessed	Performance measures
Service quality	Number of complaints Proportion of repeat bookings On-time deliveries Customer waiting time
Personnel	Staff turnover Days lost through absenteeism Days lost through accidents/sickness Training time per employee

Different industries will place a different weighting on each area depending on those most critical to their success.

7.3 Value of NFPIs

(a) **Information** can be **provided quickly** for managers (eg per shift, daily or hourly) unlike traditional financial performance reports.

(b) **Anything can be measured**/compared if it is meaningful to do so.

(c) They are **easy to calculate** and easier for non-financial managers to **understand** and use effectively.

(d) They are **less likely to be manipulated** than traditional profit-related measures.

(e) They can be **quantitative or qualitative.**

(f) They provide information about key areas such as **quality** and **customer satisfaction.**

(g) They are a better **indicator of future prospects** than financial indicators which focus on the short term.

7.4 Problems with NFPIs

(a) Too many measures can lead to **information overload** for managers, providing information which is not truly useful.

(b) They may lead managers to **pursue detailed operational goals at the expense of overall corporate strategy.**

(c) They need to be **linked with financial measures.**

(d) They need to be developed and refined over time to ensure they remain relevant.

8 The balanced scorecard

8.1 Introduction

A popular approach in current management thinking to performance measurement (for service **and** non-service organisations) is the use of what is called a 'balanced scorecard', consisting of a variety of indicators both financial and non-financial.

8.2 Balanced scorecard perspectives and measures

The balanced scorecard focuses on four different perspectives and aims to establish goals for each, together with measures which can be used to evaluate whether these goals have been achieved.

8.3 Features

(a) Traditional measures are mainly inward looking and narrow in focus, with overemphasis on financial measures and short-term goals.

(b) The balanced scorecard focuses on both internal and external factors and links performance measures to key elements of a company's strategy.

(c) It requires a balanced consideration of both financial and non-financial measures and goals to prevent improvements being made in one area at the expense of another.

(d) It attempts to identify the needs and concerns of customers in order to identify new products and markets and focuses on comparison with competitors to establish best practice.

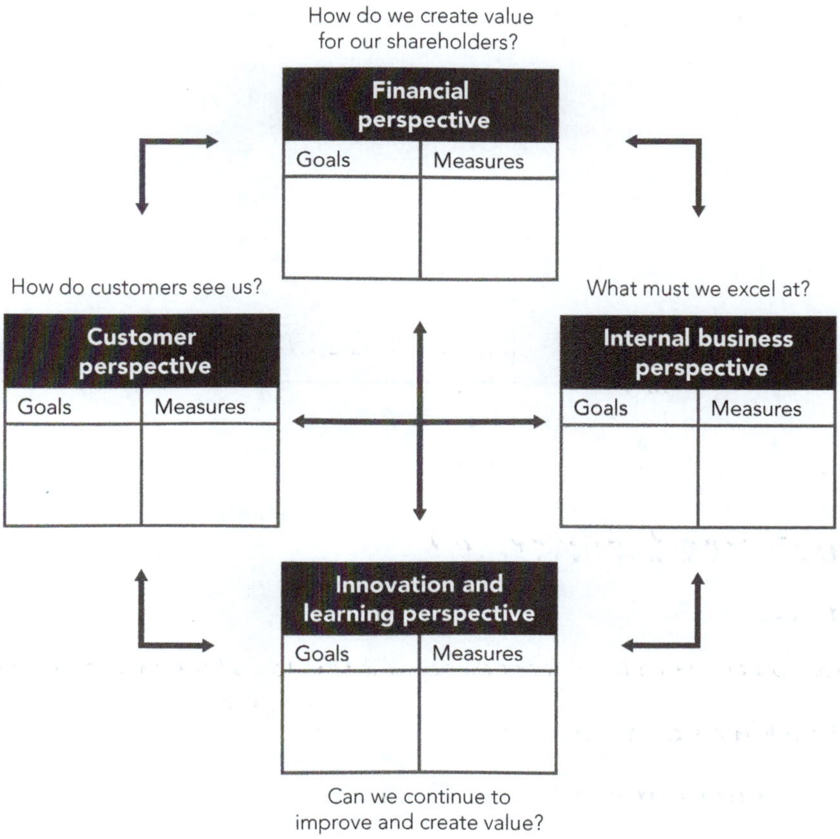

KEY TERM

Financial perspective: Performance measures determining whether the business has achieved value for shareholders.

Innovation and learning perspective: Measures to evaluate the business's capacity to maintain its competitive position through the acquisition of new skills and the development of new products.

Internal business perspective: Aims to improve internal processes and decision making.

Customer perspective: Performance measures that matter to customers.

Activity 6: Balanced scorecard measures

The following statements have been made about the use of the balanced scorecard:

(1) % of customers ordering a dessert could be used as a measure of customer satisfaction for a restaurant

(2) % of revenue from meals sold from the specials board could be used as a measure of innovation for a restaurant

Required

Which of the above statements is/are true?

- O (1) only
- O (2) only
- O Neither (1) nor (2)
- O Both (1) and (2)

Solution

Chapter summary

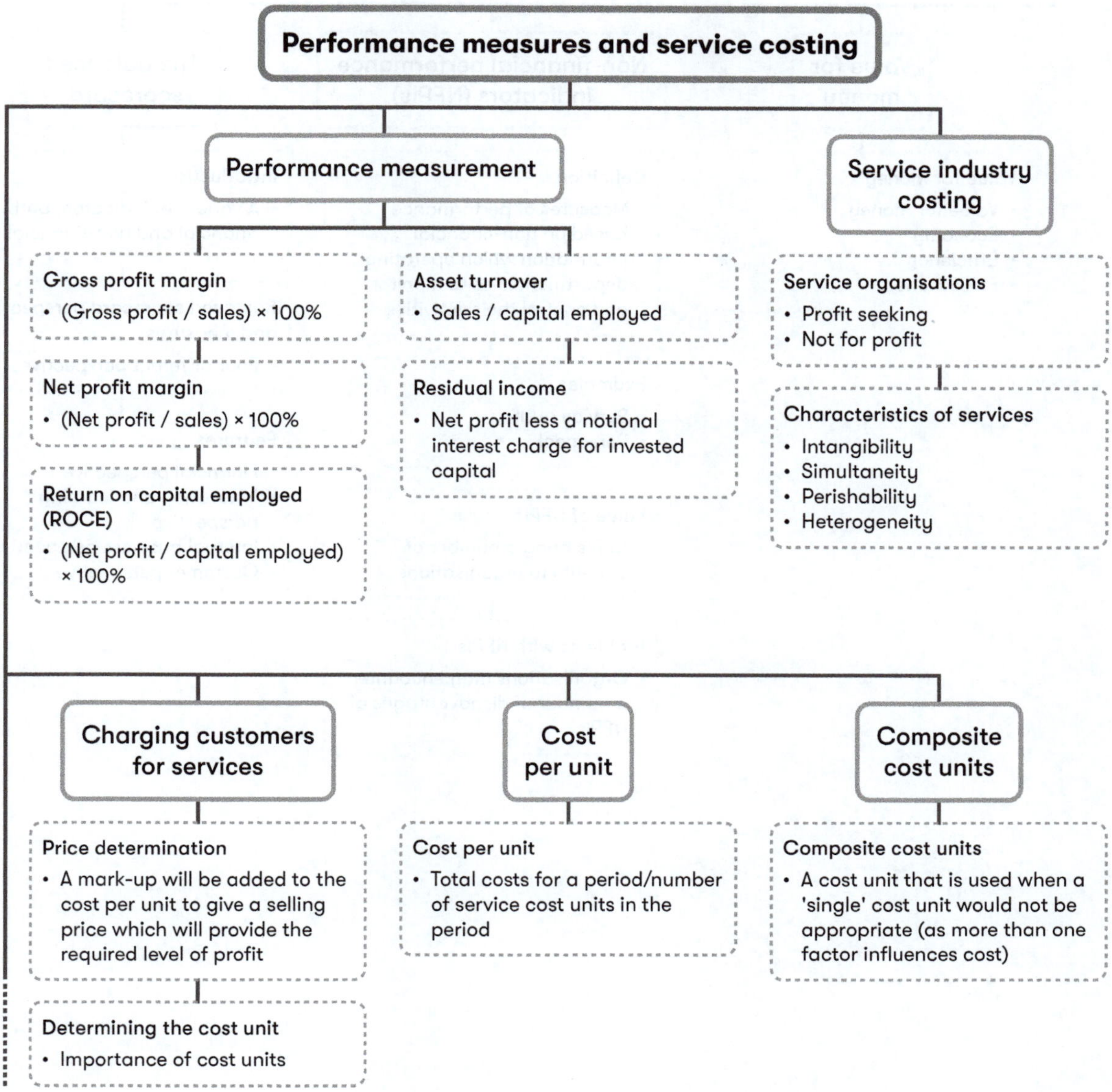

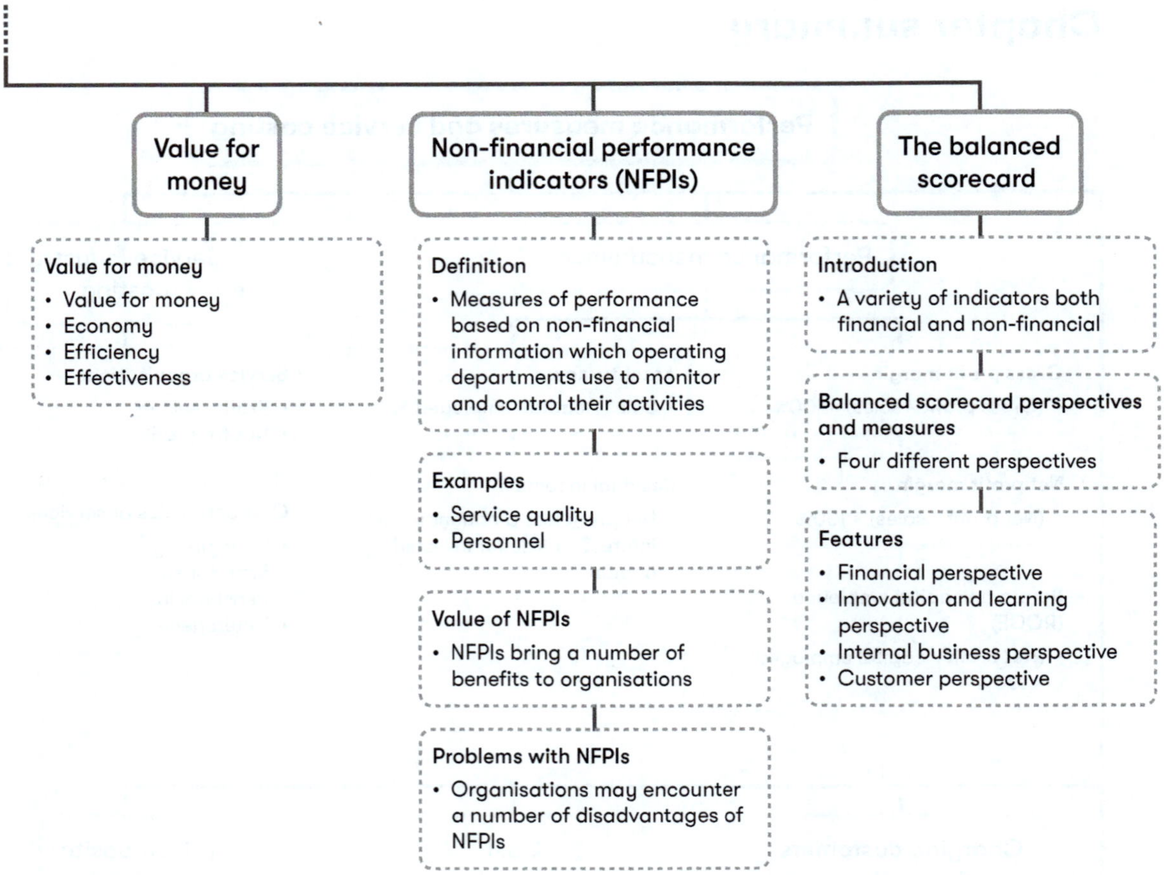
Value for money
Value for money
• Value for money
• Economy
• Efficiency
• Effectiveness
Non-financial performance indicators (NFPIs)
Definition
• Measures of performance based on non-financial information which operating departments use to monitor and control their activities
Examples
• Service quality
• Personnel
Value of NFPIs
• NFPIs bring a number of benefits to organisations
Problems with NFPIs
• Organisations may encounter a number of disadvantages of NFPIs
The balanced scorecard
Introduction
• A variety of indicators both financial and non-financial
Balanced scorecard perspectives and measures
• Four different perspectives
Features
• Financial perspective
• Innovation and learning perspective
• Internal business perspective
• Customer perspective

Key terms

Simultaneity: A service is consumed at the same time as it is produced.

Heterogeneity: Services generally vary between customers more than goods.

Intangibility: A service usually has no physical substance.

Perishability: Something that cannot be stored or worked on over time.

Composite cost unit: A cost unit that is used when a 'single' cost unit would not be appropriate (as more than one factor influences cost).

Value for money: Getting the best possible combination of services from the least resources

Economy: Purchase of inputs of appropriate quality at minimum cost.

Efficiency: Use of these inputs to maximise output.

Effectiveness: Use of these inputs to achieve organisation's goals (quality, speed of response).

These are sometimes known as the 3Es.

Non-financial performance indicators (NFPIs): Measures of performance based on non-financial information which operating departments use to monitor and control their activities.

Financial perspective: Performance measures determining whether the business has achieved value for shareholders.

Innovation and learning perspective: Measures to evaluate the business's capacity to maintain its competitive position through the acquisition of new skills and the development of new products.

Internal business perspective: Aims to improve internal processes and decision making.

Customer perspective: Performance measures that matter to customers.

Activity answers

Activity 1: Ratio calculations

	20X1	20X2
Gross profit margin	11,000/40,000 = 27.5%	15,000/50,000 = 30.0%
Net profit margin	6,000/40,000 = 15.0%	8,000/50,000 = 16.0%
ROCE	6,000/30,000 = 20.0%	8,000/40,000 = 20.0%
Asset turnover	40,000/30,000 = 1.33	50,000/40,000 = 1.25

Activity 2: Residual income

The correct answer is: $37,000

	$
Divisional profit after investment ((400,000 × 22%) + 12,000))	100,000
Notional interest (450,000 × 0.14)	(63,000)
Residual income	37,000

Activity 3: Composite cost units

Service	Cost unit
Road, rail and air transport services	Passenger/mile or tonne
Hotels	Per person per night
Education	Per student per college day (to allow for different course lengths)
Hospitals	Patient/day

Activity 4: Using composite cost units

The expected average full cost per tonne-kilometre for the week is $ 0.304

Working

Variable costs

Journey	*1*	*2*	*3*	*4*	*5*	*6*
	$	$	$	$	$	$
Loading labour	10	16	4	8	12	10
Petrol (both ways)	20	4	12	10	40	60
Repairs (both ways)	10	2	6	5	20	30
	40	22	22	23	72	100

Total costs

	$
Variable costs (total for journeys 1 to 6)	279
Loading equipment depreciation	80
Loading supervision	80
Drivers' wages	200
Vehicles depreciation	160
Drivers' supervision	120
Other costs	200
	1,119

Journey		*One-way distance*	
	Tonnes	Kilometres	Tonne-kilometres
1	5	100	500
2	8	20	160
3	2	60	120
4	4	50	200
5	6	200	1,200
6	5	300	1,500
			3,680

Activity 5: Value for money measures

Economy – The average salary for a lecturer, the cost of running the building per m^2 per month

Efficiency – Students per lecturer, students per class

Effectiveness – Pass rates, drop-out rates, percentage of graduates employed within six months of graduation

Activity 6: Balanced scorecard measures

The correct answer is: Both (1) and (2)

Both of these measures would be suitable for a restaurant and it should be possible to get the required information.

Test your learning

1 What is the main aim of performance measurement?

- O To obtain evidence in order to dismiss someone
- O To establish how well something or somebody is doing in relation to a planned activity
- O To collect information on costs
- O To award bonuses

2 Place the correct letters in the boxes.

A Profit

B Capital employed

C Sales

ROCE = [ ] / [ ] × 100%

Profit margin = [ ] / [ ] × 100%

3 Which one of the following is the correct formula for asset turnover?

- O Sales ÷ capital employed
- O Net profit ÷ sales
- O Capital employed ÷ sales
- O Sales ÷ net profit

4 With many services the cost of direct materials will be relatively high.

- O True
- O False

5 Match up the following services with their typical cost units.

Service		Cost unit
Hotels	?	Patient/day
Education		Meal served
Hospitals		Full-time student
Catering organisations		Occupied bed-night

6 What are the specific characteristics of services?

(1) Intangibility

(2) Heterogeneity

(3) Perishability

(4) Consistency

(5) Regularity

(6) Simultaneity

- O (1), (3), (5) and (6)
- O (2), (3), (4) and (5)
- O (1), (2), (3) and (6)
- O (2), (4), (5) and (6)

7 Average cost per unit of service =

[ ] / [ ]

8 Which two of the following might be characteristics of a hospital?

- ☐ Use of composite cost units
- ☐ High materials costs
- ☐ High levels of indirect costs as a proportion of total cost
- ☐ Calculation of profit per patient

9 Which of the following are characteristics of service costing?

- ☐ High levels of indirect costs as a proportion of total cost
- ☐ Cost units are often intangible
- ☐ Use of composite cost units
- ☐ Use of equivalent units

10 Which of the following would be suitable cost units for a hospital?

- ☐ Patient/day
- ☐ Operating theatre hour
- ☐ Ward
- ☐ X-ray department
- ☐ Outpatient visit

14 Cost bookkeeping

Learning outcomes

Having studied this chapter you will be able to:
• Explain the integration of the cost accounts with the financial accounting system
• Prepare a set of integrated accounts, showing standard cost variances

Chapter context

In earlier chapters we looked at how the cost of what we produce is calculated and the calculation of variances by comparing these costs with standards. This chapter looks at how these figures are actually entered into a costing system. This involves using double entry bookkeeping that is covered more extensively in Paper BA3, but if you haven't studied for this subject yet there is a basic approach that is sufficient for BA2.

Syllabus context

This chapter is part of syllabus **Section C**, which looks at **'Planning and Control'**.

This syllabus area has a weighting of **30%** and is covered by **Chapters 8 to 14**.

In the exam, you will be expected to demonstrate competence in the following areas:

- Manufacturing accounts including raw material, work-in-progress, finished goods and manufacturing overhead control accounts.
- Integrated ledgers including accounting for over and under absorption of production overhead.
- The treatment of variances in integrated ledger systems.

Chapter overview

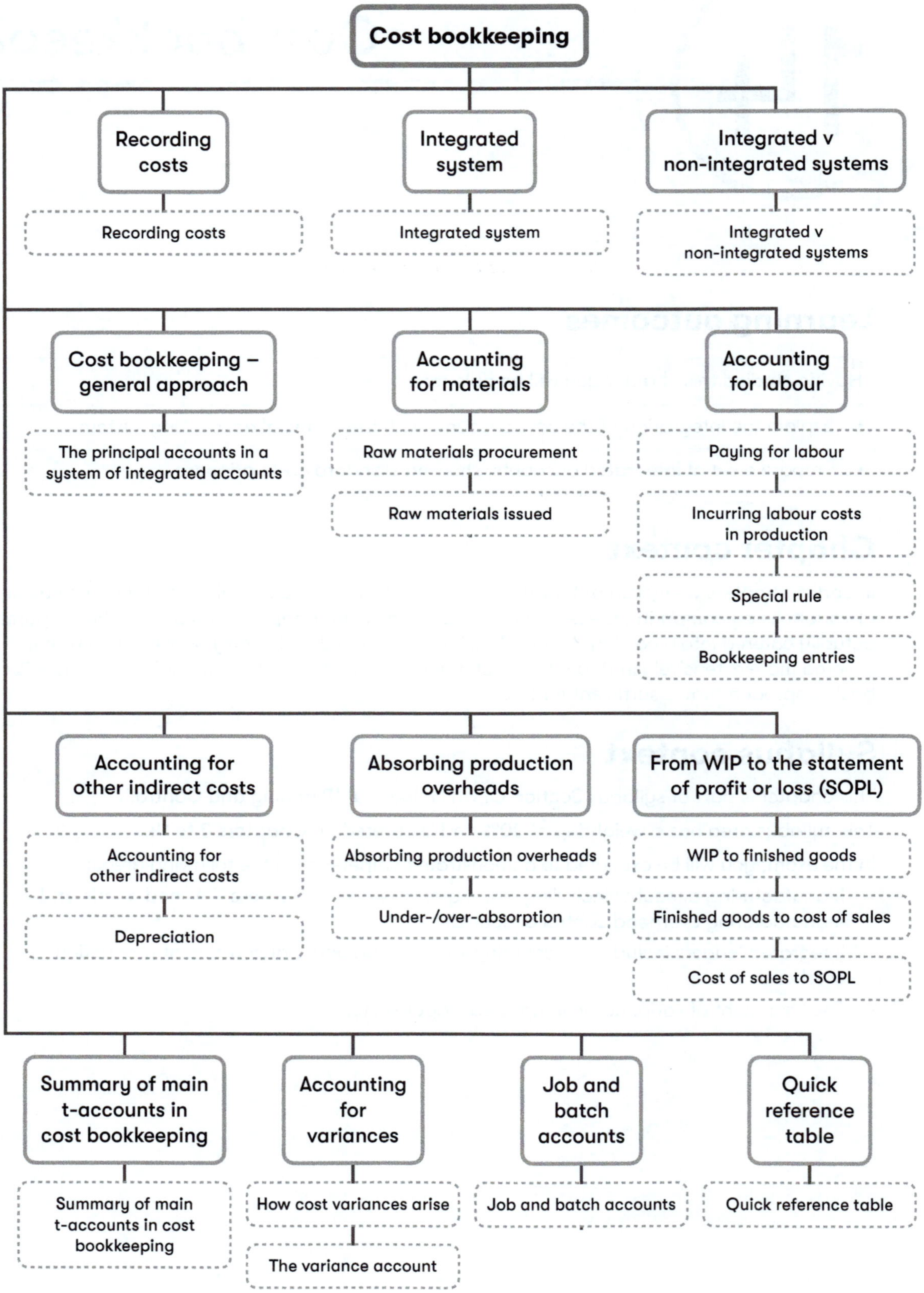

1 Recording costs

Whatever costing system is used, costs must be recorded for use in financial and management accounting.

Manufacturing businesses need details about inventories of raw materials, work in progress (WIP) and finished goods on an ongoing basis.

2 Integrated system

KEY TERM

Integrated systems: One set of accounts in which all transactions are recorded. The same system provides financial accounting and costing information.

Interlocking systems: Where one system is used for the financial accounting function and a completely separate system is used for cost/management accounting.

2.1 Integrated v non-integrated systems

Advantages of integrated systems:

(a) Saves administrative effort and expense

(b) Less confusing

Disadvantages of integrated systems:

(a) One set of books fulfils two purposes (may conflict eg inventory valuations)

(b) More detailed analysis of costs required

3 Cost bookkeeping – general approach

KEY TERM

Bookkeeping: The process of entering transactions in the books of the business, by creating equal debit and credit entries in separate ledger accounts.

A standard manufacturing process will begin with the procurement of raw materials. Labour will be employed and paid for and production overheads will be incurred in turning the raw materials into finished goods. The finished goods will be stored in a warehouse before being sold.

For each individual stage of this process, entries will be made into a cost bookkeeping system. The nature of the accounting entry will often mirror the physical 'transactions' that take place in the production environment.

3.1 The principal accounts in a system of integrated accounts

(a) The resources accounts

  (i) Materials control account or stores control account

  (ii) Wages (and salaries) control account

  (iii) Production overhead control account

  (iv) Administration overhead control account

  (v) Selling and distribution overhead control account

(b) Accounts which record the cost of production items from the start of production work through to cost of sales

  (i) Work in progress control account

  (ii) Finished goods control account

  (iii) Cost of sales control account

(c) Sales account

(d) Statement of profit or loss

In general, to correctly identify each double entry, two stages are required:

(a) Identify the two t-accounts that will be affected by the transaction

(b) Establish the debit (DR) entry and the credit (CR) entry

Note. If you are not yet familiar with debits and credits, a rule of thumb you may find useful is 'out on the right, in on the left', as this approach will be correct for all of the 'cost transactions'.

Activity 1: Double entry example

Raw materials valued at $1,500 are transferred from the material stores to the factory.

Required

Show the t-accounts and double entry required to account for this transaction.

Solution

4 Accounting for materials

Although a company can choose to structure its internal cost accounts in any way it chooses, there are several types of transactions that will always be accounted for in the same way.

4.1 Raw materials procurement

Raw materials need to be procured. This will be done either on credit or by paying cash. The double entry to record this would be as follows:

On credit:	**DR Raw materials**	**CR Trade payables**
Pay cash:	**DR Raw materials**	**CR Cash**

Either way, as the materials are procured, they are shown in the raw materials account on the left-hand side (ie as they 'come into the stores').

4.2 Raw materials issued

When they are needed, the materials will be transferred out of the stores. How this is treated in the cost accounts depends on whether the materials are direct or indirect. Direct material costs will form part of the direct cost per unit. Indirect materials will form part of the overall production overheads (ie to be absorbed separately in an absorption costing system).

Direct:	**DR WIP/Production**	**CR Raw materials**
Indirect:	**DR Production overheads**	**CR Raw materials**

Note that either way, as the materials are used, they are shown in the raw materials account on the right-hand side (ie as they 'go out of the stores').

Activity 2: Raw materials issued

Raw materials worth $6,500 are purchased on credit in a period. In the same period, $5,000 of raw materials are issued to production, and $1,500 are issued to the maintenance department.

Required

Show the t-accounts and double entries required to account for these transactions in a cost bookkeeping system.

Solution

Raw materials
D C
6500

Trade payables
D C
6500

WIP
D C

Production overheads.
D C

① D - Raw mats - 6500
C - Trade payables - 6500

② issued
D - WIP - 5000
C - Raw mats - 5000

③ - maintenance
D - prod'n o/head - 1500.
C - Raw mats - 1500

5 Accounting for labour

Cost bookkeeping for labour follows exactly the same principles as accounting for material (since it is just another resource used to make finished products). However, it is complicated by the different elements that make up an employee's wages (eg NI (social security) and income tax deductions), and the different types of labour cost that can be incurred (eg overtime and bonuses).

5.1 Paying for labour

The cost bookkeeping entries relating to the payment of wages need to account for the various deductions associated with an employee's net pay.

The gross wage will include the following items, and there will be a double entry for each:

Net pay	**DR Wages control**	**CR Cash**
PAYE (Pay As You Earn income tax)	**DR Wages control**	**CR PAYE control**
National Insurance (Employee's)	**DR Wages control**	**CR NI control**

It is important to realise that the end result of this is that the gross cost of wages has been debited to the **wages control account.**

KEY TERM

> **Wages control account:** A 'collecting place' for net wages paid and deductions made from gross pay.

Note. There is an additional labour cost to the company – Employer's NI contributions. This is paid by the company directly to the tax authorities.

5.2 Incurring labour costs in production

At the end of each period, the gross wages incurred need to be related to the work done by the employees. This will depend on whether their work should be treated as direct or indirect labour. Total gross wages will be split into two and transferred to one of two accounts – WIP account for the direct labour element and production overheads account for indirect labour. (This is the same principle as for direct and indirect materials.)

There are some general rules as to how split labour costs:

	Direct workers	Indirect workers
Normal basic pay	Direct cost	Indirect cost
General production: Overtime – Basic pay element	Direct cost	Indirect cost
General production: Overtime – O/T premium	Indirect cost	Indirect cost
General non-production: Overtime – Basic pay element	Indirect cost	Indirect cost
General non-production: Overtime – O/T premium	Indirect cost	Indirect cost
Idle time	Indirect cost	Indirect cost

Illustration 1: The wages control account

The following details were extracted from a weekly payroll for 750 employees at a factory.

	Direct workers	Indirect workers	Total
	$	$	$
Analysis of gross pay:			
Ordinary time	36,000	22,000	58,000
Overtime: basic wage	8,700	5,430	14,130
premium	4,350	2,715	7,065
Shift allowance	3,465	1,830	5,295
Sick pay	950	500	1,450
Idle time	3,200	–	3,200
	56,665	32,475	89,140
Net wages paid to employees	45,605	24,220	69,825

Required

Prepare the wages control account for the week.

Solution

(1) The **wages control account** acts as a sort of 'collecting place' for net wages paid and deductions made from gross pay. The gross pay is then analysed between direct and indirect wages.

(2) The first step is to determine which wage costs are direct and which are indirect. The direct wages will be debited to the WIP account and the indirect wages will be debited to the production overhead account.

(3) There are in fact only two items of direct wages cost in this example – the ordinary time ($36,000) and the basic overtime wage ($8,700) paid to direct workers. All other payments (including the overtime premium) are indirect wages.

(4) The net wages paid are debited to the control account, and the balance then represents the deductions which have been made for income tax, national insurance, and so on.

WAGES CONTROL ACCOUNT

	$		$
Bank: net wages paid	69,825	Work in progress – direct labour	44,700
Deductions control accounts*		Production overhead control:	
($89,140 – $69,825)	19,315	Indirect labour	27,430
		Overtime premium	7,065
		Shift allowance	5,295
		Sick pay	1,450
		Idle time	3,200
	89,140		89,140

*In practice there would be a separate deductions control account for each type of deduction made (such as income tax, National Insurance).

Activity 3: Wages control account

In April, the total gross pay to the manufacturing workforce was $55,000. PAYE deductions were $20,000 and employees' NI contributions were $5,000.

Required

Calculate the net pay in the period and show the t-accounts required to account for these transactions in a cost bookkeeping system.

Solution

5.3 Special rule

In certain circumstances, production may be carried out at the **specific request of a customer.** If this results in overtime premiums being paid, or bonuses being paid, then these 'extra' labour costs should be treated as **direct** costs because they can be identified with specific production units.

5.4 Bookkeeping entries

When the nature of the labour cost has been identified the cost bookkeeping entries will be as follows:

Direct labour:	**DR WIP/Production**	**CR Wages**
Indirect labour:	**DR Production overheads**	**CR Wages**

Activity 4: Clearing the wages control account

(Continued from Activity 3 – ie total gross wage $55,000)

An analysis of the work done in April showed the following:

	Direct workers	Indirect workers
Basic pay – ordinary hours	$35,000	$5,000
General overtime – basic element	$4,500	$2,000
– overtime premium	$2,250	$1,000
Bonus for completion of rush order (at request of customer)	$4,000	
Idle time	$1,250	

Required

Show the double entries required to account for these transactions in a cost accounting system.

Solution

Wages control account

	$		$
Cash	30,000	WIP	43500
PAYE	20,000	p/cd in o'heads	11500
NI	5,000		
	55,000		55,000

WIP

	$		$
wages	43500		

Production overhead

	$		$
Indirect labour	11500		

6 Accounting for other indirect costs

In addition to indirect materials and indirect labour, a manufacturing company will incur many other indirect production costs, such as rent, rates and insurance.

The entries for these will be:

DR Production overhead CR Rent/Rates/Other control account

6.1 Depreciation

Depreciation of machinery used in production is worthy of special attention. Note that this is treated as an indirect cost related to production, with the depreciation amount in a period accounted for as follows:

DR Production overhead CR Provision for depreciation

7 Absorbing production overheads

When all of the indirect costs have been 'collected' in the production overhead account, they will be **absorbed into production,** according to the absorption basis used by the company. The double entry for this transaction is:

DR WIP/Production CR Production overhead

The WIP/Production account will now be charged with all the costs relating to production in the period (ie all the direct costs and all the absorbed indirect costs).

Note. In a marginal costing company, the total overheads will just be transferred directly to the statement of profit or loss and treated as a period cost.

7.1 Under-/over-absorption

The production overheads account will now have been debited with all the indirect costs incurred, and credited with the amount absorbed into production.

Any remaining balance on this account will represent **under- or over-absorption.**

This balance should be transferred from the production overheads account to the statement of profit or loss, to ensure the actual profit shown is corrected for any under-/over-absorption of costs into production.

The double entry will depend on whether the company under- or over-absorbed:

Under-absorbed:

DR Statement of profit or loss   CR Production overhead

Over-absorbed:

DR Production overhead   CR Statement of profit or loss

Activity 5: Overhead absorption

Production overheads incurred in a period total $95,000.

DR prodn overheads
CR Bank.

Required

Show the t-accounts and double entries required in an absorption costing environment if profit is to be adjusted for any under-/over-absorption and the overheads absorbed into production are $88,000:

Solution

95,000 - 88,000 = 7000 under absorbed.

under absorbtion = DR statement of profit + loss 7,000. CR production overheads. 7,000

production overheads absorbed = DR WIP / production 88,000 CR production overheads. 88,000.

production overheads = DR production overheads 95,000 CR bank. 95,000

8 From WIP to the statement of profit or loss (SOPL)

8.1 WIP to finished goods

[DR Finished goods   CR WIP/Production]

At the end of the period, the cost of any finished goods will be transferred from the WIP account to the finished goods account (to reflect finished goods being transferred from the factory to the warehouse). Any unfinished WIP will remain in the WIP account as a balance carried forward to the next period.

8.2 Finished goods to cost of sales

[DR Cost of sales CR Finished goods]

Any finished goods sold during the period will have their costs transferred to the cost of sales account. Again, the cost of any closing inventory will remain in the finished goods account as a balance carried forward.

8.3 Cost of sales to SOPL

[DR SOPL CR Cost of sales]

The 'cost of goods sold' will be transferred from the cost of sales account to the statement of profit or loss (SOPL) at the end of the reporting period. At this stage it will be joined by the revenue received from selling the finished goods and any adjustments for under-/over-absorption.

Any **non-production** expenses like sales and administration will be charged to the SOPL at this time.

The resulting balance on the SOPL will represent profit (or loss) in the period.

9 Summary of main t-accounts in cost bookkeeping

9.1 Paying for resources

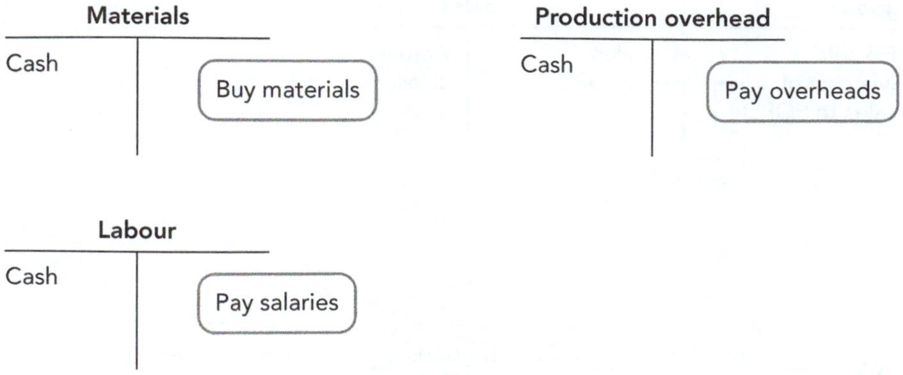

9.2 Using resources in production

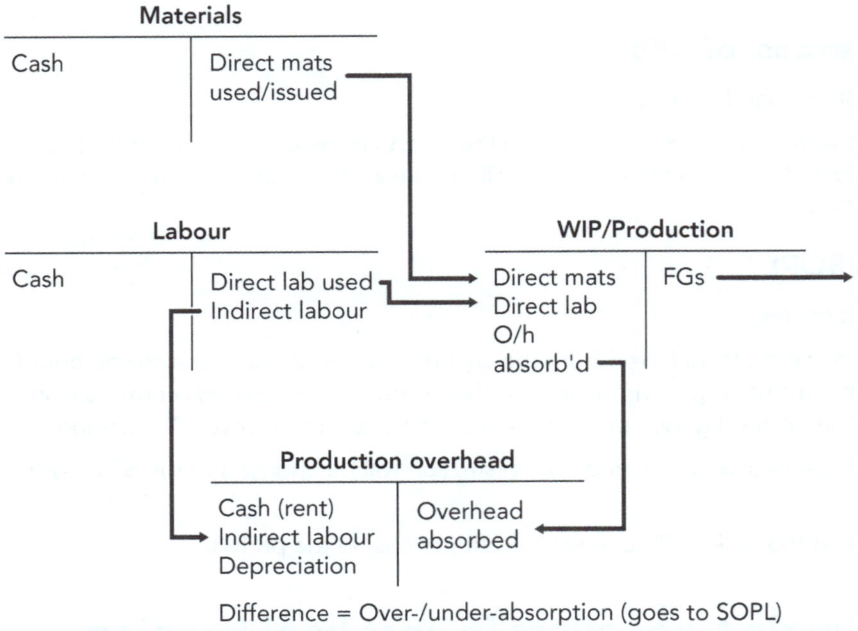

9.3 Finished goods are sold

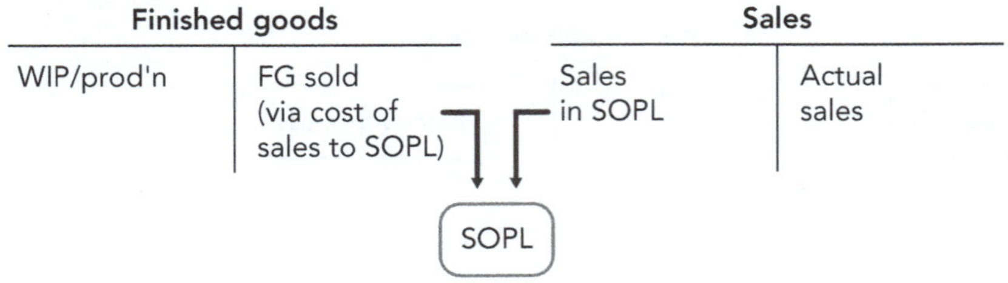

9.4 Summary

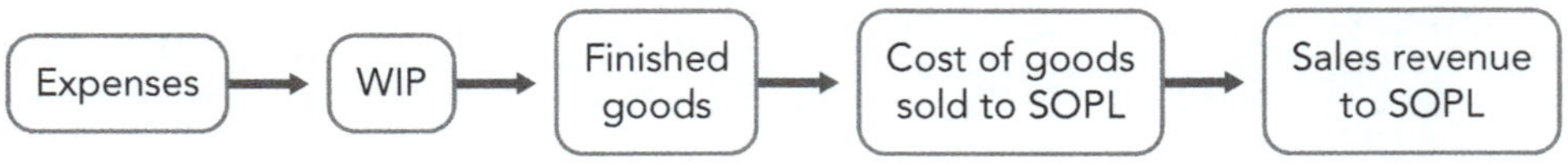

Activity 6: Bookkeeping practice

This Activity illustrates all the common 'transactions' in cost bookkeeping, and shows how the costs flow through the t-accounts, from the procurement of resources to the calculation of profit in the statement of profit or loss.

The following balances were extracted from a company's books at 30 September 2016:

	$
Raw materials inventory	9,000
WIP	8,250
Finished goods inventory	10,800

During the next three months the following transactions took place (all purchases and sales were on credit):

	$

BPP

Materials purchased	24,700
Materials issued to WIP	27,150
Materials issued to maintenance	1,000
Direct wages paid and worked (3,500 hours)	51,900
Indirect wages paid and worked	18,300
Depreciation of factory equipment	800
Other production overheads paid	13,950
Sales and distribution costs paid	7,800
Cost of sales	105,000
Sales	135,000

The closing inventory of WIP at 31 December 2016 was valued at $25,770.

Overheads are absorbed on the basis of direct labour hours at a predetermined rate of $10/hour.

Required

Complete the following ledger accounts as they would appear in an integrated system of accounting.

Solution

Raw material

	$		£
B/d	9000	WIP	27150
payables	24700	prodn overheads	1000
		c/d	5550
	33700		33700
B/d	5550		

Labour

	$		$
cash	70200	WIP	51900
		prodn o/heads	18,300
	70200		70200

Production overhead

	$		$
raw mats	1000		
indirect wages/labour	18300		
depreciation	800		

	$		$
cash	13950	WIP	35,000
SOPL	950		
	35,000		35,000

Provision for depreciation

	$		$
		Prod'n overhead	800
B/d	800		
	800		800
		B/d	800

WIP/Production

	$		$
B/d	8250	Finished goods	96,530
Raw mats	27150		
Direct wages	51900		
Production overheads	35,000	c/d	25,770
	122,300		122,300
B/d	25,770		

Finished goods inventory

	$		$
B/d	10800	Cost of sales	105,000
WIP	96,530		
		B/d	2330
	107330		107330
B/d	2330		

Sales

	$		$
SOPL	135,000	Debtors	135,000

Statement of profit or loss

	$		$
cos	105,000	sales	135,000
sales + dist	7800		
profit	23150 -	prodn o/head overabs	950
	13590		135950

Sales and distribution costs

	$		$
cash	7800	SPL	7800

Cost of sales

	$		$
finished goods	105,000		

10 Accounting for variances

10.1 How cost variances arise

The final issue that needs to be considered is how variances are accounted for. The initial payments for material, labour and overheads are entered at their actual cost but then everything is valued at standard cost each time a transaction between cost ledger accounts is recorded.

eg raw materials, labour, fixed overhead → WIP

completed production from WIP → finished goods

eg

Raw materials control a/c

	$		$
Actual cost	X	WIP (@std)	X
		Price variance	X
	-	(A)	X
		Bal c/f (@ std)	
	X		X

Direct wages control a/c

	$		$
Actual cost	X	WIP (hrs paid @ std)	X
	-	Rate variance (A)	X
	X		X

Work in progress control a/c

	$		$
Raw mat's (@std)	X	Finished goods (@ std)	X
Direct wages (@ std)	X	Mat's usage var (A)	X
Labour eff'cy var (F)	X		–
	X		X

10.2 The variance account

The result, as can be seen above, is that the price and rate variances are the balancing figures in their respective control accounts, and the usage and efficiency variances likewise in the WIP control account.

The double entry for each variance is made to a variance account, the balance on which goes to the SOPL.

Variance account

	$		$
Mat's price (A)	X	Labour efficiency (F)	X
Labour rate (A)	X		
Mat's usage (A)	X	SOPL	X
	X		X

Activity 7: Accounting for variances

A company uses raw material J in production. The standard price for material J is $3 per metre. During the month 6,000 metres were purchased for $18,600, of which 5,000 metres were issued to production.

Required

Show the t-accounts to record the above transactions.

(1) Dr raw materials 11600 Cr wages 18600

(2) → std. Dr materials 15,000 (5000 x 3) Cr WIP / production 15,000 – 5 x 3 000

(3) Dr mats 3000 Cr prod'n overheads 3000.

Solution

Activity 8: Double entry for variances

A firm uses standard costing and an integrated accounting system. The double entry for an adverse material usage variance is:

- ○ DR Stores control account CR Work in progress control account
- ○ DR Material usage variance account CR Stores control account
- ○ DR Work in progress control account CR Material usage variance account
- ○ DR Material usage variance account CR Work in progress control account

Solution

---

11 Job and batch accounts

A separate work in progress account is maintained for each individual job or batch.

Job a/c

DR	$	CR	
Raw material	X	Material transferred	X
Labour	X	Material returned to stores	X

DR	$	CR	
Overhead	X	COS (or bal c/f if incomplete)	X
	X		X

12 Quick reference table

Transaction	DR entry	CR entry	With
Procurement of materials			
Purchase raw materials	DR Materials	CR Cash or Payables	Cost of materials purchased
Materials used			
Issue materials to factory	DR WIP/Production	CR Materials	Cost of materials issued
Issue indirect materials	DR Production overhead	CR Materials	Cost of materials issued
Payment of wages			
Pay wages	DR Wages control		Gross pay
		CR Cash	Net pay
		CR PAYE control	PAYE element
		CR NI control	Employee's NI contributions
Labour used			
Direct labour worked	DR WIP/Production	CR Wages control	Cost of direct labour
Indirect labour worked	DR Production overhead	CR Wages control	Cost of indirect labour
Other indirect costs			
Pay fixed overhead (rent)	DR Production overhead	CR Cash or Rent control	Cost of rent in period
Depreciation	DR Production overhead	CR Provision for dep'n	Depreciation in period
Absorb overheads			
Absorb prod'n overheads	DR WIP/Production	CR Production overhead	Total absorbed on given basis
Under-absorption	DR Statement of profit or loss	CR Production overhead	Amount under-absorbed
Over-absorption	DR Production overhead	CR Statement of profit or loss	Amount over-absorbed
WIP to finished goods			
Complete finished	DR Finished goods	CR WIP/Production	Cost of finished goods

Transaction	DR entry	CR entry	With
goods			
Finished goods to CoS			
Sell finished goods	DR Cost of sales	CR Finished goods	Cost of goods sold
Non-production costs			
Pay non-prod'n costs	DR Non-prod'n (admin)	CR Cash	Cost of admin in the period
Statement of profit or loss			
Complete statement of profit or loss	DR Statement of profit or loss	CR Cost of sales	Final cost of sales amount
	DR Sales	CR Statement of profit or loss	Revenue in the period
	DR Statement of profit or loss	CR Non-prod'n control	Non-production costs in period

Chapter summary

Cost bookkeeping

- **Recording costs**
  - Recording costs
    - Costs must be recorded for use in financial and management accounting
- **Integrated system**
  - Integrated system
    - Integrated systems
    - Interlocking systems
- **Integrated v non-integrated systems**
  - Integrated v non-integrated systems
    - Advantages
    - Disadvantages
- **Cost bookkeeping – general approach**
  - The principal accounts in a system of integrated accounts
    - The resources accounts
    - Accounts which record the cost of production items from the start of production work through to cost of sales
    - Sales account
    - Statement of profit or loss
- **Accounting for materials**
  - Raw materials procurement
    - Accounting for raw materials
  - Raw materials issued
    - Accounting for direct materials
    - Accounting for indirect materials
- **Accounting for labour**
  - Paying for labour
    - Wages control account
  - Incurring labour costs in production
    - Direct and indirect wages
  - Special rule
    - Specific customer requests
  - Bookkeeping entries
    - Bookkeeping for labour costs

Accounting for other indirect costs

- **Accounting for other indirect costs**
  - Bookkeeping for indirect costs
- **Depreciation**
  - Bookkeeping for depreciation

Absorbing production overheads

- **Absorbing production overheads**
  - Bookkeeping for production overheads
- **Under-/over-absorption**
  - Bookkeeping for under-/over-absorption

From WIP to the statement of profit or loss (SOPL)

- **WIP to finished goods**
  - Treatment [DR Finished goods CR WIP/Production]
- **Finished goods to cost of sales**
  - Treatment [DR Cost of sales CR Finished goods]
- **Cost of sales to SOPL**
  - Treatment [DR SOPL CR Cost of sales]

Summary of main t-accounts in cost bookkeeping

- **Summary of main t-accounts in cost bookkeeping**
  - Paying for resources
  - Using resources in production
  - Finished goods are sold
  - Summary

Accounting for variances

- **How cost variances arise**
  - Double entries
- **The variance account**
  - Double entries

Job and batch accounts

- **Job and batch accounts**
  - Work-in-progress account

Quick reference table

- **Quick reference table**
  - Table of entries

Key terms

Integrated systems: One set of accounts in which all transactions are recorded. The same system provides financial accounting and costing information.

Interlocking systems: Where one system is used for the financial accounting function and a completely separate system is used for cost/management accounting.

Bookkeeping: The process of entering transactions in the books of the business, by creating equal debit and credit entries in separate ledger accounts.

Wages control account: A 'collecting place' for net wages paid and deductions made from gross pay.

Activity answers

Activity 1: Double entry example

Raw materials

	$		$
		WIP	1,500

WIP/Production

	$		$
Materials	1,500		

DR WIP/Production	$1,500	
CR Raw materials		$1,500

Activity 2: Raw materials issued

Raw materials

	$		$
Payables	6,500	WIP	5,000
		Prod o'head	1,500

Payables

	$		$
		Raw materials	6,500

WIP/Production

	$		$
Direct materials	5,000		

Production overhead

	$		$
Indirect materials	1,500		

Purchases:	DR Raw materials	CR Payables
Issue Direct Mats:	DR WIP	CR Raw materials
Issue Indirect Mats:	DR Prod overhead	CR Raw materials

Activity 3: Wages control account

Cash

	$		$
		Wages	30,000

Wages control a/c

	$		$
Cash	30,000		
PAYE	20,000		
NI	5,000		
	55,000		

PAYE control a/c

	$		$
		Wages	20,000

NI control a/c

	$		$
		Wages	5,000

Gross pay = Net pay + PAYE + Employees' NI

\$55,000 = Net pay + \$20,000 + \$5,000

Net pay = \$55,000 – (\$20,000 + \$5,000)

Net pay = \$30,000

Net pay:	DR Wages control	CR Cash
PAYE:	DR Wages control	CR PAYE control
NI:	DR Wages control	CR NI control

Activity 4: Clearing the wages control account

Wages control account

	$		$
Cash	30,000	WIP	43,500
PAYE	20,000	Prod o'head	11,500
NI	5,000		
	55,000		55,000

WIP

	$		$
Direct labour	43,500		

Production overhead

	$		$
Indirect labour	11,500		

Analysis of labour costs:

Direct labour = $35,000 + $4,500 + $4,000 = $43,500

Indirect labour = $2,250 + $1,250 + $8,000 = $11,500

Direct labour:	DR WIP	CR Wages
Indirect labour:	DR Prod o'head	CR Wages

Activity 5: Overhead absorption

Production overhead

	$		$
Incurred	95,000	Absorbed	88,000
		St of profit or loss	7,000β
	95,000		95,000

WIP/Production

	$		$
Prod overhead	88,000		

Statement of profit or loss

	$		$
Under-abs	7,000		

Absorption:	DR WIP	CR Prod overhead
Adjustment:	DR Statement of profit or loss	CR Prod overhead

Activity 6: Bookkeeping practice

Raw material

	$		£
B/d	9,000	WIP	27,150

	$		£
Creditors	24,700	Prod overheads	1,000
		c/d	5,550
	33,700		33,700
B/d	5,550		

Labour

	$		$
Cash	70,200	WIP	51,900
		Overheads	18,300
	70,200		70,200

Production overhead

	$		$
Materials	1,000	WIP (3,500 Hrs × $10/hr)	35,000
Indirect Labour	18,300		
Depreciation	800		
Cash (other production overhead)	13,950		
SOPL (over absorption)	950		
	35,000		35,000

Provision for depreciation

	$		$
		Prod o'head	800
C/d	800		
	800		800
		B/d	800

WIP/Production

	$		$
B/d	8,250	Finished goods	96,530
Materials	27,150		
Labour	51,900		
Overhead	35,000	c/d	25,770
	122,300		122,300
B/d	25,770		

Finished goods inventory

	$		$
B/d	10,800	Cost of sales	105,000
WIP	96,530		
		C/d	2,330
	107,330		107,330
B/d	2,330		

Sales

	$		$
SoPOL	135,000	Debtors	135,000

Statement of profit or loss

	$		$
Cost of sales	105,000	Sales	135,000
Sales and distribution costs	7,800		
Profit	23,150	Over absorption	950
	135,950		135,950

Sales and distribution costs

	$		$
Cash	7,800	SoPOL	7,800

Cost of sales

	$		$
Finished Goods	105,000	I/S	105,000

Activity 7: Accounting for variances

Raw material

	$		$
Cash/payables (actual)	18,600	WIP (5,000 × $3)	15,000
		Raw material variance ($3.10 – $3) × 6,000	600

	$		$
		Balance c/d (1,000 × $3)	3,000

WIP

	$		$
Raw materials	15,000		

Raw material variance

	$		$
Raw materials	600		

Activity 8: Double entry for variances

The correct answer is: DR Material usage variance account CR Work in progress control account

The usage variance arises during production therefore the correct account to be credited is work in progress. The fourth option is correct.

An adverse variance is debited to the relevant variance account. Therefore we can eliminate the first and third options, which are incorrect.

The second option has the correct debit entry for the adverse variance but the credit entry is incorrect.

Test your learning

1 What is the double entry for the following in an integrated accounts system?

(1) Production overhead absorbed in the cost of production

(2) Completed work transferred from the production process to inventory

2 GF Co bought $100,000 worth of materials and issued $75,000 to production. An entry was made to trade payables for the purchase

Required

Which **three** of the following entries completes the correct bookkeeping treatment?

☐ DR Raw materials $75,000

☐ DR Raw materials $100,000

☐ CR Work in progress $75,000

☐ CR Raw materials $75,000

☐ CR Raw materials $100,000

☐ DR Work in progress $75,000

☐ DR Work in progress $100,000

3 The wages control account for X Co for October looks like this.

WAGES CONTROL ACCOUNT

	$'000		$'000
Bank	110	Work in progress	101
		Production overhead	7
		Balance c/d	2
	110		110

Required

Indicate whether the following statements are true or false.

	True / False
(1) Total wages incurred during October was $110,000	
(2) Indirect wages incurred during October was $7,000	
(3) Wages accrued at the end of October were $2,000	

4 The material usage variance is recorded in the raw materials control account.

O True

O False

5 Indicate whether the following statements are true or false.

	True / False
(1) Integrated systems conform to statutory requirements	
(2) Integrated systems are preferable to two systems because they conform to statutory requirements	
(3) Integrated systems reduce the number of account reconciliations	
(4) Systems with separate cost and financial accounting systems can aid provision of internal management information	

6 Which **three** of the following variances are recorded in the work in progress control account in a standard cost bookkeeping system?

- ☐ Material price variance
- ☐ Material usage variance
- ☐ Labour rate variance
- ☐ Variable overhead efficiency variance
- ☐ Sales variance
- ☐ Idle time variance

7 A company operates an integrated accounting system. The accounting entries for the issue to production of indirect materials from inventory would be:

- O DR Work in progress account; CR Stores control account
- O DR Stores control account; CR Overhead control account
- O DR Overhead control account; CR Stores control account
- O DR Cost of sales account; CR Stores control account

8 Which of the following descriptions correctly describes a control account?

- O An account for pooling costs before they are recharged
- O Contra to cash
- O An account which records total cost as opposed to individual costs
- O A type of suspense account

9 In a cost bookkeeping system what would be the entry for the absorption of production overhead?

- O DR Cost ledger control account; CR Production overhead account
- O DR Production overhead account; CR Work in progress account
- O DR Work in progress account; CR Cost ledger control account
- O DR Work in progress account; CR Production overhead account

15 Risk and probability

Learning outcomes

Having studied this chapter you will be able to:

- Explain the concepts of risk and uncertainty
- Demonstrate the use of expected values and joint probabilities in decision making

Chapter context

In this chapter we start to look at a key function of management; that of making decisions. All decisions carry some element of risk or uncertainty. We distinguish between these, and then look at ways of dealing with risk by looking at the concept of probability, linking probability to expected values, and finally how decisions can be made based on expected values.

Syllabus context

This chapter is part of syllabus **Section D**, which looks at **'Decision Making'**.

This syllabus area has a weighting of **35%** and is covered by **Chapters 6 and 7 and 15 to 17**.

In the exam, you will be expected to demonstrate competence in the following areas:

- Risk and uncertainty.
- Probability and its relationship with proportions and percentages.
- Expected values and expected values tables.
- Limitations of expected values.

Chapter overview

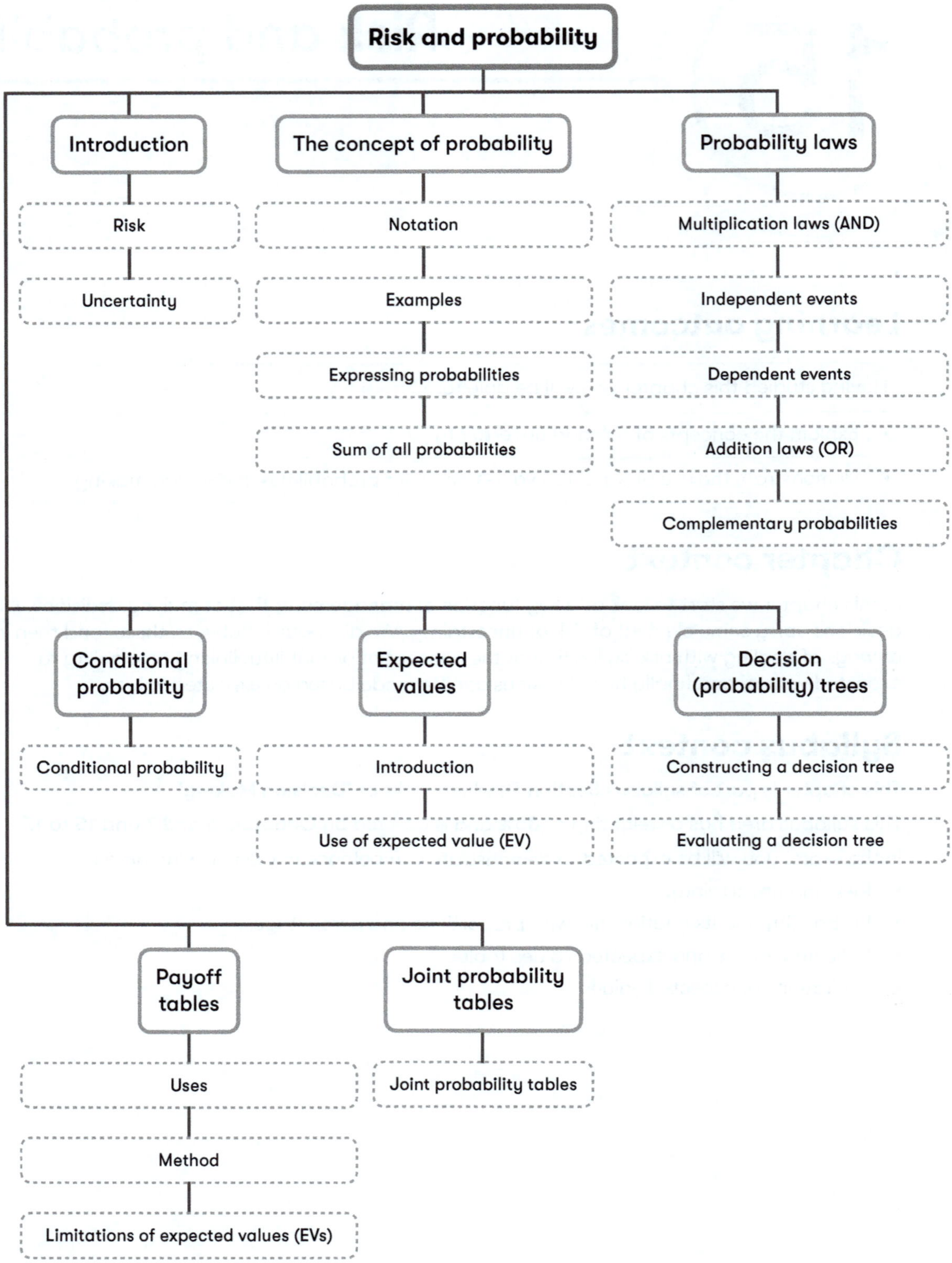

1 Introduction

Decision making involves making decisions now which will affect future outcomes and it is unlikely that future cash flows will be known with certainty.

1.1 Risk

KEY TERM

> **Risk:** Exists where a decision maker has knowledge that several possible future outcomes are possible, usually **due to past experience.**

This past experience enables a decision maker to estimate the probability of the likely occurrence of each potential future outcome. Risk can be **quantified.**

1.2 Uncertainty

KEY TERM

> **Uncertainty:** Exists when the future is unknown and the decision maker has **no past experience** on which to base predictions.

Uncertainty **cannot be quantified** but techniques can be adopted to reduce uncertainty.

These might include:

- Market research
- Focus groups

2 The concept of probability

KEY TERM

> **Probability:** The likelihood of a particular outcome from a given **event.**

There are three types of probability:

- **Exact** – applies to a population, such as the probability of drawing a red ball out of a bag of differently coloured balls.
- **Empirical** – derived from recorded historical observations, such as the probability of a certain number of customers visiting a shop in a day.
- **Subjective** – based on judgement, such as the probability of finding diamonds in a particular geological area.

2.1 Notation

> **Formula to learn**
>
> P[X]= The probability of outcome occurring.
>
> $$P[X] = \frac{\text{The number of ways in which X can occur}}{\text{The total number of possible outcomes}}$$

2.2 Examples

(a) Consider a ten-horse race where each horse has an equal chance of winning and there can only be one winner. The probability or likelihood of selecting the winner is one in ten (1/10).

(b) Consider a six-sided dice showing the numbers 1 to 6. Assuming each side has an equal chance of being thrown, the probability of throwing a six is one in six (1/6).

(c) Consider a standard pack of playing cards. The probability of selecting a red card at random is 26 possibilities from 52 cards (possible outcomes) (26/52).

So, given that a red card has been picked from a packet of 52 cards, what is the probability of it being a 10?

There are 26 red cards in the pack and of these, two will be 10s:

Solution:

$$P(10) = \frac{2}{26} = \frac{1}{13} = 0.077 = 7.7\%$$

2.3 Expressing probabilities

Probability can be expressed as a proportion or a percentage.

If an event has a probability of 1 it is said to be certain.

	Certainty	Impossibility
Decimal	1	0
Percentage	100%	0%
Fraction	1	0

2.4 Sum of all probabilities

$\sum p = 1$ always (note the $\sum$ (sigma) symbol means 'the sum of')

For example, toss a coin once

p(head) = ½, p(tail) = ½

p(all outcomes) = p(head) + p(tail) = 1

KEY TERM

Mutually exclusive outcomes (OR): The outcome of one event cannot happen at the same time as the outcome of another.

Eg a student can only have one country of birth.

(single event)

Non-mutually exclusive outcomes (OR): Both outcomes can occur at the same time.

Eg a student can be studying for an accountancy qualification and their country of birth is the UK.

Independent events (AND): One outcome has nothing to do with another.

Eg asking two unrelated students where they were born.

Dependent events (AND): One outcome depends upon something else taking place either with a proviso regarding the first event or given it has happened.

Eg asking twins where they were born.

(successive events)

3 Probability laws

3.1 Multiplication laws (AND)

Here we consider the outcomes of successive events.

3.2 Independent events

Here we acknowledge that the outcome of one event has no impact on the outcome of another event.

Formula to learn

The probabilities of two events are multiplied as follows:

P[X and Y] = P[X] × P[Y]

P[X∩Y] = P[X] × P[Y]

Note. (the ∩ (intersect) symbol means objects that 'belong' in both set X and set Y)

Activity 1: Independent events

What is the probability of getting two heads in two throws of a coin?

Solution

P(H and H)

$\frac{1}{2} \times \frac{1}{2} = \frac{1}{4}$

3.3 Dependent events

Here the probability of one event is dependent on the outcome of a **previous** event.

Formula to learn

P[X **and** Y] = P[X] × P[Y|X]

where P[Y|X] is the probability of Y occurring given that X has already occurred.

Note. the vertical line means 'given'.

Activity 2: Dependent events

A class contains 16 male students and 14 female. What is the probability of the first two to arrive in the morning being male?

Solution

1st student, 2nd student

$\frac{16}{30} \times \frac{15}{29} = \frac{240}{870} = \frac{8}{29}$

3.4 Addition laws (OR)

Consider all the possible outcomes of a single event. The addition laws are relevant when we are interested in considering a specific group of potential outcomes against all the possible outcomes.

(a) **Mutually exclusive outcomes** – The outcome of one event cannot happen at the same time as the outcome of another. Here we add the probabilities of the outcomes.

Formula to learn

P[X or Y] = P[X] + P[Y]

This can be illustrated in the form of a Venn diagram.

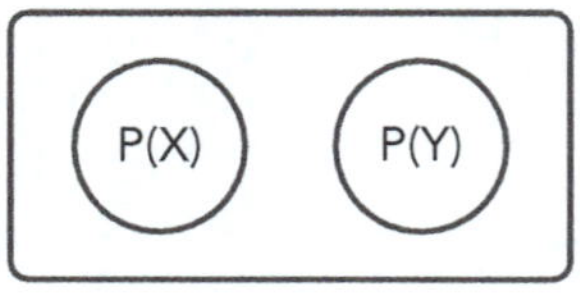

Activity 3: Mutually exclusive events

What is the probability that a person's birthday falls in June or July?

Solution

$1/12 + 1/12 = 2/12 = 1/6$

(b) **Non-mutually exclusive outcomes** – Both outcomes can occur at the same time.

Formula to learn

P[X or Y] = P[X] + P[Y] – P[X and Y]

This can be illustrated in the form of a Venn diagram.

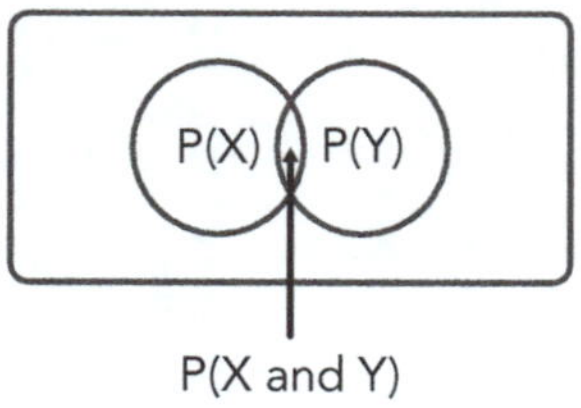

Activity 4: Non-mutually exclusive events

What is the probability of a person's birthday falling in May or having been born on a Sunday?

Solution

3.5 Complementary probabilities

Using complementary probabilities is a possible shortcut when an event is repeated a number of times, such that calculating the probability of the combination of successive events becomes unwieldy.

It may be possible to split the event ultimately between two outcomes, success and failure. As we must have either success or failure then P(success) + P(failure) = certainty = 1

> **Formula to learn**
>
> Rearranging the equation
>
> **P (success) = 1 – P (failure)**
>
> **Examples**
>
> (a) P[at least one success in n attempts] = 1 – P[failure in all attempts]
>
> (b) P[at least one six in 10 throws of a dice] = 1 – P[no sixes in 10 throws of dice]

Activity 5: Complementary probabilities

A coin is tossed four times.

Required

What is the probability of getting at least one head?

Solution

4 Conditional probability

Conditional probability relates to the chance of an event occurring given other events have already taken place.

A contingency table is helpful in calculating these probabilities.

Illustration 1: Conditional probability

A cosmetics company has developed a new anti-dandruff shampoo which is being tested on volunteers. Seventy per cent of the volunteers have used the shampoo whereas others have used a normal shampoo, believing it to be the new anti-dandruff shampoo. Two-sevenths of those using the new shampoo showed no improvement whereas one-third of those using the normal shampoo had less dandruff.

Required

A volunteer shows no improvement. What is the probability that they used the normal shampoo?

Solution

The problem is solved by drawing a contingency table, showing 'improvement' and 'no improvement', volunteers using normal shampoo and volunteers using the new shampoo.

Let us suppose that there were 1,000 volunteers (we could use any number). We could depict the results of the test on the 1,000 volunteers as follows.

	New shampoo	Normal shampoo	Total
Improvement	***500	****100	600
No improvement	**200	*** 200	400
	*700	300	1,000

* 70% × 1,000   ** $\frac{2}{7}700$

*** Balancing figure   **** $\frac{1}{3} \times 300$

We can now calculate P (shows no improvement)

$$\text{P (shows no improvement)} = \frac{400}{1{,}000}$$

$$\text{P (used normal shampoo| shows no improvement)} = \frac{200}{400} = \frac{1}{2}$$

Other probabilities are just as easy to calculate.

$$\text{P (shows improvement| used new shampoo)} = \frac{500}{700} = \frac{5}{7}$$

$$\text{P (used new shampoo| shows improvement)} = \frac{500}{600} = \frac{5}{6}$$

Activity 6: Conditional probability

A sample of 100 university students have been analysed by the subjects they are studying and whether they pay their tuition fees promptly. The sample has been cross-tabulated into arts students/science students against fast payers/slow payers.

60 of the students sampled were classified as arts students, of which 40 are slow payers. In total, 30 of the students are fast payers.

Required

Calculate the probability that a student chosen at random is a fast-paying science student.

Solution

	Arts	science	total
fast payers	20	10	30
slow payers	40	30	70
	60	40	100

$10/100 = 0.1 = 1/10$

10 %

5 Expected values

5.1 Introduction

When the final outcome is unknown and a range of possible future outcomes has been quantified (for example, best, worst and most likely) probabilities can be assigned to these outcomes and a weighted average **(expected value)** of those outcomes calculated.

$EV = \sum px$

where p is the probability of the outcome occurring and x is the value of the outcome (profit or cost).

KEY TERM

Expected value (EV): A weighted average, based on probabilities.

5.2 Use of expected value (EV)

Expected value can be used in situations where there are a number of possible outcomes from a single event and it is not known with certainty what will actually happen. Each outcome is assigned a probability.

6 Decision (probability) trees

A decision tree (also known as a probability tree) is a pictorial method of showing a sequence of interrelated decisions and their expected outcomes. They can incorporate both the probabilities and value of expected outcomes, and are used in decision-making.

Decision trees are most useful when there are several decisions and ranges of outcome.

6.1 Constructing a decision tree

Constructing a tree requires all the choices and outcomes to be drawn and the numbers (probabilities, outcomes and EVs) to be entered.

6.2 Evaluating a decision tree

Once drawn the optimal decision can be calculated using rollback analysis.

Evaluate the tree from **right to left.**

- Calculate expected values at outcome points (indicated by a **circle**)
- Take highest benefit at decision points (indicated by a **square**)

Illustration 2: Decision trees

Captain Co runs its business through a number of centres. One of its centres is suffering from declining sales and management has a range of options:

(1) To shut down the site and sell it for $5 million

(2) To undertake a major refurbishment

(3) To undertake a cheaper refurbishment

In the past 2/3 of such refurbishments have achieved good results, the other 1/3 being less successful, achieving poor results.

The major refurbishment will cost $4,000,000 now. Estimates of the outcomes are as follows.

(1)	Good results	PV =	$13,500,000
(2)	Poor results	PV =	$6,500,000

The cheaper refurbishment, costing $2,000,000 now would have the following outcomes:

(1)	Good results	PV =	$8,500,000
(2)	Poor results	PV =	$4,000,000

Required

1 Complete the labels on the decision tree (below) for Captain Co by:

(1) Entering the probabilities on to the relevant branches of the tree

(2) Calculating the expected value at points B and C

2 Evaluate the decision tree at point A and recommend what action should be taken.

Solution

1

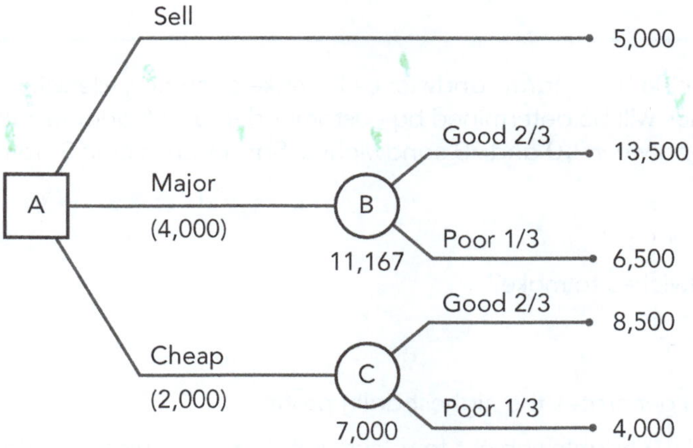

The expected value at point B = (2/3 × \$13,500) + (1/3 × \$6,500) = \$11,167

The expected value at point C is = (2/3 × \$8,500) + (1/3 × \$4,000) = \$7,000

2 The decision at A is:

The expected values of the options are:

(1)	Sell	\$5,000,000	
(2)	Major refurb	\$7,167,000	(\$11,167,000 – \$4,000,000)
(3)	Cheap refurb	\$5,000,000	(\$7,000,000 – \$2,000,000)

Captain Co should undertake the major refurbishment as this will result in the highest EV of \$7,167,000.

7 Payoff tables

7.1 Uses

Expected value concepts can be used to make decisions under conditions of uncertainty. We must consider the outcome of each choice against an uncontrollable event.

7.2 Method

(a) Set up payoff table – profit/loss for each combination of variables.

Questions usually involve two variables:

(i) The **variable subject to uncertainty** (probability distribution given in question)

(ii) The **decision variable** (for example, which order quantity)

KEY TERM

Decision variable: The different options a manager has to choose between.

(b) Apply probabilities to calculate expected value (EV).

EV = ∑np(x)

where:

n = various profits under an option

p(x) = chance of each profit occurring

Be prepared to interpret your findings. Decision rules are as follows:

- A project with a positive EV should be accepted.
- A project with a negative EV should be rejected.

- When faced with a number of alternative decisions, the one with the **highest EV** should be chosen.

Illustration 3: Payoff tables

A sandwich shopkeeper will determine how many sandwiches to make each day (decision variable). Sales of those sandwiches will be determined by customer demand (variable subject to uncertainty) which lies in a range between 40 and 70 sandwiches. Sandwiches cost $1 to make and sell at $2.

Required

What is the optimum level of sandwiches to make?

Solution

Clearly this will be the order which generates the highest daily profit.

Set up a grid of 'Decision variable' v 'Variable subject to uncertainty' and calculate the daily profit in each case (revenue less cost).

An expected value can then be determined for each decision variable using the expected value formula.

The order level with the highest expected profit will be selected.

Demand	*Make 40*	*Make 50*	*Make 60*	*Make 70*
40 (20% probability)	$40	$30	$20	$10
50 (30% probability)	$40	$50	$40	$30
60 (30% probability)	$40	$50	$60	$50
70 (20% probability)	$40	$50	$60	$70
Expected value	$40	**$46**	**$46**	$40

The shopkeeper will be indifferent between an order of 50 or 60 sandwiches.

Activity 7: Payoff tables

In an internal audit of 400 invoices, the following numbers of errors per invoice were discovered:

Number of errors per invoice:	0	1	2	3	4	5	6
Number of invoices:	180	38	80	40	40	20	2

Required

1 Calculate the percentage of invoices with errors.

2 Calculate the expected value of the number of errors per invoice (to 3 decimal places). (Hint: probability calculation = number of invoices ÷ total number of invoices)

Solution

7.3 Limitations of expected values (EVs)

(a) **EV is a long-term average,** so the EV will not be reached in the short term and is therefore not suitable for one off decisions.

(b) The results are dependent on the accuracy of the probability distribution. In particular, it uses discrete variables rather than continuous variables (ie variables are point estimates rather than a continuous range). This may not accurately model the real situation.

(c) EV **takes no account of the risk** associated with a decision.

(d) The EV itself may **not represent a single possible outcome.**

8 Joint probability tables

KEY TERM

Joint probability table: Records the range of possible outcomes where there are two variables that are uncertain or risky.

If there are two variables that are uncertain or risky it may be helpful to record the range of possible outcomes in a joint probability table.

Analysis could take the form of EVs or the data table could be used to give management an overview of the decision it is facing.

Activity 8: Joint probability table

Brown Co has developed a new product.

The company is confident that demand for the product will be 30,000 units at a selling price of $25, but both the variable cost per unit and the specific fixed costs associated with this product are uncertain.

Brown Co believes that the following circumstances could occur.

VC per unit	*Probability*	*FC*	*Probability*
$		$	
12	0.2	100,000	0.4

13	0.35	110,000	0.5
14	0.45	120,000	0.1

Required

1 Construct a two-way data table for profit generated.

2 Using the joint probabilities for each combination of fixed cost and variable cost, calculate the expected value of Brown Co's profit.

Solution

1 **Profit generated ($'000)**

	Fixed costs		
	$100,000	$110,000	$120,000
VC $12	290,000	280,000	270,000
VC $13	260,000	250,000	240,000
VC $14	230,000	220,000	210,000

2 **Joint probability table**

		Fixed costs		
		$100,000	$110,000	$120,000
	Prob	0.4	0.5	0.1
VC $12	0.2	0.2×0.4 = 0.08	0.1	0.02
VC $13	0.35	0.14	0.175	0.035
VC $14	0.45	0.18	0.225	0.045

Expected value of profit

	Fixed costs		
	$100,000	$110,000	$120,000
VC $12	23,200	28,000	5400
VC $13	36,400	43,750	8400
VC $14	41,400	49,500	9450

EV of profit = sum of probability × outcome.

245,500.

Chapter summary

Risk and probability

Introduction

Risk
- Exists where a decision maker has knowledge that several possible future outcomes are possible, usually due to past experience

Uncertainty
- Exists when the future is unknown and the decision maker has no past experience on which to base predictions

The concept of probability

Notation
- The probability of outcome x occurring
- The number of ways x can occur/ the total number of possible outcomes

Examples
- Examples

Expressing probabilities
- Probability can be expressed as a proportion or a percentage

Sum of all probabilities
- $\sum p = 1$ always
- Mutually exclusive outcomes
- Non-mutually exclusive outcomes
- Independent events
- Dependent events

Probability laws

Multiplication laws (AND)
- The outcomes of successive events

Independent events
- The outcome of one event has no impact on the outcome of another event

Dependent events
- The probability of one event is dependent on the outcome of a previous event

Addition laws (OR)
- All the possible outcomes of a single event

Complementary probabilities
- A possible shortcut when an event is repeated a number of times

Conditional probability

Conditional probability
- Relates to the chance of an event occurring given other events have already taken place
- Contingency table

Expected values

Introduction
- Expected value (EV) – a weighted average, based on probabilities

Use of expected value (EV)
- Used in situations where there are a number of possible outcomes from a single event and it is not known with certainty what will actually happen

Decision (probability) trees

Constructing a decision tree
- Requires all the choices and outcomes to be drawn and the numbers (probabilities, outcomes and EVs) to be entered

Evaluating a decision tree
- Rollback analysis
- Evaluate the tree from right to left

Payoff tables

Uses

- Make decisions under conditions of uncertainty

Method

- Set up payoff table
- Apply probabilities to calculate expected value (EV)
- Decision variable – the different options a manager has to choose between

Limitations of expected values (EVs)

- Long-term average
- Depends on accuracy of probability distribution
- EV takes no account of the risk associated with a decision
- The EV itself may not represent a single possible outcome

Joint probability tables

Joint probability tables

- Joint probability table – records the range of possible outcomes where there are two variables that are uncertain or risky

Key terms

Risk: Exists where a decision maker has knowledge that several possible future outcomes are possible, usually **due to past experience.**

Uncertainty: Exists when the future is unknown and the decision maker has **no past experience** on which to base predictions.

Probability: The likelihood of a particular outcome from a given **event.**

Mutually exclusive outcomes (OR): The outcome of one event cannot happen at the same time as the outcome of another.

Eg a student can only have one country of birth.

(single event)

Non-mutually exclusive outcomes (OR): Both outcomes can occur at the same time.

Eg a student can be studying for an accountancy qualification and their country of birth is the UK.

Independent events (AND): One outcome has nothing to do with another.

Eg asking two unrelated students where they were born.

Dependent events (AND): One outcome depends upon something else taking place either with a proviso regarding the first event or given it has happened.

Eg asking twins where they were born.

(successive events)

Expected value (EV): A weighted average, based on probabilities.

Decision variable: The different options a manager has to choose between.

Joint probability table: Records the range of possible outcomes where there are two variables that are uncertain or risky.

Activity answers

Activity 1: Independent events

P[H and H] = ½ × ½ = ¼

Activity 2: Dependent events

$$P[\text{Male and Male}] = \frac{16}{30} \times \frac{15}{29} = \frac{8}{29}$$

Activity 3: Mutually exclusive events

$$P[\text{June or July}] = \frac{1}{12} + \frac{1}{12} = \frac{1}{6}$$

Activity 4: Non-mutually exclusive events

Assume four Sundays per month

$$P[\text{May or Sunday}] = \frac{1}{12} + \frac{1}{7} - \frac{1}{12} \times \frac{1}{7} = \frac{3}{14}$$

Activity 5: Complementary probabilities

P[No heads]

$$= P[\text{T, T, T and T}] = ½ \times ½ \times ½ \times ½ = \frac{1}{16}$$

$$\therefore P[\text{G 1 head}] = 1 - \frac{1}{16} = \frac{15}{16}$$

Activity 6: Conditional probability

	Arts	*Science*	*Total*
Fast payer	20	10	30
Slow payer	40	30	70
	60	40	100

$$\text{Probability} = \frac{10}{100} = 0.1$$

Activity 7: Payoff tables

1 Percentage of invoices with errors:

Total number of invoices	=	400
Number without errors	=	180
Number with errors	=	400 – 180

$$\text{Percentage with errors} = \frac{220}{400} \times 100 = 55\%$$

2

Number of errors per invoice:	0	1	2	3	4	5	6
Number of invoices:	180	38	80	40	40	20	2
Probability:	0.45	0.095	0.2	0.1	0.1	0.05	0.005

$$\left(\text{Probability calculation} = \frac{\text{No. of invoices}}{\text{Total no. of invoices}}\right)$$

Expected value of number of errors per invoice

= (0 × 0.45) + (1 × 0.095) + (2 × 0.2) + (3 × 0.1) + (4 × 0.1) + (5 × 0.05) + (6 × 0.005)

= 0 + 0.095 + 0.4 + 0.3 + 0.4 + 0.25 + 0.03

= 1.475 errors.

Activity 8: Joint probability table

1 **Profit generated ($'000)**

	Fixed costs		
	$100,000	$110,000	$120,000
VC $12	290	280	270
VC $13	260	250	240
VC $14	230	220	210

2 **Joint probability table**

		Fixed costs		
		$100,000	$110,000	$120,000
	Prob	0.4	0.5	0.1
VC $12	0.2	0.08	0.1	0.02
VC $13	0.35	0.14	0.175	0.035
VC $14	0.45	0.18	0.225	0.045

Expected value of profit

	Fixed costs		
	$100,000	$110,000	$120,000
VC $12	23,200	28,000	5,400
VC $13	36,400	43,750	8,400
VC $14	41,400	49,500	9,450

	$
EV profit = $\sum px$	245,500

Test your learning

1 An analysis of 480 working days in a factory shows that on 360 days there were no machine breakdowns. Assuming that this pattern will continue, what is the probability that there will be a machine breakdown on a particular day?

- O 0%
- O 25%
- O 35%
- O 75%

2 A production director is responsible for overseeing the operations of three factories – North, South and West. He visits one factory per week. He visits the West factory as often as he visits the North factory, but he visits the South factory twice as often as he visits the West factory.

Required

What is the probability that in any one week he will visit the North factory?

- O 0.17
- O 0.20
- O 0.25
- O 0.33

3 A project may result in profits of $15,000 or $20,000, or in a loss of $5,000. The probabilities of each profit are 0.2, 0.5 and 0.3 respectively.

Required

What is the expected profit? $ [ ]

4 ABC Co is considering launching a new product. The new product will have a selling price of $6 per unit. Fixed costs are expected to be $2,500. Expected sales volumes and variable costs are as follows.

Sales units	Probability	Variable cost per unit	Probability
1,500	0.8	$2.30	0.65
2,500	0.2	$2.50	0.35

Required

What is the expected profit? $ [ ]

5 How is expected value calculated?

- O $\sum px$
- O $p\sum x$
- O $e\sum px$
- O $x\sum p$

6 Tick the correct boxes to indicate the usefulness of expected values as a guide to decision making in the following decisions.

		Most useful	Not as useful
(a)	Whether to change the logo painted on the window of 700 retail outlets		
(b)	Whether to purchase machine X or machine Y		
(c)	Whether to launch product A		
(d)	Deciding on the optimum daily purchases of a perishable item		

16 Averages and the normal distribution

Learning outcomes

Having studied this chapter you will be able to:
• Calculate summary measures of central tendency and dispersion for both grouped and ungrouped data.
• Demonstrate the use of the normal distribution

Chapter context

It is vital for management to be able to summarise raw data into useful information. This chapter contains mathematical methods of summarising data.

We use sampling in the business world to make assumptions about populations. Rather than carrying out a full census, we gather data that is representative of the whole population. Using normal distribution we can start to attach probabilities and percentages to the likelihood of events and attributes, for decision making.

Syllabus context

This chapter is part of syllabus **Section D**, which looks at **'Decision Making'**.

This syllabus area has a weighting of **35%** and is covered by **Chapters 6 and 7 and 15 to 17**.

In the exam, you will be expected to demonstrate competence in the following areas:

- Arithmetic mean, median, mode, range, variance, standard deviation and coefficient of variation for both ungrouped and grouped data.
- Graphs/diagrams and use of normal distribution tables.

Chapter overview

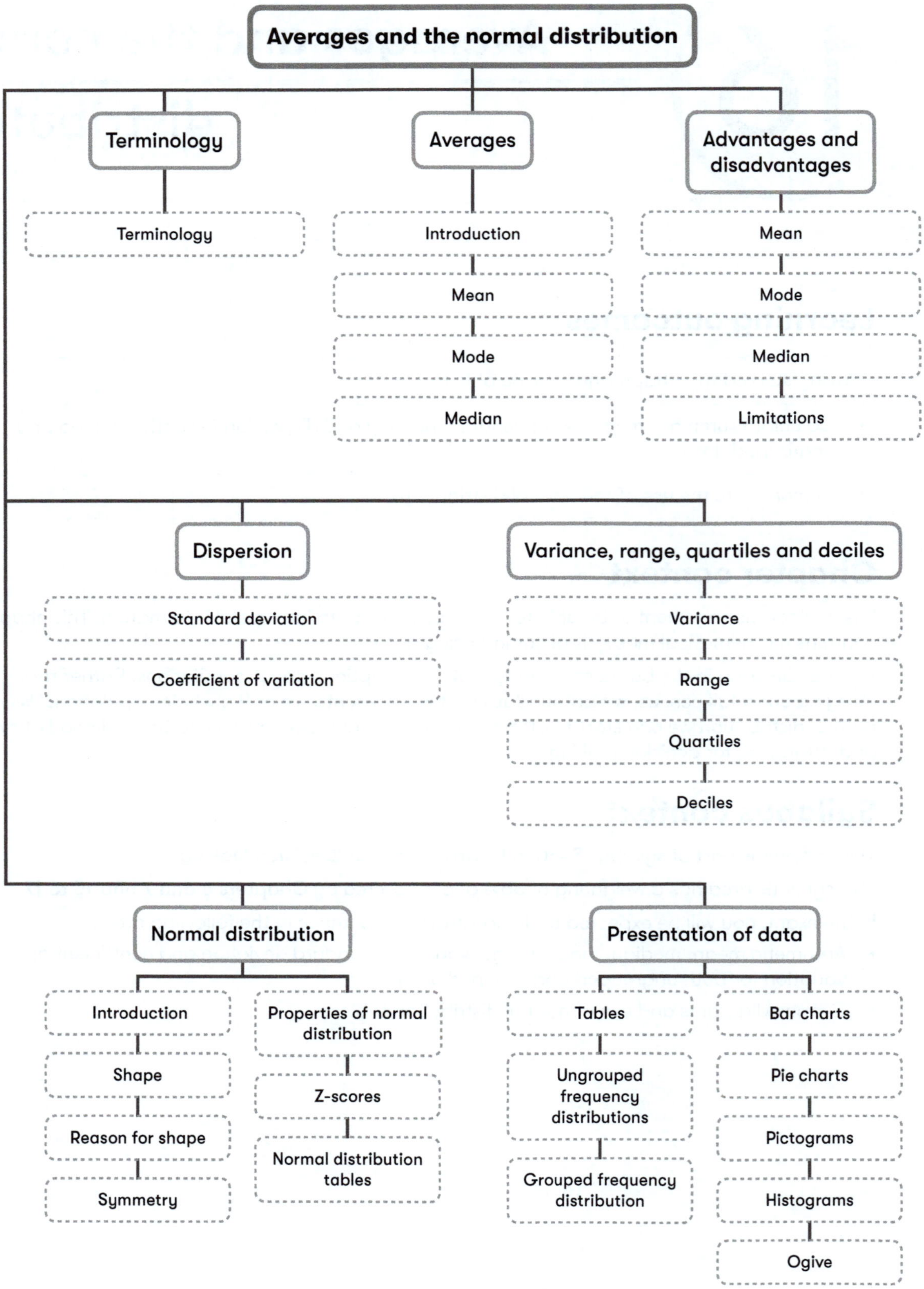

1 Terminology

KEY TERM

> **Grouped data:** Where the frequency is shown in terms of a range. Known as continuous data.
>
> **Ungrouped data:** Discrete data, where the frequency is shown in terms of a specific measure/value.

2 Averages

2.1 Introduction

The example below will be used throughout the chapter in order to calculate the three averages; the **mean, median** and **mode.**

In the small town of Brum Brum, a survey of 1,600 out of 100,000 car owners was performed to find out about annual mileage travelled. The results were as follows:

			Mid-point mileage		No. cars
			x	f	fx
		< 2,000	1,000 *	10	
2,000	–	< 4,000	3,000	14	
4,000	–	< 6,000	5,000	154	
6,000	–	< 8,000	7,000	292	
8,000	–	< 10,000	9,000	493	
10,000	–	< 12,000	11,000	404	
12,000	–	< 14,000	13,000	164	
14,000	–	< 16,000	15,000	48	
		≥ 16,000	17,000 *	21	
				1,600	

* assume same size as adjacent intervals

2.2 Mean

KEY TERM

> **Arithmetic mean:** The best known type of average and is widely understood. It is used for further statistical analysis.

> **Formula to learn**
>
> **Ungrouped data:**
>
> $$\text{Mean} = \frac{\text{Sum of values of items}}{\text{number of items}}$$

Example: The arithmetic mean for ungrouped data

The demand for a product on each of 20 days was as follows (in units).

3 12 7 17 3 14 9 6 11 10 1 4 19 7 15 6 9 12 12 8

The arithmetic mean of daily demand is $\bar{x}$.

$$\bar{X} = \frac{\text{Sum of demand}}{\text{Number of days}} = \frac{185}{20} = 9.25 \text{ units}$$

In this example, demand on any one day is never actually 9.25 units. The arithmetic mean is merely an **average representation** of demand on each of the 20 days.

Grouped data:

$$\bar{X} = \frac{\sum fx}{n} \quad \text{or} \quad \bar{X} = \frac{\sum fx}{\sum f} \text{(frequency distribution)}$$

where x = value

y = frequency

To calculate the arithmetic mean of grouped data we need to decide on **a value which best represents all of the values in a particular class interval**. This value is known as the **mid-point**.

Activity 1: Calculating the mean

Using the information in 2.1, calculate the mean annual mileage for these 1,600 cars.

Solution

2.3 Mode

KEY TERM

Mode: The most frequently occurring item.

Ungrouped data: the most frequently occurring item in the list.

Grouped data: we cannot say what the most frequently occurring item is; however, we can estimate the mode using the following method.

To find the mode using a histogram:

(a) Draw the frequency histogram and identify the highest frequency class

(b) Draw a diagonal line from the top of the block either side of the highest class

(c) The intercept is the estimated modal value, read from the x axis

Example: Finding the mode using a histogram

(using the data from the previous example)

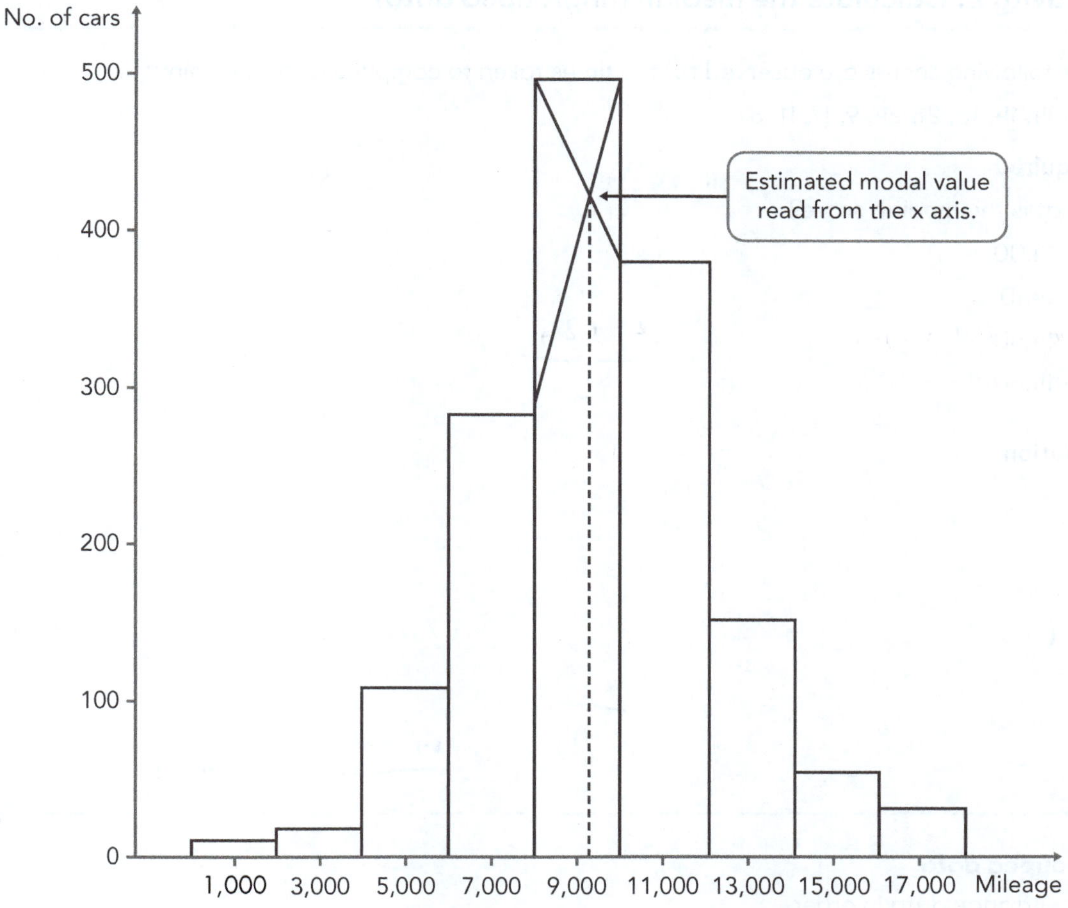

Reading from the histogram the **mode** is approximately **9,250 miles.**

You cannot draw a histogram in a computer-based assessment so questions may ask you to interpret a diagram.

2.4 Median

KEY TERM

Median: The value of the middle item.

Ungrouped data (odd number)

(a) Arrange data in order

(b)

$$\text{Calculate middle (median) rank } \frac{(n+1)}{2} = \text{ nth item in the list}$$

(c) Median value = the entry corresponding to the median rank

Ungrouped data (even number)

(a) Arrange the data in order

(b) Calculate the mean of the two median ranks

The mean of $\frac{n}{2}$ th and $\frac{n}{2}$ + 1 th

Activity 2: Calculate the median (ungrouped data)

The following scores are observed for the times taken to complete a task, in minutes.

12, 34, 14, 15, 21, 24, 9, 17, 11, 8

Required

What is the median score?

10 even 5

- ○ 14.00
- ○ 14.10
- ● 14.50
- ○ 14.60

$\frac{21 + 24}{2}$ =

Solution

$\frac{10}{2}$ = 5 6

re-order !

8, 9, 11, 12, 14, 15, 17, 21, 24, 34

$\frac{21}{10}$

$\frac{14 + 15}{2}$ = 14.5

Grouped data

(a) Arrange data in order

(b) Calculate middle (median) rank (note whether even or odd)

(c) Estimate median using ogive (cumulative frequency distribution graph – see section 7.8)

Finding the median from an ogive (using data from Activity 1)

$$\text{Median rank} = \frac{1{,}600}{2} = 800\text{th}$$

We can now look up the 800th item on our ogive.

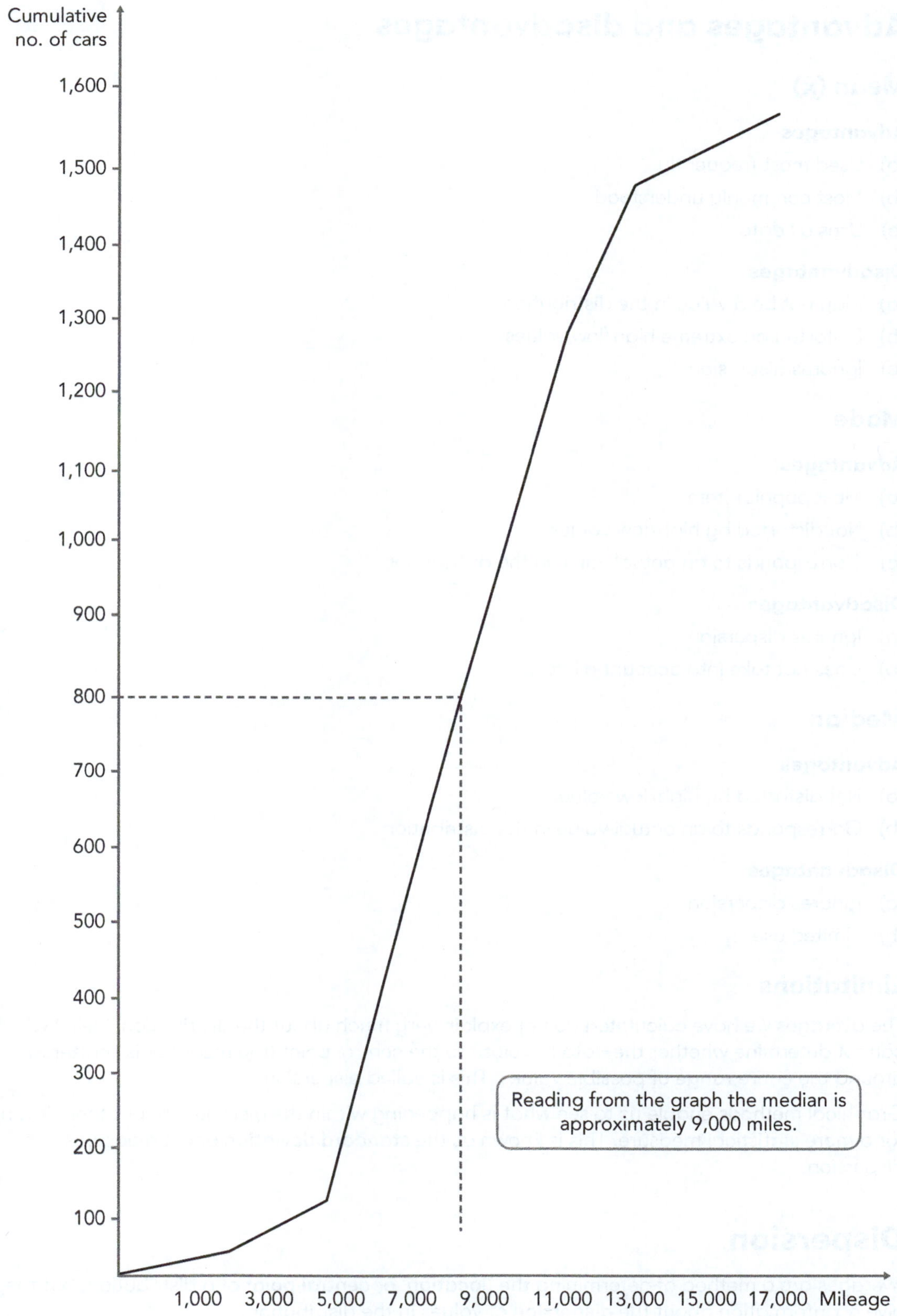
Cumulative no. of cars
1,600
1,500
1,400
1,300
1,200
1,100
1,000
900
800
700
600
500
400
300
200
100
1,000
3,000
5,000
7,000
9,000
11,000
13,000
15,000
17,000
Mileage
Reading from the graph the median is approximately 9,000 miles.

3 Advantages and disadvantages

3.1 Mean ($\bar{x}$)

Advantages

(a) Used most frequently

(b) Most commonly understood

(c) Uses all data

Disadvantages

(a) May not be a value in the distribution

(b) Distorted by extreme high/low values

(c) Ignores dispersion

3.2 Mode

Advantages

(a) Most popular item

(b) Not distorted by high/low values

(c) Corresponds to an actual value in the distribution

Disadvantages

(a) Ignores dispersion

(b) Does not take into account all data

3.3 Median

Advantages

(a) Not distorted by high/low values

(b) Corresponds to an actual value in the distribution

Disadvantages

(a) Ignores dispersion

(b) Limited use

3.4 Limitations

The averages we have calculated do not explain very much about the distribution itself. We cannot determine whether the data lies close to the central point (the mean) or is scattered around the entire **range** of possible values. This is called dispersion.

Graphical methods enable us to see what is happening within the distribution, but there is a need for a more statistical measure. This is known as the **standard deviation** and it measures dispersion.

4 Dispersion

Averages are a method of determining the **'location'** or **central point** of a distribution, but they give no information about the **dispersion** of values in the distribution.

Measures of dispersion give some idea of the **spread of a variable about its average (mean).**

4.1 Standard deviation

KEY TERM

Standard deviation: One of the most important measures of dispersion. The standard deviation measures the spread of data around the mean.

In general, the larger the standard deviation value in relation to the mean, the more dispersed the data.

Formula to learn

$$\sigma = \sqrt{\frac{\sum(x-\bar{x})^2}{n}}$$

For a frequency distribution the formula becomes

$$\sigma = \sqrt{\frac{\sum fx^2}{\sum f} - \bar{x}^2}$$

where	σ	= standard deviation
	x	= value
	$\bar{x}$	= mean
	f	= frequency
	n	= $\sum f$

Note that σ is the Greek letter sigma (in lower case).

Advantages

(a) Uses all data

(b) Gives 'weight' to values that lie far away from mean

Example: Standard deviation

The hours of overtime worked in a particular quarter by the 60 employees of ABC Co are as follows.

grouped data.

Hours		*Frequency*
More than	*Not more than*	
0	10	3
10	20	6
20	30	11
30	40	15
40	50	12
50	60	7
60	70	6
		60

Using the formula provided in the assessment, the standard deviation calculation is as follows.

↗ frequency distribution.

Mid-point x	*f*	*fx*	*x²*	*fx²*
5	3	15	25	75
15	6	90	225	1,350
25	11	275	625	6,875
35	15	525	1,225	18,375

Mid-point x	f	fx	x^2	fx^2
45	12	540	2,025	24,300
55	7	385	3,025	21,175
65	6	390	4,225	25,350
	$\sum f$ = 60	$\sum fx$ = 2,220		$\sum fx^2$ = 97,500

$$\text{Mean} = \frac{\sum fx}{\sum f} = \frac{2{,}220}{60} = 37$$

Variance = the square of the standard deviation:

$$\frac{\sum fx^2}{\sum f} - \left(\frac{\sum fx}{\sum f}\right)^2 = \frac{97{,}500}{60} - (37)^2$$

$$= 256 \text{ hours}$$

$$\text{Standard deviation} = \sqrt{256} = 16 \text{ hours}$$

Activity 3: Standard deviation calculation

Complete the following table and calculate σ.

	Mid-point mileage x ('000)	*No. of cars* f	fx	x^2	fx^2
< 2	1	10			
2 – < 4	3	14			
4 – < 6	5	154			
6 – < 8	7	292			
8 – < 10	9	493			
10 – < 12	11	404			
12 – < 14	13	164			
14 – < 16	15	48			
≥ 16	17	21			
		1,600			

$\bar{x}$ = 9,347.5 miles

Solution

4.2 Coefficient of variation

This measures the standard deviation as a percentage of the mean. It is particularly useful when comparing the dispersion of two distributions.

The higher the percentage, the higher the dispersion.

Formula to learn

$$\text{Coefficient of variation} = \frac{\sigma}{\bar{x}}$$

For example, suppose that two sets of data, A and B, have the following means and standard deviations.

	A		B
Mean	120		125
Standard deviation	50		51
Coefficient of variation (50/120)	0.417	(51/125)	0.408

Although B has a higher standard deviation in absolute terms (51 compared to 50), its relative spread is less than A's since the coefficient of variation is smaller.

Activity 4: Coefficient of variation

Calculate the coefficient of variation for Activity 3.

Solution

The standard deviation's main properties are as follows.

(a) It is based on **all the values in the distribution** and so is more comprehensive than dispersion measures based on **quartiles,** such as the quartile deviation (see Section 5.3).

(b) It is suitable for **further statistical analysis.**

(c) It is **more difficult to understand** than some other measures of dispersion.

The importance of the standard deviation lies in its **suitability for further statistical analysis.** (We shall consider this further when we study the **normal distribution**.)

5 Variance, range, quartiles and deciles

5.1 Variance

KEY TERM

Variance: Defined as the square of the standard deviation (σ^2)

Watch out for questions where you are given a variance but need a standard deviation for your calculation.

Formula to learn

$$\text{Variance} = \sigma^2$$

$$\text{Standard deviation } \sigma = \sqrt{\text{variance}}$$

5.2 Range

KEY TERM

Range: A measure of spread; the difference between the highest and lowest possible values or, where data is grouped, it will be the difference between the upper interval limit and the lowest interval limit.

5.3 Quartiles

KEY TERM

Quartiles: Divide a distribution into quarters. In other words, the **quartiles** and the **median** divide the population into four groups of equal size.

(a) Lower quartile (Q1) – defined as the value below which 25% of the observations fall.

(b) Median (Q2) – lies at the mid-point (50%) between the upper and lower quartiles and is defined as the value below which 50% of the observations fall.

(c) Upper quartile (Q3) – defined as the value above which 25% of the observations fall.

(d)

KEY TERM

Inter-quartile range: The difference between the upper and lower quartiles (Q3–Q1).

(e) Quartile deviation (or semi-interquartile range) is calculated as:

$$\frac{1}{2}(\text{upper quartile} - \text{lower quartile})$$

Activity 5: Quartile deviation

The lower and upper quartiles of a distribution are given as 44 and 62. Calculate the quartile deviation. Q1 Q3

Solution

½ (62 - 44)

9

5.4 Deciles

Deciles divide a distribution into tenths (1/10ths).

6 Normal distribution

6.1 Introduction

KEY TERM

Normal distribution (or probability distribution): A frequency distribution which is important because it arises frequently in 'real life'. It is any distribution that is symmetrical around the mean.

It has been found that **many probability distributions are close enough to a normal distribution** to be treated as one without any significant loss of accuracy. This means that the normal distribution can be used as a tool in business decision making involving probabilities.

For example, if we take the population of the UK and look at the distribution of the height of all adults it would almost certainly follow a normal distribution. In fact, most data distributions follow a normal distribution where the majority of items lie near to the average.

6.2 Shape

The normal distribution is often described as a 'bell-shaped' curve. The normal curve for the height of adults might look like this.

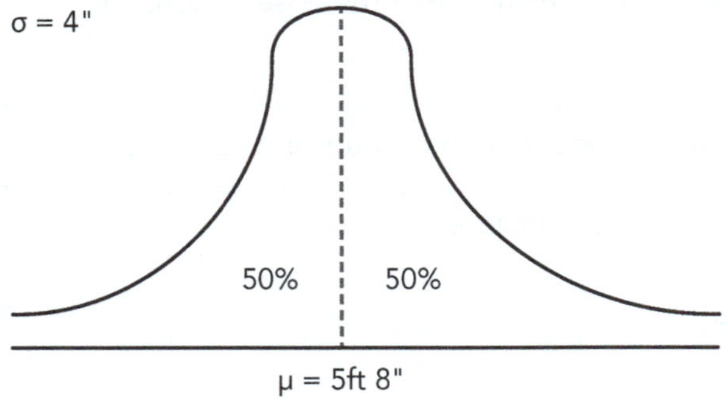

When using the normal distribution we will use the μ (pronounced mew) to define the mean and σ to define standard deviation.

Here μ = 5ft 8" and standard deviation, σ = 4"

6.3 Reason for shape

As the majority of people's heights lie on or near to the average height (the mean), there is a higher concentration of occurrences the closer we get to the mean.

As you get further away from the mean, the number of people with these heights gets smaller and smaller, hence the curve gets lower and lower.

6.4 Symmetry

When attempting questions, it is important to note the normal distribution is always symmetrical around the mean. Consequently, the area either side of the mean represents 50%.

6.5 Properties of normal distribution

(a) The curve is symmetrical centred on μ (mean).

In our example, 50% of people are taller than 5ft 8" and 50% are shorter than 5ft 8".

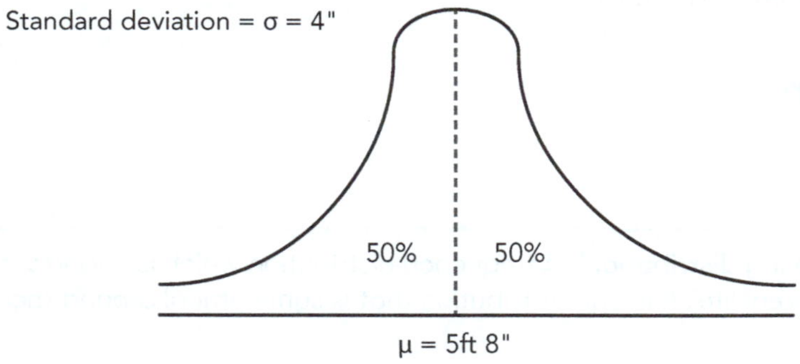

(b) The total area under the curve = 1 or 100% of the population.

(c) The width of the curve is measured in terms of the standard deviation (σ).

(d) For practical purposes the range of the normal distribution is six standard deviations

ie heights of adults range between

$\mu - 3\sigma$ = 5ft 8" – (3 × 4") = 4ft 8"

and $\mu + 3\sigma$ = 5ft 8" + (3 × 4") = 6ft 8"

There will be occasional exceptions but on the whole heights will be in this range.

(e) The most useful feature of the normal curve is that, at a point a certain number of standard deviations from the mean, the area under the curve will always represent the same percentage of the population (no matter what normal curve is being considered).

Normal distribution examples

(a)

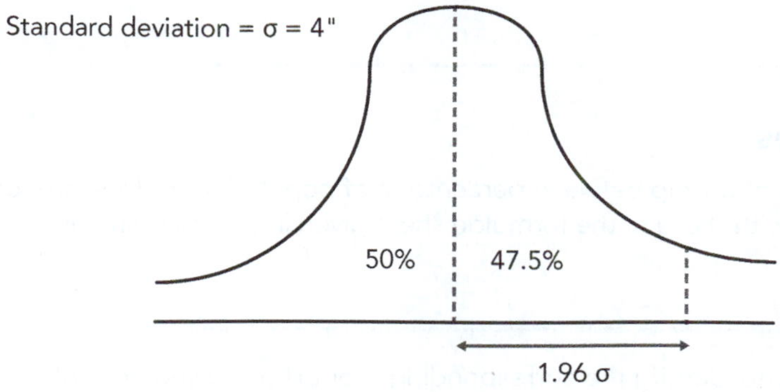

In the height example this would mean that 2.5% of the population are taller than 5ft 8" + 1.96 × 4" = 6ft 3.84".

(b)

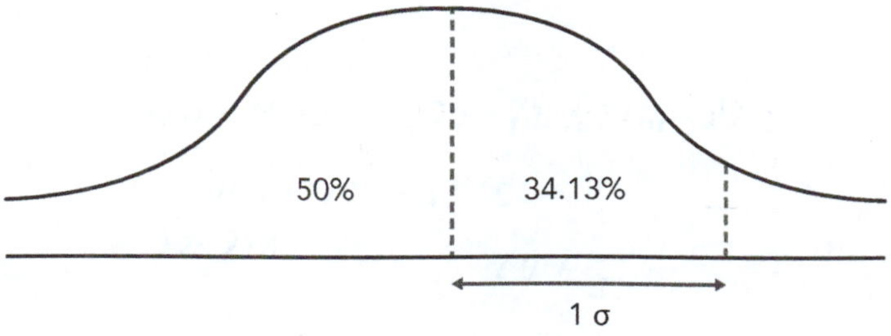

Here we are measuring a range one standard deviation from the mean ie 5ft 8" + 1 × 4" = 6ft.

This would mean that 84.13% of the population are shorter than 6ft and 15.87% of the population are taller than 6ft.

(c)

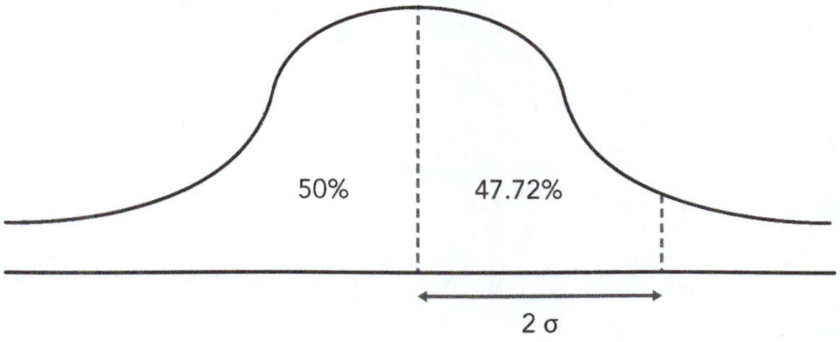

Here we are measuring a range two standard deviations from the mean ie 5ft 8" + (2 × 4") = 6ft 4".

This would mean that 97.72% of the population are shorter than 6ft 4" and 2.28% of the population are taller than 6ft 4".

We need a method to translate distances from the mean into probabilities ie areas under the curve. We do this with a combination of **z-scores** and normal distribution tables.

6.6 Z-scores

KEY TERM

Z-score: Distances from the mean in the normal distribution, measured by the number of standard deviations they represent.

Formula provided

$$z = \frac{x - \mu}{\sigma}$$ (formula on normal distribution table)

6.7 Normal distribution tables

These are tables which give the relationship between percentage of population and z score for any z score. You will be provided with these in the formulae sheet given in the assessment.

Illustration 1: Calculating z

Calculate the following z-scores and identify the corresponding proportions using normal distribution tables.

1 $x = 100$, $\mu = 200$, $\sigma = 50$

2 $x = 1{,}000$, $\mu = 1{,}200$, $\sigma = 200$

Solution

1

$$z = \frac{x - \mu}{\sigma}$$

$$= \frac{100 - 200}{50}$$

$$= 2$$

A z-score of 2 corresponds to a proportion of 0.4772 or 47.72%.

2

$$z = \frac{x - \mu}{\sigma}$$

$$= \frac{1{,}000 - 1{,}200}{200}$$

$$= 1$$

A z-score of 1 corresponds to a proportion of 0.3413 or 34.13%.

Activity 6: Using the normal distribution

The average number of litres of water consumed in three months by accountancy students is 251. The standard deviation is 15 litres.

Assume a normal distribution.

Required

Calculate the likelihood that a student will drink:

1 More than 285 litres

2 Less than 200 litres

3 Between 220 and 255 litres

Solution

Exam focus point

It is important to recognise that you may need to manipulate the z-score calculation to answer questions. For example, you may need to work backwards from a percentage of population to calculate the z-score and then the x value.

Illustration 2: Calculating x

A normal distribution has a mean of 120 and a standard deviation of 15. 75% of the population is therefore below what value?

Solution

50% of the population is below 120.

A further 25% of the population is below x.

From the normal distribution table, a value of 0.25 equates to a z value of 0.67.

$$z = \frac{x-\mu}{\sigma}$$

$$0.67 = \frac{x-120}{15}$$

$0.67 \times 15 = x - 120$

$10.05 = x - 120$

$x = 10.05 + 120$

$= 130.05$

75% of the population is below 130.05.

Activity 7: Manipulating the z-score

A normal distribution has a mean of 150 and a standard deviation of 20.

80% of the population is therefore below what value?

Solution

50 –

$\frac{x - 150}{20} =$

30%.

50% – below

30% – below.

= 0.300

0.300

20% – 0.2 =

$x - 150 = 10.4$

0.52

160.4

below

0.85 = $\frac{x - 150}{20} =$

$0.52 = \frac{x - 150}{20}$

$x - 150 = 17$

167.

---

7 Presentation of data

Data and information can be presented in a number of ways. The most common include the following.

7.1 Tables

Table guidelines

(a) Include a title

(b) Label all columns

(c) Include subtotals where appropriate

(d) Total column at right/bottom

Types of tables

(a) **Array** – values are placed in ascending/descending order

(b) **Tally marks** – a simple way of presenting data where each mark represents one item of data.

0	卌 卌	10
1	卌 111	8
2	卌 卌 卌 卌	20
3	卌 卌 11	12
		50

7.2 Ungrouped frequency distributions

A discreet or ungrouped frequency distribution is a sample of data containing items of data, each with a definitive value. Here, items of data are **not** sorted in ranges. This is useful if a particular value appears more than once in a group/distribution.

Consider the age of CIMA BA2 students on a course:

19	20	24	19
21	22	19	21
21	21	22	23

Here, data can be formulated into an Ungrouped Frequency Distribution as follows:

Age of student	*Frequency*
19	3
20	1
21	4
22	2
23	1
24	1
	12

7.3 Grouped frequency distribution

A grouped frequency distribution is useful where each value of data is different. Here data is measured instead of counted and can be sorted into convenient ranges. Consider the following distribution:

Heights of a group of 12 toddlers:

64 cm	65 cm
70 cm	68 cm
62 cm	71 cm
72 cm	69 cm
74 cm	73 cm
65 cm	67 cm

Put in classes where the class size is 2cm:

Heights	No. of toddlers
62 - < 64	1
64 - < 66	3
66 - < 68	1
68 - < 70	2
70 - < 72	2
72 - < 74	2
74 - < 76	1
	12

∴ A grouped frequency distribution is good for continuous variables (measured data against a continuous scale).

7.4 Bar charts

Data is represented by bars of equal width, the height of which corresponds to the value of the data.

(a) **Simple bar chart** – Consider the profits for Douglas Co by year

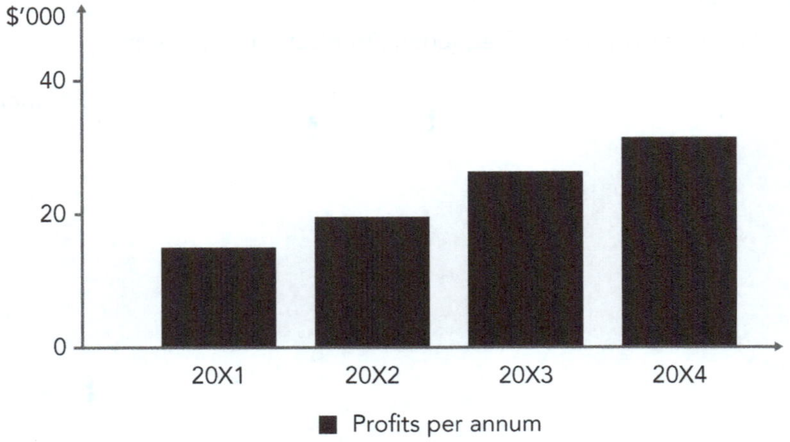

(b) **Component bar chart** – total sales by product breakdown

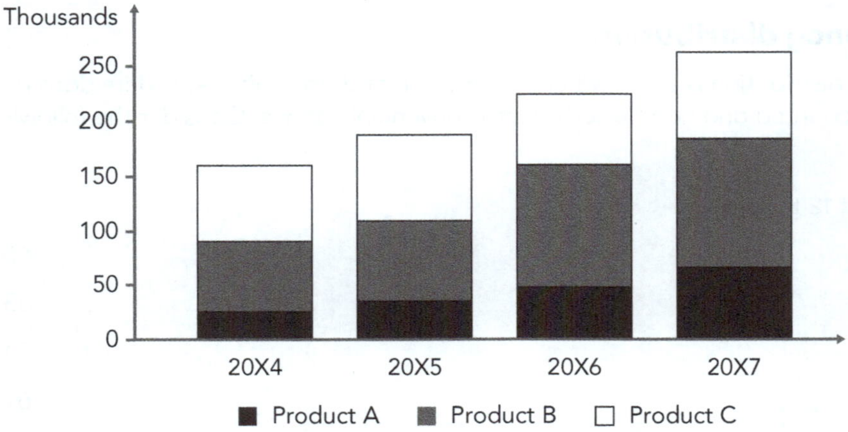

(c) **Multiple bar chart** – Each colour bar represents a product type whose height represents product sales in the year. Notice total sales information for the year is sacrificed.

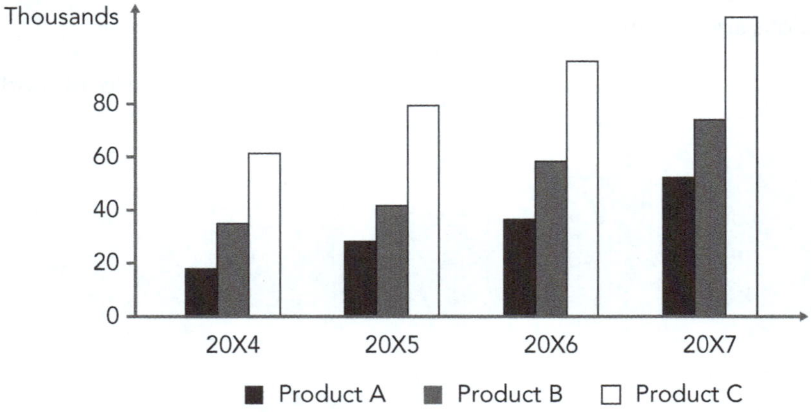

BPP

(d) % **Bar chart** – Each bar represents 100% of total sales. A breakdown into component sales is represented as a % of total sales.

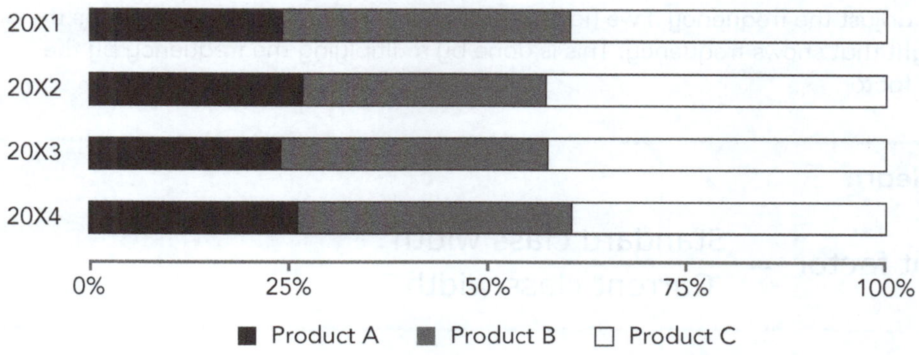

7.5 Pie charts

Pie charts show the relative size of the components of a total.

(a) Draw a circle, split into sections (number of degrees in a circle = 360)

(b) Each sector is proportional to the component it represents

Example

Employment – Destination of UK graduates in 20X6

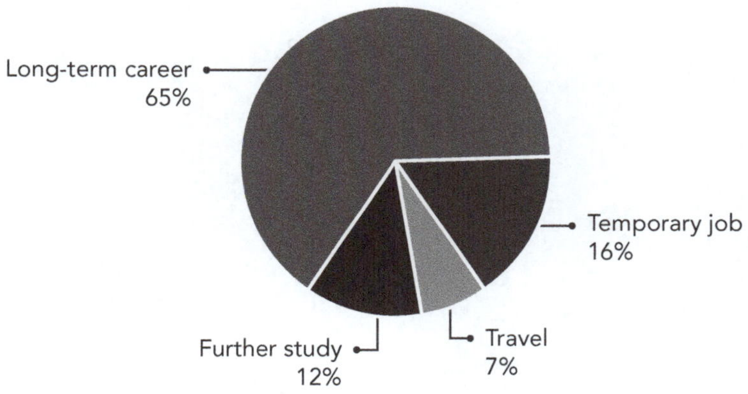

7.6 Pictograms

Difference in values are shown by the use of symbols or pictures. Values are represented by pictures of the same size. An increase in the number of pictures, demonstrates an increase in value.

Example

7.7 Histograms

(a) Good for continuous variables and grouped frequency distributions

(b) **Area** of bars represent frequencies/number of observations, not **heights**

(c) Width of bar proportionate to size of interval

(d) Height = frequency if **all** intervals are of the same size

(e) Pick a standard class size to begin

(f) We need to adjust the frequency if we have varying class interval sizes because it is the area, not the height that shows frequency. This is done by multiplying the frequency by the adjustment factor.

Formula to learn

$$\text{Adjustment factor} = \frac{\text{Standard class width}}{\text{Current class width}}$$

7.8 Ogive

The **Ogive** or **Cumulative Frequency Curve** will show graphically the total number of items less than a certain value.

Example

	Frequency	*Cumulative Frequency*
110 ≤ 115	2	2
115 ≤ 125	2	4
125 ≤ 135	4	8
135 ≤ 145	4	12
145 ≤ 155	2	14
155 ≤ 165	1	15

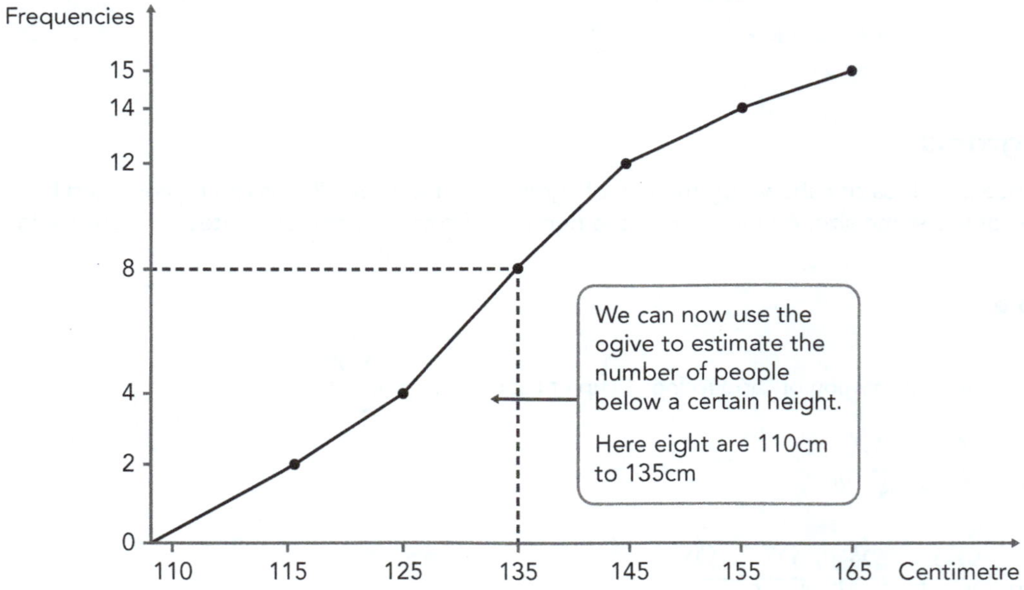

Chapter summary

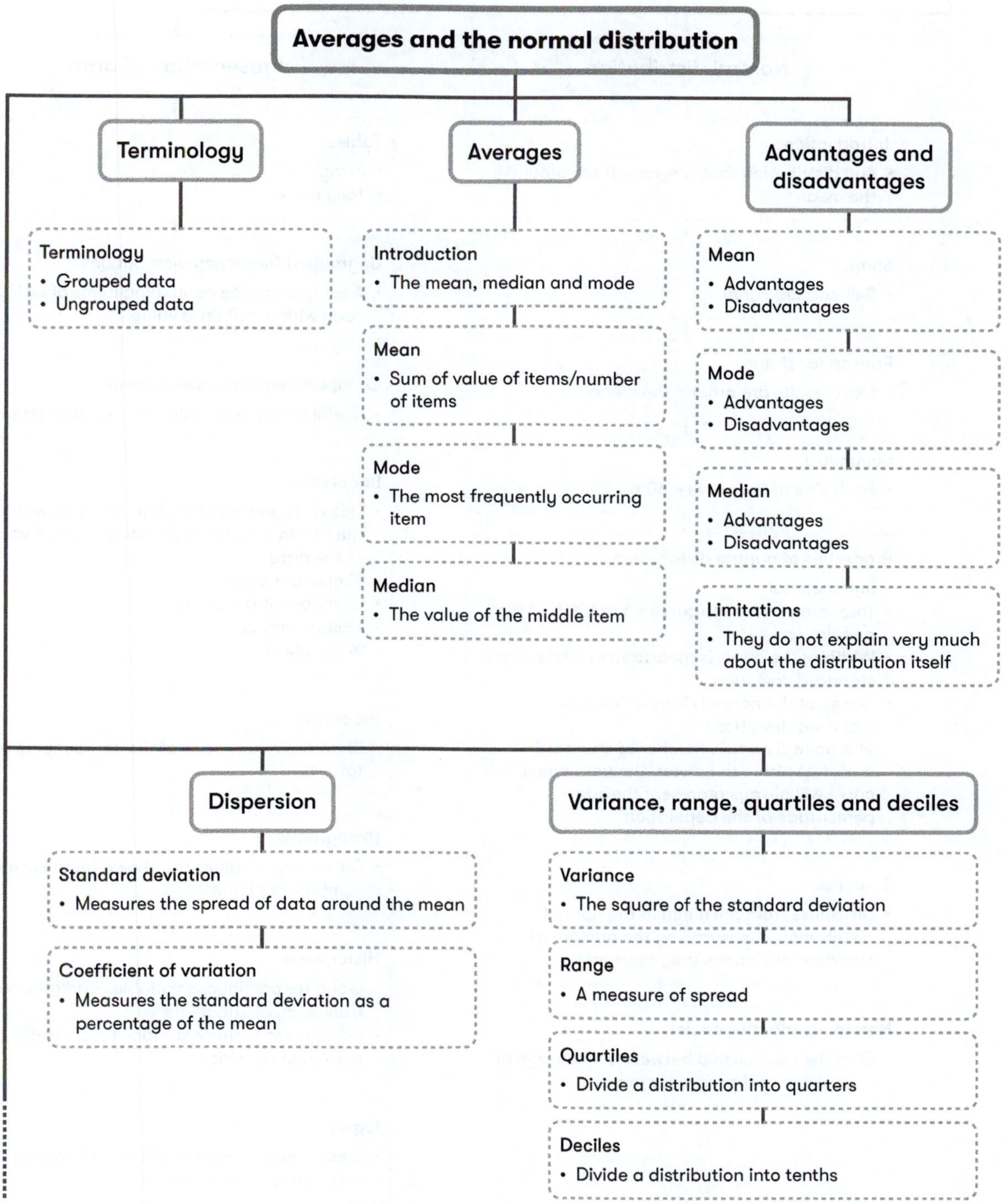

Normal distribution

Introduction
- Any distribution that is symmetrical around the mean

Shape
- Bell-shaped curve

Reason for shape
- Most results are around the mean

Symmetry
- Each side of the curve = 50%

Properties of normal distribution
- Symmetrical
- Total area under the curve = 1 or 100% of the population
- Width of the curve is measured in terms of the standard deviation
- Range of the normal distribution is six standard deviations
- At a point a certain number of standard deviations from the mean, the area under the curve will always represent the same percentage of the population

Z-scores
- Distances from the mean in the normal distribution, measured by the number of standard deviations they represent

Normal distribution tables
- Give the relationship between percentage of population and z score for any z score

Presentation of data

Tables
- Array
- Tally marks

Ungrouped frequency distributions
- A sample of data containing items of data, each with a definitive value

Grouped frequency distribution
- Useful where each value of data is different

Bar charts
- Data is represented by bars of equal width, the height of which corresponds to the value of the data
- Simple bar chart
- Component bar chart
- Multiple bar chart
- % Bar chart

Pie charts
- Show the relative size of the components of a total

Pictograms
- Difference in values are shown by the use of symbols or pictures

Histograms
- Good for continuous variables and grouped frequency distributions
- Adjustment factor = standard class width / current class width

Ogive
- Shows graphically the total number of items less than a certain value

Key terms

Grouped data: Where the frequency is shown in terms of a range. Known as continuous data.

Ungrouped data: Discrete data, where the frequency is shown in terms of a specific measure/value.

Arithmetic mean: The best known type of average and is widely understood. It is used for further statistical analysis.

Mode: The most frequently occurring item.

Median: The value of the middle item.

Standard deviation: One of the most important measures of dispersion. The standard deviation measures the spread of data around the mean.

Variance: Defined as the square of the standard deviation (σ^2)

Range: A measure of spread; the difference between the highest and lowest possible values or, where data is grouped, it will be the difference between the upper interval limit and the lowest interval limit.

Quartiles: Divide a distribution into quarters. In other words, the **quartiles** and the **median** divide the population into four groups of equal size.

Inter-quartile range: The difference between the upper and lower quartiles (Q3–Q1).

Normal distribution (or probability distribution): A frequency distribution which is important because it arises frequently in 'real life'. It is any distribution that is symmetrical around the mean.

Z-score: Distances from the mean in the normal distribution, measured by the number of standard deviations they represent.

Activity answers

Activity 1: Calculating the mean

			Mid-point	*No. of cars*	*Mileage*
			xf	f	fx
	<	2,000	1,000	10	10,000
2,000	<	4,000	3,000	14	42,000
4,000	<	6,000	5,000	154	770,000
6,000	<	8,000	7,000	292	2,044,000
8,000	<	10,000	9,000	493	4,437,000
10,000	<	12,000	11,000	404	4,444,000
12,000	<	14,000	13,000	164	2,132,000
14,000	<	16,000	15,000	48	720,000
	≥	16,000	17,000	21	357,000
				1,600	14,956,000

$$\text{Mean} = \frac{\Sigma fx}{\Sigma f}$$

$$= \frac{14,956,000}{1,600}$$

$$= 9,347.5$$

The mean annual mileage of these car owners is 9,347.5 miles.

Activity 2: Calculate the median (ungrouped data)

The correct answer is: 14.50

The first thing to do is to arrange the scores in order of magnitude.

8, 9, 11, 12, 14, 15, 17, 21, 24, 34

There are ten items, and so median is the arithmetic mean of the fifth and sixth items.

$$= \frac{14 + 15}{2} = \frac{29}{2} = 14.50$$

The correct answer is therefore the third option.

Activity 3: Standard deviation calculation

	Mid-point mileage	*No. of cars*			
	x	f	fx	x^2	fx^2
	('000)				
< 2	1	10	10	1	10
2 – < 4	3	14	42	9	126
4 – < 6	5	154	770	25	3,850

	Mid-point mileage x	No. of cars f	fx	x^2	fx^2
6 – < 8	7	292	2,044	49	14,308
8 – < 10	9	493	4,437	81	39,933
10 – < 12	11	404	4,444	121	48,884
12 – < 14	13	164	2,132	169	27,716
14 – < 16	15	48	720	225	10,800
≥ 16	17	21	357	289	6,069
		1,600	14,956		151,696

$$\sigma = \sqrt{\frac{\Sigma fx^2}{\Sigma f} - \bar{x}^2}$$

$$= \sqrt{\frac{151,696}{1,600} - 9.3475^2}$$

Note. Calculations using '000s of miles.

= 2.72658........ (measured in '000s)

ie standard deviation = 2,727 miles (nearest mile)

Activity 4: Coefficient of variation

$$\text{Coefficient of variation} = \frac{\sigma}{x}$$

$$= \frac{2,727}{9,347.5}$$

= 0.292 (3 dp)

ie, 29.2%

Activity 5: Quartile deviation

$$\text{The quartile deviation} = \frac{(Q_3 - Q_1)}{2} = \frac{62-44}{2} = \frac{18}{2} = 9$$

Activity 6: Using the normal distribution

1

$\bar{x} = 25$
$\sigma = 15$

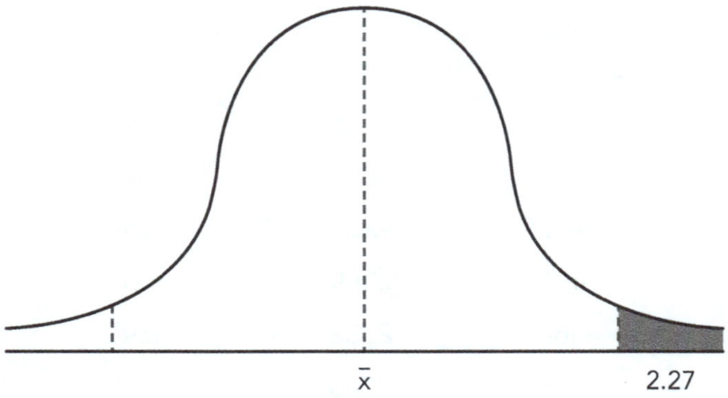

$$z(285) = \frac{285-251}{15} = 2.27 \Rightarrow (0.5-0.4884)$$
$$\Rightarrow 0.0116$$

∴ probability of a student drinking more than 285 litres is 0.0116 or 1.16%.

2

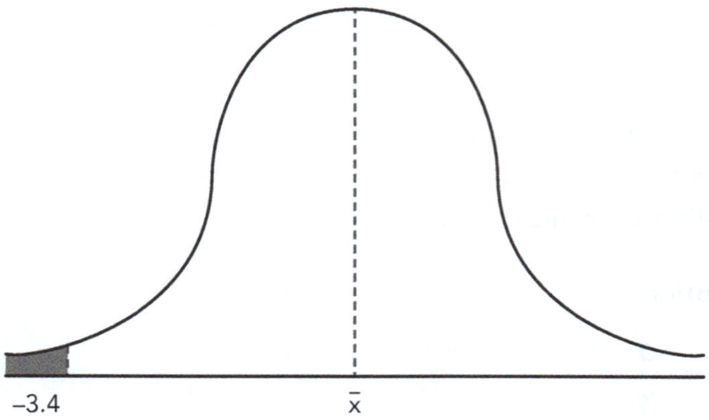

$$z(200) = \frac{200-251}{15} = -3.4 \quad \Rightarrow (0.5 - 0.49966)$$
$$\Rightarrow 0.00034$$

∴ probability of a student drinking less than 200 litres in 3 months is 0.00034 (0.034%) ie negligible.

3

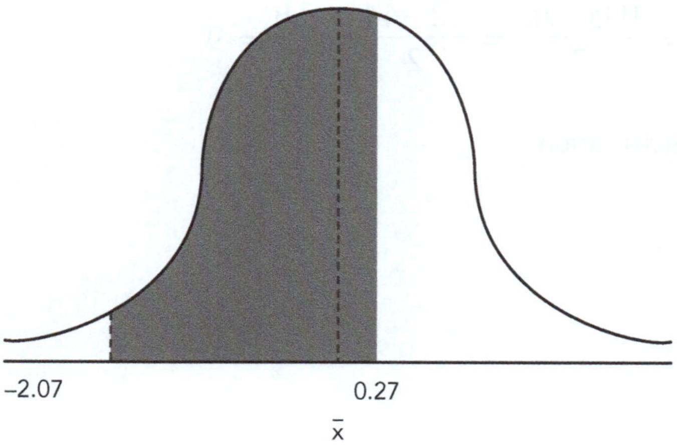

$$z(220) = \frac{220-251}{15} = -2.07 \Rightarrow 0.4808$$

$$z(255) = \frac{225-251}{15} = 0.27 \Rightarrow 0.1064$$

∴ probability that a student will drink between 220 and 255 litres in 3 months = 0.4808 + 0.1064 = 0.5872 or 58.72%.

Activity 7: Manipulating the z-score

50% are below 150

Need to find 30% (30% from the tables gives a z of 0.84)

$$\frac{x-150}{20} = 0.84 \Rightarrow x = 166.8$$

80% of the population is under 166.8.

Test your learning

1 Insert the formulae in the bullets below into the correct position.

(1) The arithmetic mean of ungrouped data =

(2) The arithmetic mean of grouped data = or

- $\frac{\sum x}{n}$
- $\frac{\sum fx}{n}$
- $\frac{\sum fx}{\sum f}$

2 What is the name given to the average which means 'the most frequently occurring value'?

- O Arithmetic mean
- O Median
- O Mode

3 The mean weight of a group of components has been calculated as 133.5. The individual weights of the components were 143, 96, x, 153.5, 92.5, y, 47. When y = 4x;

Required

What is the value of x?

[ ]

4 Calculate the mid-points for both discrete and continuous variables in the table below.

Class interval	*Mid-point (Discrete data)*	*Mid-point (Continuous data)*
25 < 30		
30 < 35		
35 < 40		
40 < 45		
45 < 50		
50 < 55		
55 < 60		
60 < 65		

5 Fill in the blanks using the pull down list:

The mode of a grouped frequency distribution can be found from a(n) [▼].

The median of a grouped frequency distribution can be found from a(n) [▼].

Pull down list

- Histogram

- Ogive

6 A group of children have the following ages in years: 10, 8, 6, 9, 13, 12, 7, 11.

Required

What is the median age? [ ]

7 Fill in the blanks in the statements below using the words in the box.

Upper	Above	Below	Lower

(1) [ ] quartile = Q1 = value [ ] which 25% of the population fall.

(2) [ ] quartile = Q3 = value [ ] which 25% of the population fall.

8 Complete the following sentence:

The area under the curve of a normal distribution = [ ] which represents [ ] % of all probabilities.

9 (a) The formula for the semi-interquartile range is:

(b) The semi-interquartile range is also known as the [ ]

10 A normal distribution has a mean of 80 and a variance of 16. What is the upper quartile of this distribution?

17 Investment appraisal

Learning outcomes

Having studied this chapter you will be able to:
• Explain the time value of money
• Apply financial mathematics
• Calculate the net present value, internal rate of return and payback for an investment or project

Chapter context

One of the key roles of the management accountant is providing information to help make better decisions. This chapter looks at long-term decision making. It starts by addressing the time value of money and methods to factor the time value of money into calculations. It then covers several techniques that can be used to help make a particularly difficult decision: which long-term projects should be invested in to increase the wealth of the owners of the business?

Syllabus context

This chapter is part of syllabus **Section D**, which looks at **'Decision Making'**.

This syllabus area has a weighting of **35%** and is covered by **Chapters 6 and 7 and 15 to 17.**

In the exam, you will be expected to demonstrate competence in the following areas:

- The time value of money.
- Discounting, compounding, annuities and perpetuities.
- Net present value, internal rate of return and payback.

Chapter overview

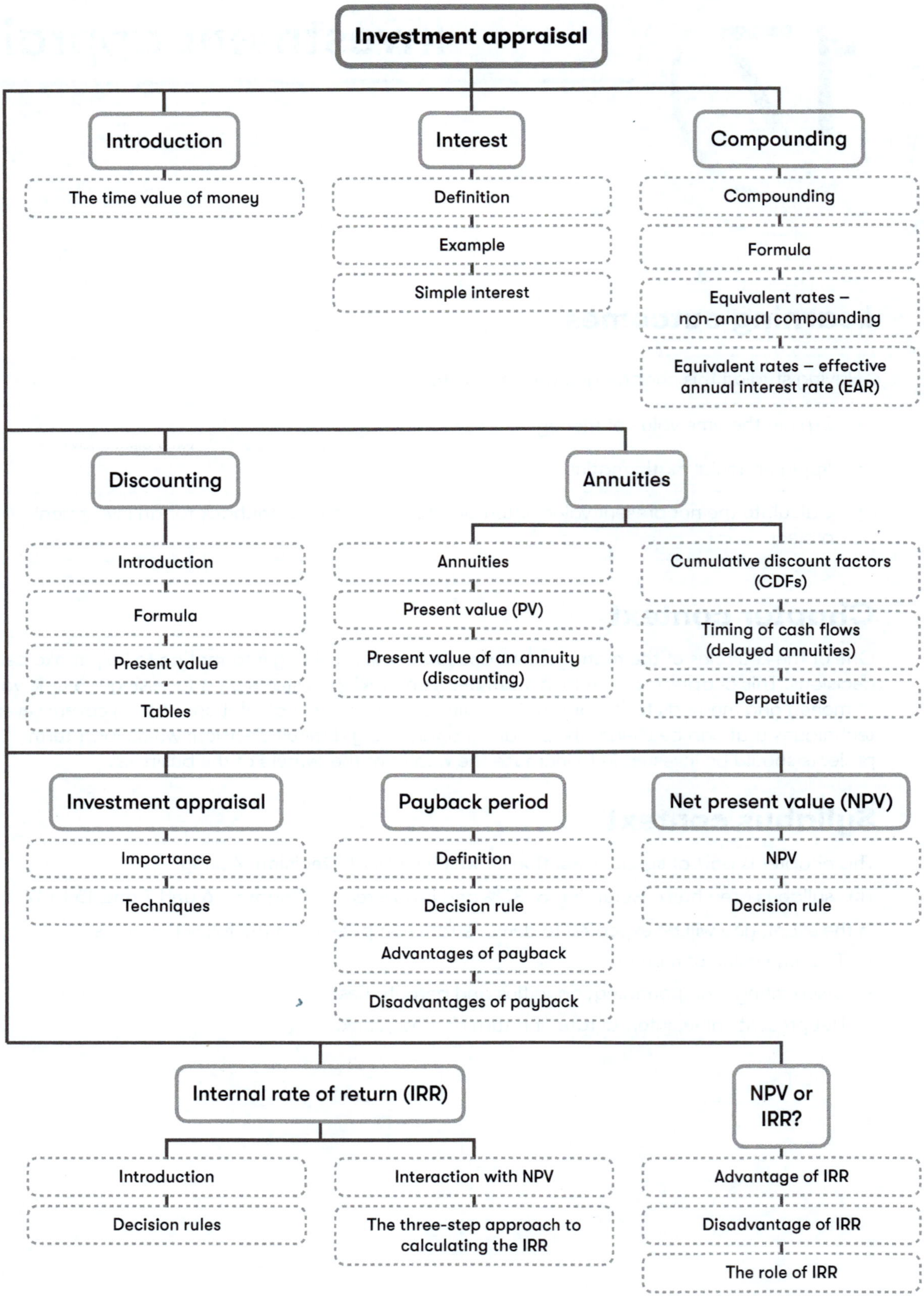

1 Introduction

1.1 The time value of money

For long-term decision making an important factor is the time value of money. This is the idea that money today is worth more than the same amount of money in the future.

Illustration 1: Time value of money

1. Given a choice between receiving $600 now, or $200 per year for 3 years starting in one year's time, which would you choose? Why?
2. Would your answer change if you were offered only $500 now? How much of a drop would be required for you to decide to accept the future payments instead of the immediate payment?

Solution

1. It is common sense to prefer the immediate payment of $600. Three annual payments of $200 are not as attractive as $600 received today. This is the meaning of the term **'time value of money'**. The **logic** behind rejecting the future cash flows is that you would be better off if you took the $600 now and put it into a bank account and invested it. Future cash flows are also uncertain (more risky) and their purchasing power is lower in periods of inflation.
2. It is more difficult to judge when the immediate cash flow is of a lower nominal value. We cannot make this decision objectively without some form of analysis to take into account the time value of money. The standard approach to dealing with situations like this is to use 'discounting' techniques and we will look at these later.

2 Interest

2.1 Definition

Interest is the amount of money which an investment earns over time.

2.2 Example

How much will an investor have after 5 years if they invest $1,000 at 10% simple interest per annum?

Final sum = $1,000 + (5 × 0.1 × $1,000) = $1,500

2.3 Formula

Formula to learn (simple interest)

$$S = X + rXn$$

Where S = final sum

X = amount invested

r = interest rate as a decimal

n = number of periods investment is held for

Activity 1: Simple interest

$500 is invested in a savings account earning simple interest of 0.1% per **month.**

Required

Calculate the final value in the account after two years.

Solution

3 Compounding

KEY TERM

> **Compounding:** Interest is normally calculated by means of compounding.
>
> Compound interest is where interest is calculated and paid on capital plus any interest paid or payable earned up to that point.

This means that, as interest is earned, it is added to the original investment and starts to earn interest itself.

3.1 Formula

> **Formula to learn (compound interest)**
>
> $$s = x(1 + r)^n$$
>
> Where s = final sum
>
> x = amount invested
>
> r = interest as a decimal
>
> n = number of periods investment is held for

Example: Compound interest

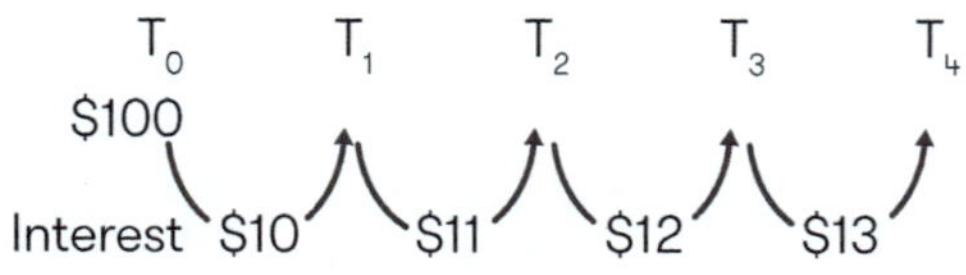

ie	S1	=	$100 (1 + 0.1) = $110	
	S2	=	S1 +0.1S1 = S1 (1 + 0.1)	= 100 (1 + 0.1) (1 + 0.1)
				= 100 (1 + 0.1)2
				= $121

BPP

Activity 2: Compound interest

1 $500 is invested in a savings account earning compound interest of 10% p.a. How much will the investment have grown to in five years' time?

0.1

2 $1,750 is invested for 20 years at 6% compound interest. What is the final value of the investment?

3 A house is purchased for $200,000. If house price growth is 1.2% per annum for 8 years, how much will the house be worth in 8 years' time? (To the nearest whole number)

Solution

1) 500 × (1 + 0.1)^5 = 805

2) 1750 × (1 + 0.06)^{20} = 5612

3) 200,000 × (1 + 0.012)^8 = 220,026.

3.2 Equivalent rates – non annual compounding

In the previous activities, interest has been calculated **annually,** but this isn't always the case. Interest may be compounded **daily, weekly, monthly** or **quarterly**.

For example, $10,000 invested for 5 years at an interest rate (called a **nominal rate**) of 2% per month will have a final value of $10,000 × (1 + 0.02)60 = $32,810. Notice that n relates to the number of periods (5 years × 12 months) that r is compounded.

Activity 3: Non-annual compounding

$1,000 initial investment, 6% **six-monthly** interest rate.

Required

Calculate the value of the investment after one year and how much interest is earned.

Solution

1000 × (1 + 0.06)^2

= 1123.60

interest = 1000 − 1123.60 =

123.60.

3.3 Equivalent rates – effective annual interest rate (EAR)

Formula to learn

The non-annual compounding interest rate can be converted into an annual equivalent using the following formula. (This formula is **not** given in the assessment.)

$$(1 + R) = (1 + r)^n$$

Where R = effective annual rate

r = period rate

n = number of periods in a year

The effective annual interest rate (EAR) is also called the annual percentage rate (APR) by banks, building societies and credit companies.

Activity 4: EAR

If the quarterly rate of interest is 3.9%, what is the annual percentage rate?

Solution

(1 + R) = (1 + 0.039)⁴

R = 0.165

16.5 %

4 Discounting

4.1 Introduction

Discounting: The opposite of compounding. Here we are evaluating an equivalent value of money at an earlier point in time. We are, in effect, taking account of the 'time value of money'.

The basic principle of discounting is that if we wish to have $S in n years' time, we need to invest a certain sum now (Year 0) at an interest rate of r% in order to obtain the required sum of money in the future.

4.2 Formula

Earlier we saw, for compounding, the future value of an amount is given by the formula:

$$S = x(1 + r)^n$$

Rearranging the formula for x, the present value, we have:

$$x = \frac{S}{(1 + r)^n}$$

Activity 5: Discounting a single cash flow

We need $1,610 at the end of 5 years from now.

Required

Assuming we could earn 10% pa, how much should be invested now?

Solution

$$\frac{1610}{(1+0.1)^5} = 999.68 = 1000$$

4.3 Present value

KEY TERM

> **Present value:** The value, in today's prices, of a future cash flow.

$1,000 is the present value (PV) of $1,610 @ 10% in 5 years.

In purely monetary terms we would be indifferent between receiving $1,000 now or $1,610 in 5 years. In order to maintain the same purchasing power, we would require $1,610 in 5 years' time to purchase goods costing $1,000 now.

4.4 Discount factor

Formula provided

$$\frac{1}{(1 + r)^n}$$

This is known as a discount factor - DFn

It can also be presented as $(1 + r)^{-n}$

Therefore present value = Sn × DFn

We can take any future cash flow and discount it back to what it is equivalently worth today.

4.5 Tables

Some discount factors are available in tables. The tables range from discount (interest) rates of between 1% and 20% and between 1 and 20 periods. Should interest rates or periods fall outside these ranges then use the formula to derive the answer.

Activity 6: Discounting a single cash flow using tables

We need $5,000 at the end of 3 years.

Required

Assuming we could earn interest at 8% pa, how much should we invest now?

$$\frac{5000}{(1+0.08)^3} = 3970$$

Solution

Activity 7: Discounting with changing interest rates

If the interest rate is currently 10% but in 2 years' time will change to 15%, what is the 5-year discount factor?

Solution

Discount factor =

$$\frac{1}{(1+0.1)^2 \times (1+0.15)^3} = 0.543$$

$$\frac{1}{(1+x)^1} = 0.83 = 10\%\ 2\ \text{yrs}$$

$= 0.997.$

5 Annuities

KEY TERM

> **Annuity:** A constant sum of money paid or received each and every period for a given number of periods.

5.1 Present value (PV)

The present value (PV) of an annuity is the discounted value of each annuity payment over the period of the investment. A practical example of this would be someone about to retire, who wants to 'buy' a pension of $X per year for Y years. The cost of this pension is the PV of the annuity.

5.2 Present value of an annuity (discounting)

The present value of an annuity represents that amount you would be prepared to receive now to make you indifferent between future receipts from the annuity and a cash lump sum at T0 (ie now).

Activity 8: Present value of annuity (timeline)

An investment is made of $100 now and at the end of each of the next 3 years with a discount rate of 10% per annum.

Required

What is the present value of this investment?

Solution

5.3 Cumulative discount factors (CDFs)

To make the calculations easier we can use cumulative discount factors (CDFs) to calculate the **PV** of an annuity.

$\$100 \times (1 + DF_1 + DF_2 + DF_3)$

The CDF is a sum of the annual discount factors for the period concerned.

$CDF_{1-3} = DF_1 + \ldots\ldots + DF_3$

A selection of these are given in the tables. The following formula must be used for an annuity > 20 periods.

Formula provided

$$CDF_{1-n} = \frac{1}{r}\left[1 - \frac{1}{(1+r)^n}\right]$$

It can also be presented as:

$$\frac{1-(1+r)^{-n}}{r}$$

Formula to learn

Timing

(a) Present value of an annuity starting at time 1 = a × CDF_n

(b) Present value of an annuity starting at time 0 (ie now) = a × (1 + CDF_n)

Activity 9: Present value of annuity (tables and formula)

1 What is the present value of an annuity that pays $12,000 at the end of each year for 10 years, assuming an interest rate of 6%?

2 What is the present value of an annuity that pays $10,000 at the end of each year for 25 years, assuming an interest rate of 7.5%?

3 What is the present value of $1,500 invested now and at the end of each of the next 4 years at an interest rate of 6%?

Solution

5.4 Timing of cash flows (delayed annuities)

If the annuity payment does not start until a future period, we need to take this into account when calculating the present value of an annuity.

We do this by taking the CDF for years 1 – n (where n is the last payment or receipt made) and deduct the CDF for the years **prior** to the start of the annuity.

Activity 10: Delayed annuity

Calculate the present value of an annuity of $3,000 per annum, using a discount rate of 6% per annum.

The annuity starts at the end of the third year and finishes at the end of the tenth year.

Solution

5.5 Perpetuities

KEY TERM

Perpetuity: An annuity, commencing at T1 which continues to be paid/received at regular intervals forever.

A perpetuity therefore has no end. For example, you might receive an entry to a competition offering you $1,000 per year for the remainder of your life.

Formula to learn

$$\text{PV of \$1 per annum in perpetuity} = \frac{1}{r}$$

For the formula to work, the timing of the first cash flow must be in one year's time (ie at T_1).

Activity 11: Perpetuity calculations

1 If the interest rate is 10%, what would you pay for a perpetuity of $1,000 starting in 1 year's time?

2 What would you pay if the same perpetuity starts now?

3 What would you pay if the same perpetuity starts in 4 years' time?

Solution

a) 1000 x 1/0.1 = 10,000

b) PV = 10,000 + 1000 = 11,000

c) Delayed perpetuity

PV = 10,000

PV formula.

3 yrs DF

10,000 x 0.751

= 7513

6 Investment appraisal

6.1 Importance

To be successful organisations need to make long-term investments. These investments may be, for example, in new machinery, new products, new production facilities, or refurbishing retail outlets.

Proper appraisal of projects involving capital expenditure is important for the following reasons.

(a) A relatively significant amount of the resources of the business will be involved.

(b) A capital investment decision may be difficult to reverse, and on any reversal considerable costs may have been incurred for little benefit.

(c) Investment decisions need to be considered in the light of strategic and tactical decisions of the company. The decision made should be consistent with the company's long-term objective, which will usually be the maximisation of the wealth of shareholders.

(d) Future benefits need detailed evaluation since they are often difficult to predict. Consequently, there may be a high degree of risk and uncertainty.

6.2 Techniques

Businesses need techniques to help them decide which investments are worth making. The assumption made is that the key criteria in making the decision is whether the investment will increase the wealth of the owners of the business.

There are three investment appraisal techniques that you need to be able to use in BA2.

All three techniques are based on relevant cash flows.

7 Payback period

7.1 Definition

KEY TERM

> **Payback period:** A measure of how many years it takes for the **cash flows affected by the decision to invest** to repay the cost of the original investment.

A long payback period is considered risky because it relies on cash flows that are in the distant future.

Activity 12: Payback period

GA Co is considering purchasing a new machine for $250,000. Cash flow projections from the project (which can be assumed to accrue evenly) are shown below.

same amt of money each mth in a yr.

Year	*Net cash flows*
	$
1	60,000
2	60,000
3	80,000
4	100,000
5	100,000

After 5 years the machine will be scrapped. The scrap value of the machine is included in the year 5 cash flow shown above.

Required

Calculate the payback period for the project, in years, to 1 decimal place.

Solution

time	cashflow	cumulative cashflow
0	(250,000)	(250,000) + 60,000
1	60,000	(190,000) + 60,000
2	60,000	(130,000) + 80,000
3	80,000	(50,000) + 100,000
4	100,000	50,000

50,000 / 100,000 = 0.5 + 3 = 3.5

identify time to break even.

payback period 3.5 yrs

7.2 Decision rule

The decision rule is to accept all projects with a payback period within the company's target payback period.

7.3 Advantages of payback

(a) A simple way of **screening out** projects that look too risky

(b) Useful when a company has cash flow problems

7.4 Disadvantages of payback

(a) Ignores the timing of the cash flows within the payback period

(b) Ignores the cash flows outside the payback period

(c) Ignores the time value of money

8 Discounted cash flow techniques: net present value (NPV)

8.1 NPV

We need a technique that allows us to take into account the timing of cash flows when deciding whether to accept a project.

KEY TERM

> **Net present value (NPV) technique:** A comparison of the discounted value of the future cash flows with the cost of setting up a project today.

Many **projects** involve investing money now and receiving returns on the investment in the future; so the timing of a project's cash flows need to be analysed to see if they offer a better return than the return an investor could get if they invested their money in other ways.

The process of adjusting a project's cash flows to reflect the return that investors could get elsewhere uses the **discounting** principles we saw earlier in this chapter. **The cash flows** of the project are discounted to present value and compared to the cash outlay taking place.

Illustration 2: NPV

Dog Co is considering whether to spend $5,000 on an item of equipment. The 'cash profits', the excess of income over cash expenditure, from the project would be $3,000 in the first year and $4,000 in the second year. The company will not invest in any project unless it offers a return in excess of 15% per annum.

Required

Assess whether the investment is worthwhile, or 'viable'.

Solution

In this example, an outlay of $5,000 now promises a return of $3,000 **during** the first year and $4,000 **during** the second year. It is a convention in discounted cash flow, however, that cash flows spread over a year are assumed to occur **at the end of the year,** so that the cash flows of the project are as follows.

	$
Year 0 (now)	(5,000)
Year 1 (at the end of the year)	3,000
Year 2 (at the end of the year)	4,000

A net present value (NPV) statement could be drawn up as follows.

Year	Cash flow $	Discount factor 15%	Present value $
0	(5,000)	1.000	(5,000)
1	3,000	0.870	2,610
2	4,000	0.756	3,024
		Net present value	+634

The project has a positive NPV, so it is acceptable.

Activity 13: Net present value (1)

If a project involved the outlay of $1,000 today and provided a definite return of $1,001 in 1 year's time, would you accept it if you could get a return of 5% on investments of similar risk?

Solution

8.2 Decision rule

If the discounted value of the future cash flows are higher than the cost of setting up a project today, then the project has a **positive NPV** and should be **accepted**.

Activity 14: Net present value (2)

1 If a project involved the outlay of $1,000 today and provided a definite return of $1,000 per year for 2 years starting in 1 year's time, would you accept it if you could get a return of 5% on investments of similar risk?

2 If a project involved the outlay of $1,000 today and provided a definite return of $1,000 per year, for the foreseeable future starting in 1 year's time, would you accept it? (Again assume that you could get a return of 5% on investments of similar risk.)

Solution

Annuity: A series of equal cash flows. Use the annuity table or discount each cash flow separately, whichever you prefer (the annuity table is quicker).

Cost of capital: the return required by the company's investors (5% in the activity. If required this will always be provided in the assessment).

Activity 15: NPV – GA Co

We earlier calculated the payback for GA's proposed investment, the details of which are reproduced below.

GA Co is considering purchasing a new machine for $250,000. Cash flow projections from the project are shown below.

Year	*Net cash flows*
	$
1	60,000
2	60,000
3	80,000
4	100,000
5	100,000

After 5 years the machine will be scrapped. The scrap value of the machine is included in the Year 5 cash flow shown above. GA's cost of capital is 10%.

Required

Calculate the NPV for the project.

Solution

Advantages of NPV	Disadvantages of NPV
Shareholder wealth is **maximised**.	It can be difficult to identify an **appropriate discount rate**.
It takes into account the **time value of money**.	For simplicity, cash flows are sometimes all assumed to occur at **year ends**: this assumption may be unrealistic.
It is based on **cash flows** which are less subjective than profit.	Some managers are **unfamiliar** with the concept of NPV.
Shareholders will **benefit** if a project with a positive NPV is accepted.	

9 Discounted cash flow techniques: Internal rate of return (IRR)

9.1 Introduction

KEY TERM

> **Internal rate of return (IRR):** A discounted cash flow technique that calculates the annual percentage return given by a project.

9.2 Decision rules

If the internal rate of return (IRR) is greater than the cost of capital then the project should be accepted. If it earns a **lower rate of return**, it is not worthwhile (and its **NPV** would be **negative**).

9.3 Interaction with NPV

IRR is also the discount rate where the **NPV of the project = 0.**

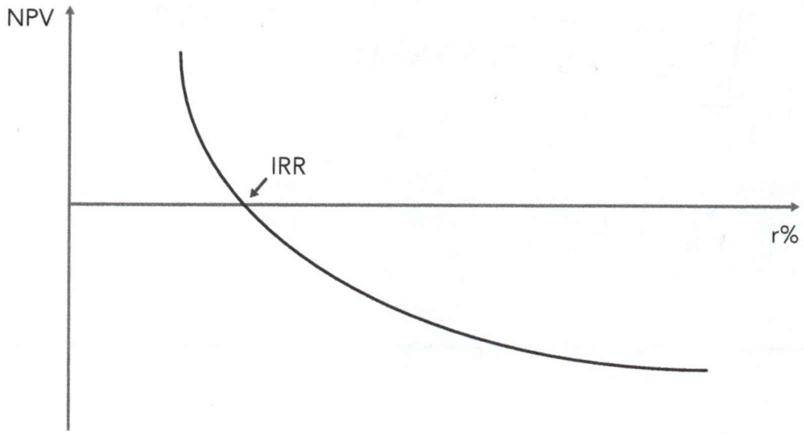

For most investments the NPV of a project will decrease as the discount rate (the required rate of return) increases as demonstrated by the illustration above.

9.4 The three-step approach to calculating the IRR

Step 1 **Calculate the NPV of the project at the first rate (usually the cost of capital given in the question)**

Step 2 **Calculate the NPV of the project at a second rate**

If the first NPV is positive then use a higher rate whereas if the first NPV is negative then use a lower rate.

Step 3 **Calculate the IRR using the formula**

Note. You will need to learn the formula for the assessment.

The formula will work whether you have two positive NPVs, two negative NPVs, or a positive and a negative NPV.

Formula to learn

$$IRR = a + \frac{NPVa}{NPVa - NPVb}(b - a)$$

Where a is the lower discount rate giving NPVa

b is the second discount rate giving NPVb

Activity 16: IRR – GA Co

Calculate the internal rate of return (to 1 decimal place) for GA's project shown in the previous activity.

Note. Step 1 is complete – we already know from Activity 15 that the NPV at 10% is + $44,580.

Solution

NPV at 10% = 44,580 (a)

Discount cashflow at higher rate

step 2 - 20% = (23,660)

$a + \left[\frac{NPVa}{NPVa - NPVb}\right](b - a)$

a = 10% b = 20%

$IRR = 10 + \left[\frac{44,580}{44580 - (-23660)}\right](20-10)$

16.533 %

10 NPV or IRR?

Both NPV and IRR are superior methods for appraising investments compared to payback because:

(a) They account for the time value of money

(b) They look at the cash flows over the whole life of the project

10.1 Advantage of IRR

IRR gives the annual percentage return of a project. This concept **is easy** for non-financial managers **to understand** and for financial managers to calculate because it does not require the calculation of a cost of capital.

10.2 Disadvantage of IRR

IRR can result in **dysfunctional behaviour**. This is best illustrated by looking at an example.

Activity 17: Dysfunctional behaviour

You are given the opportunity to invest in one of two mutually exclusive projects (ie you can invest in either project A or project B but not both).

Project	Initial investment $	Project return %
A	10	50
B	1,000	1

Required

Which project should you invest in if your objective is to maximise your wealth?

Solution

one or other.

IRR = Higher %. return = decision would be A

However,

A : $5

B : $ 10

Disadvantage	Explanation
Mutually exclusive projects	A smaller project might be chosen over a larger project because it has a higher IRR. NPV would choose the larger project because it deals in $, not %.
A change in direction of the cash flows	If there is another year of negative cash flows, there may be more than 1 IRR. This means that IRR becomes confusing.

Conclusion – NPV is a better technique.

10.3 The role of IRR

NPV does not have any of the problems of IRR. The role of IRR is to act as a tool for explaining the benefits of an investment to non-financial managers. It should not be used as the financial analysis used to justify the investment decision.

This is not to say that NPV is perfect. Like any financial technique, there is the danger that the **non-financial benefits** of an investment are ignored.

Chapter summary

Investment appraisal

Introduction

The time value of money
- The idea that money today is worth more than the same amount of money in the future

Interest

Definition
- The amount of money which an investment earns over time

Example
- Example

Simple interest
- $S = X + rXn$

Compounding

Compounding
- Where interest is calculated and paid on capital plus any interest paid or payable earned up to that point

Formula
- $S = X(1 + r)^n$

Equivalent rates – non-annual compounding
- Interest may be compounded daily, weekly, monthly or quarterly

Equivalent rates – effective annual interest rate (EAR)
- $(1+R) = (1+r)^n$

Discounting

Introduction
- Taking account of the 'time value of money'

Formula
- $X = S / (1/R)^n$

Present value
- The value, in today's prices, of a future cash flow
- Present value = Sn × DFn

Tables
- Discount factors are available in tables

Annuities

Annuities
- A constant sum of money paid or received each and every period for a given number of periods

Present value (PV)
- The discounted value of each annuity payment over the period of the investment

Present value of an annuity (discounting)
- The amount you would be prepared to receive now to make you indifferent between future receipts from the annuity and a cash lump sum at T_0 (ie now)

Cumulative discount factors (CDFs)
- The CDF is a sum of the annual discount factors for the period concerned

Timing of cash flows (delayed annuities)
- Timing of cashflows depending on receiving them at the start or end of a period

Perpetuities
- An annuity, commencing at T_1 which continues to be paid/received at regular intervals forever

Investment appraisal

Importance
- Significant amount of resources used
- Capital investment decisions may be difficult to reverse
- Decisions must be consistent with the company's long-term objective
- Future benefits difficult to predict

Techniques
- Payback period
- Net present value (NPV)
- Internal rate of return (IRR)

Payback period

Definition
- A measure of how many years it takes for the cash flows affected by the decision to invest to repay the cost of the original investment

Decision rule
- Accept all projects with a payback period within the company's target payback period

Advantages of payback
- Simple
- Useful when cashflow is limited

Disadvantages of payback
- Ignores timing of payments within the payback period
- Ignores cash flows outside the payback period
- Ignores time value of money

Net present value (NPV)

NPV
- A comparison of the discounted value of the future cash flows with the cost of setting up a project today

Decision rule
- If the project has a positive NPV it should be accepted

Internal rate of return (IRR)

Introduction
- A discounted cash flow technique that calculates the annual percentage return given by a project

Decision rules
- If the internal rate of return (IRR) is greater than the cost of capital then the project should be accepted
- If it earns a lower rate of return, it is not worthwhile (and its NPV would be negative)

Interaction with NPV
- IRR is the discount rate where the NPV of the project = 0

The three-step approach to calculating the IRR
- Calculate the NPV of the project at the first rate
- Calculate the NPV of the project at a second rate
- Calculate the IRR using the formula

NPV or IRR?

Advantage of IRR
- Easy for non-finance managers to understand

Disadvantage of IRR
- Can result in dysfunctional behaviour

The role of IRR
- To act as a tool for explaining the benefits of an investment to non-financial managers

Key terms

Compounding: Interest is normally calculated by means of compounding.

Compound interest is where interest is calculated and paid on capital plus any interest paid or payable earned up to that point.

Discounting: The opposite of compounding. Here we are evaluating an equivalent value of money at an earlier point in time. We are, in effect, taking account of the 'time value of money'.

Present value: The value, in today's prices, of a future cash flow.

Annuity: A constant sum of money paid or received each and every period for a given number of periods.

Perpetuity: An annuity, commencing at T1 which continues to be paid/received at regular intervals forever.

Payback period: A measure of how many years it takes for the **cash flows affected by the decision to invest** to repay the cost of the original investment.

Net present value (NPV) technique: A comparison of the discounted value of the future cash flows with the cost of setting up a project today.

Annuity: A series of equal cash flows. Use the annuity table or discount each cash flow separately, whichever you prefer (the annuity table is quicker).

Cost of capital: the return required by the company's investors (5% in the activity. If required this will always be provided in the assessment).

Internal rate of return (IRR): A discounted cash flow technique that calculates the annual percentage return given by a project.

Activity answers

Activity 1: Simple interest

Final value = 500 + (0.001 × 500 × 24)

= \$512

Activity 2: Compound interest

1 $500\,(1 + 0.1)^5 = \$805.26$

2 $1{,}750 \times (1 + 0.06)^{20} = \$5{,}612.49$

3 $200{,}000 \times (1 + 0.012)^8 = \$220{,}026$

Activity 3: Non-annual compounding

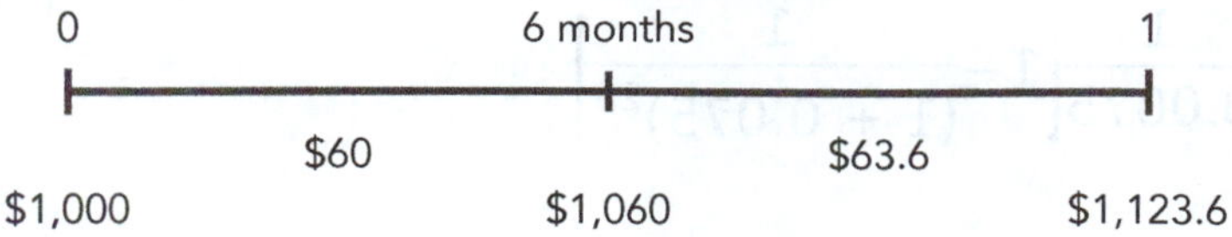

Alternative

$s_2 = \$1{,}000(1.06)^2$

$= \$1{,}123.6$

Activity 4: EAR

$1 + R = (1 + 0.039)^4$

$1 + 4 = 1.165$

$R = 16.5\%$

Activity 5: Discounting a single cash flow

$$s_1 = \frac{\$1{,}610}{(1.1)^5} = \$1{,}000$$

Activity 6: Discounting a single cash flow using tables

$DF_3 = 0.794$

$\therefore$ PV = \$5,000 × 0.794 = \$3,970

Activity 7: Discounting with changing interest rates

$$DF_5 = \frac{1}{(1.1)^2(1.15)^3} = 0.543$$

Activity 8: Present value of annuity (timeline)

$$PV = 100 + \frac{100}{(1 + 0.1)} + \frac{100}{(1 + 0.1)^2} + \frac{100}{(1.01)^3}$$

$$= \$348.69$$

Activity 9: Present value of annuity (tables and formula)

1 Using tables, annuity factor is 7.360. Make sure you can find this figure in the annuity discount tables. You need to look up 6% for period 10.

PV = 12,000 × 7.36 = $88,320

Using formula:

$$PV \quad = \quad 12{,}000 \times \frac{1}{0.06}\left[1 - \frac{1}{(1 + 0.06)^{10}}\right]$$

$$= \$88{,}321$$

Always use the discount tables if you can.

2

$$PV \quad = \quad \$10{,}000 \times \frac{1}{0.0075}\left[1 - \frac{1}{(1 + 0.075)^{25}}\right]$$

$$= \$10{,}000 \times 11.147$$

$$= \$111{,}470$$

3 Using tables:

PV = 1,500 × (1 + 3.465)

= 6,697.50

Using formula:

$$PV = 1{,}500 + 1{,}500 \times \frac{1}{0.06}\left[1 - \frac{1}{(1 + 0.06)^{4}}\right]$$

PV = 1,500 + 5,197.66 = $6,697.66

Activity 10: Delayed annuity

PV of annuity for 3–10 years

CDF = (CDF 1 to 10) minus (CDF 1 to 2)

Using tables: @ 6% = 7.360 – 1.833

3,000 × (7.360 – 1.833) = $16,581

Activity 11: Perpetuity calculations

1

$$\frac{1{,}000}{0.1} = \$10{,}000$$

2 PV = a × (1 + 1/r)

PV = 1,000 × (1+ 1/10%)

PV = $11,000

3 CDF = 1/r – CDF1-3

CDF = 1/10% – 2.487

CDF = 7.513

PV = a × CDF

PV = 1,000 × 7.513

PV = $7,513

Activity 12: Payback period

Time	*Net cash flows*	*Cumulative cash flow*
	$	$
0	(250,000)	(250,000)
1	60,000	(190,000)
2	60,000	(130,000)
3	80,000	(50,000)
4	100,000	50,000

Assuming that the cash flows occur evenly during Year 4, payback will be 3 + 50,000/100,000 = 3.5 years.

Activity 13: Net present value (1)

Time	Cash flow	*Discount factor (5%)*	*Present value*
0	(1,000)	1.000	(1,000)
1	1,001	0.952	953
		NPV	(47)

A negative NPV means that the investment does not give a 5% return and therefore should be rejected.

Activity 14: Net present value (2)

1

Time	*Cash flow*	*Discount factor (5%)*	*Present value*
0	(1,000)	1.000	(1,000)
1	1,000	0.952	952
2	1,000	0.907	907
		NPV	859

or

Time	*Cash flow*	*Discount factor (5%)*	*Present value*
0	(1,000)	1.000	(1,000)
1–2	1,000	1.859	1,859
		NPV	859

A positive NPV means that the investment gives more than a 5% return and therefore should be accepted.

2

Time	*Cash flow*	*Discount factor (5%)*	*Present value*

0	(1,000)	1.000	(1,000)
1+	1,000	20.000*	20,000
		NPV	19,000

A positive NPV means that the investment gives more than a 5% return and therefore should be accepted.

* The discount factor for a cash flow that occurs every year (a perpetuity) starting in one year's time is 1/r =1/0.05 = 20.

Activity 15: NPV – GA Co

Time	*Cash flow*	*Discount factor (10%)*	*Present value*
0	(250,000)	1.000	(250,000)
1	60,000	0.909	54,540
2	60,000	0.826	49,560
3	80,000	0.751	60,080
4	100,000	0.683	68,300
5	100,000	0.621	62,100
		NPV	44,580

Activity 16: IRR – GA Co

Step 1 **Step 1 is complete** – we already know from Activity 15 that the NPV at 10% is + $44,580.

Step 2 As the NPV is positive at 10% the IRR must be higher than this, therefore try 15% (but any rate higher than 10% could have been used).

Time	*Cash flow*	*Discount factor (15%)*	*Present value*
0	(250,000)	1.000	(250,000)
1	60,000	0.870	52,200
2	60,000	0.756	45,360
3	80,000	0.658	52,640
4	100,000	0.572	57,200
5	100,000	0.497	49,700
		NPV	7,100

Step 3

$$IRR = a + \frac{NPVa}{NPVa - NPVb}(b-a)$$

a = 10, NPVa = 44,580

b = 15, NPVb = 7,100

$$IRR = 10 + \frac{44,580}{44,580 - 7,100}(15-10) = 15.9\%$$

Activity 17: Dysfunctional behaviour

Project	*Initial investment*	*Project return*	*Project return*
	$		$
A	10	50%	5.00
B	1000	1%	10.00

Even though it produces a lower percentage return, it is investment B that increases your wealth more in absolute terms (ie $) and therefore it is this investment that should be accepted.

Test your learning

1 An investor has been offered two deals:

Option 1	1.1% compounded every 3 months
Option 2	3.2% compounded every 6 months

Required

Which option offers the best APR? [ ]

2 A machine will cost $25,000 to replace in 25 years' time. The rate of interest is 8.5% per annum.

Required

What is the present value of the replacement cost of the machine? (To the nearest $) $ [ ]

3 A project requiring an investment of $120,000 is expected to generate returns of $40,000 in years 1 and 2 and $35,000 in years 3 and 4.

Required

If the NPV is $22,000 at 9% and –$4,000 at 10%, what is the IRR for the project? (To 2 decimal places) [ ]

4 Fill in the blank:

What is the present value of an annuity of $5,000 per annum discounted at 7% if it starts at the end of the third year and finishes at the end of the tenth year? [ ]

5 What is the yardstick for acceptance of projects when using the net present value method?

- ○ Accept if a profit is made
- ○ Accept if the present value of future cash flows is positive
- ○ Accept if payback occurs within an reasonable time frame
- ○ Accept if the discount rate that achieves a breakeven return is greater than the company's cost of capital

6 Tick the correct box to indicate whether or not the following items are included in the cash flows when determining the net present value of a project.

	Included	Not included
(1) The disposal value of equipment at the end of its life		
(2) Depreciation charges for the equipment		
(3) Research costs incurred prior to the appraisal		
(4) Interest payments on the loan to finance the investment		

Test your learning answers

Chapter 1

1 The correct answer is: False

Management accounting is mainly concerned with the preparation of management accounts for internal managers of an organisation. Financial accounts are prepared for individuals external to an organisation eg shareholders and customers.

2 The correct answer is: Implementing

The purpose of management information is to help managers to manage resources efficiently and effectively by planning and controlling operations and by allowing informed decision making.

3 Management accounting is increasingly being viewed as supporting [management] rather than being part of the [finance] function.

4 Management information is used for planning, control and [decision making].

5 The correct answer is: True

The management accountant may frequently have to take into account non-financial information.

Chapter 2

1

(1) A [cost unit] is a unit of product or service to which costs can be related. It is the basic control unit for costing purposes.

(2) A [cost centre] acts as a collecting place for certain costs before they are analysed further.

(3) A [cost object] is anything that users of accounting information want to know the cost of.

2 In practice, most cost accounting systems use [historical cost] as a measurement basis.

3 The correct answer is: Classification by nature

4

(1) [Direct] and [indirect] (or overhead) costs

(2) [Functional] costs (production costs, distribution and selling costs, administration costs and financing costs)

5 The correct answer is: A stores assistant in a factory store

The others are direct labour.

6 The correct answer is: To establish how well something or somebody is doing in relation to a planned activity

Note that the question said 'the **main** aim'. Performance measurement may well be used to decide on bonus levels, but this is not the main aim.

7 The correct answer is: Direct expense

The royalty cost can be traced in full to the company's product, therefore it is a direct expense.

Chapter 3

1 The correct answer is: False

They will rise.

2

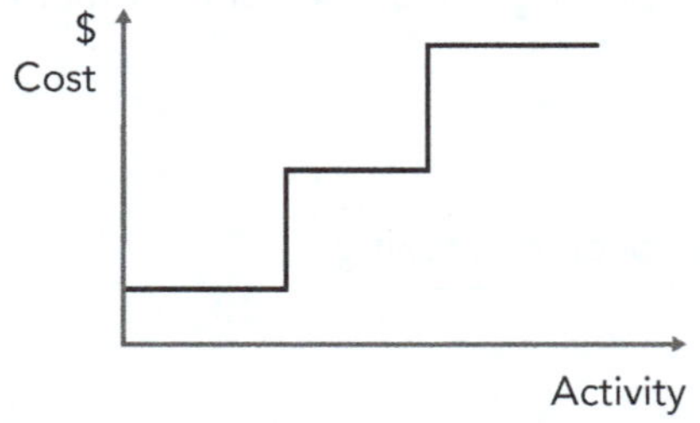

Graph of a stepped cost. Example: rent, supervisors' salaries

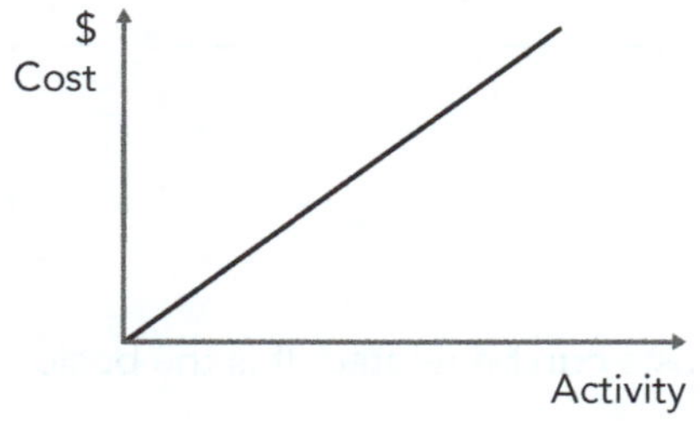

Graph of a Variable cost. Example: raw materials, direct labour

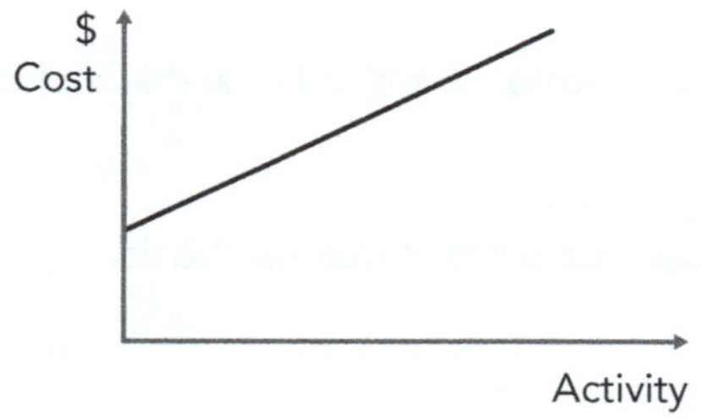

Graph of a Semi-variable cost. Example: electricity and telephone

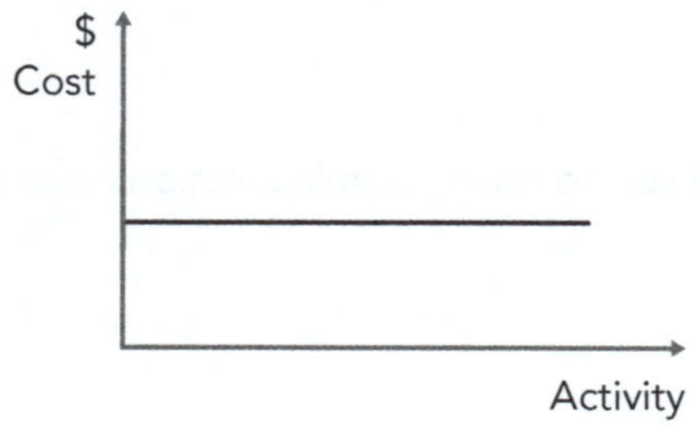

Graph of a Fixed cost. Example: rent, depreciation (straight line)

3 The correct answer is: True

4 Variable cost (per employee month) = $ 50 per employee per month

Fixed cost per month = $ 10,000 per month

Working

	Activity	*Cost*
		$
High	1,300	75,000
Low	1,175	68,750
	125	6,250

Variable cost per employee = $6,250/125 = $50

For 1,175 employees, total cost = $68,750

Total cost	= variable cost + fixed cost
$68,750	= (1,175 × $50) + fixed cost
∴ Fixed cost	= $68,750 – $58,750
	= $10,000

5 The costs could be subdivided into variable costs of $14 per unit and fixed costs of:

$ 187,000 per month.

Using the high-low method we have:

	Units	Costs
		$
Highest	9,500	320,000
Lowest	4,700	252,800
Difference	4,800	67,200

Variable costs = 67,200/4,800 = $14/unit

Fixed costs = Total cost – variable cost

At 9,500 units, fixed cost = $320,000 – (9,500 × $14) = $187,000

6 The correct answer is: Variable

Make sure you read the question carefully. Note that the $5 is **per staff member** so 100 staff would mean $500 in expenditure.

7 The correct answer is: Fixed cost

The difference between variable cost and total cost = fixed cost.

8 The correct answer is: Fixed

The name given to cost unaffected by increases and decreases in the volume of output is fixed costs.

9 The correct answer is: Telephone bill

Telephone bills usually have a fixed element (the line rental) and a variable element (the charge per call made). The first, second, and fourth options are all usually fixed costs.

10 The correct answer is: Decrease by less than 10%

Only part of the cost is variable so a 10% increase in activity will lead to a less than 10% increase in the overall cost. Cost per unit will therefore decrease by less than 10%.

Chapter 4

1 The correct answer is: False

It is the process whereby whole cost items are charged direct to a cost unit or cost centre.

2

Overhead	Basis of apportionment
Depreciation of equipment	Book value of equipment
Heat and light costs	Floor area
Canteen	Number of employees
Insurance of equipment	Book value of equipment

3

Department	Involved in production ✔
Finished goods warehouse	
Canteen	
Machining department	✔
Offices	
Assembly department	✔

4

Description	Step
Apportion fixed costs over departments	2
Establish the overhead absorption rate	4
Choose fair methods of apportionment	1
Apply the overhead absorption rate to products	5
Reapportion service departments costs	3

5 In order to recognise the work service departments do for each other, the Repeated distribution method or algebraic method methods of reapportioning service department overheads should be used.

6 The correct answer is: Labour-intensive

7 The correct answer is: True

8 Traditional costing systems tend to allocate [too great] a proportion of overheads to high volume products and [too small] a proportion of overheads to low volume products.

9 (a) The correct answer is: True

It is generally the case that overheads increase with time therefore a time-based approach is considered most sensible.

(b) The correct answer is: True

This method is not particularly logical.

10 The correct answer is: $110,000 under-absorbed

$$\text{OAR} = \frac{\text{Budgeted overheads}}{\text{Budgeted labour hours}} = \frac{\$600{,}000}{120{,}000} = \$5 \text{ per labour hour}$$

Overheads absorbed = 110,000 hours × $5
= $550,000

Overheads absorbed – actual overheads = $550,000 – $660,000
= $110,000

∴ overheads were under-absorbed by $110,000

Chapter 5

1 Sales value – marginal cost of sales = [Contribution]

2

		A or M
(a)	Closing inventories valued at marginal production cost	M
(b)	Closing inventories valued at full production cost	A
(c)	Cost of sales include some fixed overhead incurred in previous period in opening inventory values	A
(d)	Fixed costs are charged in full against profit for the period	M

3 The correct answers are:

- It is simple to operate.
- There is no under- or over-absorption of overheads.
- Fixed costs are the same regardless of activity levels.
- The information from this costing method may be used for decision making.

All are arguments in favour of marginal costing.

4 The full cost of product B is $ [400]

Required return = 12% × $1,000,000 = $120,000

Expected revenue = 1,200 × $500 = $600,000

Expected cost = expected revenue – required return

∴ Expected cost = $(600,000 – 120,000) = $480,000

∴ Full cost per unit = $480,000/1,200 = $400

5 (a) The correct answer is: $739.20

$255.70 + $483.50 = $739.20

Selling costs are never included in inventory valuations. The valuation under absorption costing is the full production cost so it is the sum of the fixed production cost and the variable production cost.

(b) The correct answer is: $483.50

Selling costs are never included in inventory valuations. The valuation under a variable costing system is the variable production cost.

6 The correct answer is: Absorption costing profits will be higher and closing inventory valuations higher than those under marginal costing

Closing inventory valuation under absorption costing will always be higher than under marginal costing because of the absorption of fixed overheads into closing inventory values.

The profit under absorption costing will be greater because the fixed overhead being carried forward in closing inventory is greater than the fixed overhead being written off in opening inventory.

7 A fixed cost.

8 The correct answer is: (3) and (4)

If inventory levels decrease, marginal costing will report the higher profit. If inventory levels increase, absorption costing will report the higher profit. The profit figures will be the same where inventory levels are unchanged.

9 The correct answer is: The profit for the period is $540 higher.

200 units × ($7.50 – $4.80)/unit

10 The correct answer is: would be lower would be lower

Under marginal costing, closing inventory will be valued lower than under absorption costing. If production is greater than sales the inventory level has increased during the month. Absorption costing would therefore produce a higher profit than marginal costing.

Chapter 6

1 (a)

$$\text{Breakeven point (sales units)} = \frac{\text{Fixed costs}}{\text{Contribution per unit}}$$

$$\text{or} = \frac{\text{Contribution required to break even}}{\text{Contribution per unit}}$$

(b)

$$\text{Breakeven points (sales revenue)} = \frac{\text{Fixed costs}}{\text{C/S ratio}}$$

$$\text{or} = \frac{\text{Contribution required to break even}}{\text{C/S ratio}}$$

2 The correct answer is: False

The P/V ratio is a measure of how much **contribution** is earned from each $1 of sales.

3 The correct answer is: False

At the breakeven point there is no profit.

4 At the breakeven point, total contribution = fixed costs .

5 The total contribution required for a target profit = fixed costs + required profit .

6 The correct answer is: (1), (3) and (4)

The fixed cost line runs parallel to the horizontal axis and the breakeven point is the intersection of the sales line and the total costs line.

7 On a breakeven chart, the distance between the breakeven point and the expected (or budgeted) sales, in units, indicates the Margin of safety .

8 The correct answer is: Cannot say without more information

The sales revenue can be calculated as $157,500/0.35 = $450,000. The number of units cannot be calculated with the information supplied.

9 The correct answer is: $135,000

$$\text{Breakeven point} = \frac{\text{Fixed costs}}{\text{Contribution/unit}}$$

$$\therefore \text{70,000 units} = \frac{\text{Fixed costs}}{\$4.50}$$

$$\therefore \text{Fixed costs} = \text{70,000 units} \times \$4.50$$

$$\text{Margin of safety} = \frac{\text{Budgeted sales units} - \text{Breakeven sales units}}{\text{Budgeted sales units}}$$

$$\therefore 0.3 = \frac{\text{Budgeted sales units} - 70{,}000}{\text{Budgeted sales units}}$$

Let X = budgeted sales units

$$0.3 = \frac{X - 70{,}000}{X}$$

$\therefore$ 0.3X = X – 70,000

$\therefore$ 70,000 = X – 0.3X

$\therefore$ 70,000 = 0.7X

$\therefore$ X = 100,000 = budgeted sales units

Total profit = contribution – fixed costs

= (100,000 units × $4.50) £315,000

= $135,000

10

- It assumes fixed costs are constant at all levels of output.
- It assumes that variable costs are the same per unit at all levels of output.
- It assumes that sales prices are constant at all levels of output.
- It assumes production and sales are the same (inventory levels are ignored).
- It ignores the uncertainty in the estimates of fixed costs and variable cost per unit.

You may also have thought:

- A breakeven chart may be time consuming to prepare.

Chapter 7

1 Step 1 [Confirm that the limiting factor is something other than sales]

Step 2 [Calculate contribution per unit of limiting factor for each product]

Step 3 [Make products in rank order until scarce resource is used up (optimal production plan)]

2 When there is just one limiting factor, the product with the [biggest] contribution earning ability per unit of limiting factor should be produced first.

3 The correct answer is: Profit

Limiting factors are resources or demand.

4 The correct answer is: Milk

Milk (0.5 × 100 + 0.4 × 200 + 0.25 × 75) = 148.75 litres, but only 140 are available

5 The correct answer is: 82 CE, 200 TD and 75 SS

(contribution per litre for CE = $20, for TD is $22.50 and for SS is $24)

Note. Always round down the last unit unless divisible.

Chapter 8

1 A standard cost is a [planned] [unit] cost.

2 The correct answer is: False

It has a number of uses including:

(1) To value inventory and cost production for cost accounting purposes

(2) To act as a control device by establishing standards and highlighting activities that are not conforming to plan and bringing these to the attention of management

3 The correct answer is: Standard costing

4 The correct answer is: False

They can be used in marginal costing too.

5 (1) Ideal

(2) Attainable

(3) Current

(4) Basic

6 The formula for standard material cost per unit =

standard material usage × standard material price

7 Three of:

(1) Deciding how to incorporate **inflation** into planned unit costs
(2) Agreeing on a **performance standard** (attainable or ideal)
(3) Deciding on the **quality** of materials to be used (a better quality of material will cost more, but perhaps reduce material wastage)
(4) Estimating materials **prices** where seasonal price variations or bulk purchase discounts may be significant
(5) Finding sufficient **time** to construct accurate standards as standard setting can be a **time consuming process**
(6) Incurring the **cost of setting up and maintaining a system** for establishing standards
(7) Dealing with possible **behavioural problems,** managers responsible for the achievement of standards possibly resisting the use of a standard costing control system for fear of being blamed for any adverse variances

8 The correct answers are:

- Standards are an aid to more accurate budgeting.
- Cost consciousness is stimulated
- The principle of management by exception can be operated.

If standards are planned carefully they can be an aid to more accurate budgeting. Cost consciousness can be stimulated when a target of efficiency is set for employees. Variances enable the principle of management by exception to be operated by setting tolerance limits.

Chapter 9

1

(1) At the planning stage, a flexible budget can show what the effects would be if the actual outcome differs from the prediction.
(2) At the end of each period, actual results may be compared with the relevant activity level in the flexible budget as a control procedure.
(3) Master budgets are fixed budgets.

2 The correct answer is: True

3 Budget cost allowance = [budgeted fixed cost] + ([number of units] × [variable cost per unit])

4 Using a fixed budget at the planning stage means that only one activity level scenario is planned for. Management is not forced to think of contingency plans for different activity levels.

When actual results are compared against a fixed budget the variances that are due to different activity levels can produce a misleading impression of performance.

5 A fixed budget is a budget which is designed to remain unchanged regardless of the volume of output or sales achieved.

A flexible budget is a budget which, by recognising different cost behaviour patterns, is designed to change if volumes of output change.

6 A fixed budget profit might differ from an actual profit because costs were higher or lower than expected given the actual output and/or sales volumes were different to the level expected.

7 A flexible budget is a budget which, by recognising [cost behaviour patterns], is designed to [flex/change] as the level of activity changes.

8 The correct answer is: A budget which by recognising different cost behaviour patterns is designed to change as the volume of activity changes

A flexible budget shows the budgeted costs and revenues at different levels of activity. The budgeted variable costs and revenues are **increased or decreased in line with changes in activity**, and the budgeted fixed cost remains **unaltered**.

9 The correct answers are:

- A budget which is most generally used for planning purposes
- A budget for a single level of activity

Fixed budgets are prepared for a single level of activity and do not include any provision for the event that actual volumes may differ from the budget. They are generally used for planning purposes because they use a single level of activity for co-ordination and resource allocation.

Chapter 10

1

(1) To [Co-ordinate] the activities of different departments towards a single plan

(2) To [Communicate] targets to managers responsible for achieving them

(3) To establish a system of [Control] by comparing budgeted and actual results

(4) To compel [Planning]

2 The correct answer is: Selling overhead budget

3 The correct answer is: (1), (2) and (3)

4 1st [Sales]

2nd Production

3rd Material usage

4th Material purchase

5th Cash

5

Short-term surplus	Increase credit terms to customers
Long-term surplus	Replace/update non-current assets
Short-term shortfall	Pay suppliers later
Long-term shortfall	Issue share capital

6 The correct answer is: False

Only cash flow items are included in cash budgets. Depreciation is not a cash flow and so is not included in a cash budget.

7 The correct answer is: (1), (2) and (3)

8 The correct answer is: $42,000

	Jan	*Feb*
	$	$
Sales	60,000	80,000
Gross profit (@ 40%)	24,000	32,000
Cost of sales (sales – GP)	36,000	48,000
Closing trade payables (@ 50%)	18,000	24,000

	$
Feb opening payables	18,000
Increase in amounts owing (COS)	48,000
Feb closing payables	(24,000)
Amount paid in Feb	42,000

9 $ 7,300,000

Jay Co needs to produce 100,000 + 20,000 = 120,000 units in September.

Labour hours required = 120,000 units × 3 hours

= 360,000 hours

Only 340,000 hours are usually worked so there will need to be overtime of 360,000 – 340,000 = 20,000 hours.

	$
360,000 hours at basic rate (× $20)	7,200,000

20,000 hours at premium (× $20 × 25%)	100,000
Budgeted labour cost	7,300,000

10 When preparing a production budget, the quantity to be produced is equal to sales [minus] opening inventory [plus] closing inventory.

Chapter 11

1

(1) Price
    Usage
(2) Rate
    Efficiency
(3) Expenditure
    Efficiency

2 The correct answer is: (1), (2) and (3)

Unforeseen discounts received would lead to a favourable price variance.

3 (a) The correct answer is: $124

	$
6,200 kg should have cost (× 50c)	3,100
But did cost	3,224
	124 (A)

(b) The correct answer is: Adverse

4 The correct answer is: Operating statement

5 The correct answer is: True

The variance is favourable if the actual price is higher than standard.

6 The correct answer is: False

Favourable material price and adverse material usage variances might be interdependent, for example.

7 The sales volume variance considers the difference between [budgeted] sales volume and [actual] sales volume.

8 The correct answer is: 1,650 kg

First we write out the way we would normally calculate the material efficiency variance and fill in the figures that we know.

2,200 units should have used (× 1,500 kg/3,000 units)	1,100	kg
But did use		(Q)
Material efficiency variance in kg		(P)
× standard cost per kg	x $3	
	$1,650	(A)

Working backwards we can see that the efficiency variance in kg (box (P))

= 1,650 ÷ $3

= 550 kg

Now that we know the efficiency variance in kg, we can work out the number of kg that were actually used (box (Q)).

= 550 kg + 1,100 kg

= 1,650 kg

9 The correct answer is: $5,775

1,650 kg should have cost (× $3)	4,950	
But did cost		
Materials price variance	825	(A)

Working backwards we can see that the actual cost must have been 825 + 4,950 = $5,775.

Chapter 12

1 The correct answer is: (1) and (2) only

Homogeneous means 'all the same'. Jobs are usually on customer request and therefore are all different.

2 (a) If profit is 25% of the job cost, the price of the job = $ 125,000

$100,000 + (25% × $100,000) = $100,000 + $25,000 = $125,000

(b) If there is a 25% margin, the price of the job = $ 133,333

Profit is 25% of the selling price, therefore selling price should be written as 100%:

	%
Selling price	100
Profit	25
Cost	75

∴ Price = $100,000 × 100/75 = $133,333.

3 The correct answer is: An architect designing a new school

A pizza manufacturer would probably use batch costing. Sugar and screws are both homogenous items so do not need job costing.

4 A group of similar articles which maintains its identity during one or more stages of production and is treated as a cost unit.

5

$$\frac{\text{Total batch cost}}{\text{Number of units in the batch}}$$

6 The correct answer is: $8,400

(630 ÷ 0·9 hours) × $12/hour) = $8,400.

Closing work in progress value = 61,894 + 3,190

= $65,084

7 Assuming that only 90% of her time worked will be chargeable to customers, her charge for each hour of writing (to the nearest cent) should be $ [28.94]

Charge for each hour of writing (to the nearest cent) should be $28.94

Weeks worked per year = 52 – 4 = 48

Hours worked per year = 48 × 40 hrs

= 1,920

Hours chargeable to clients = 1,920 × 90% = 1,728

Total expenses = $10,000 + $40,000 = $50,000

$$\text{Hourly rate} = \frac{\$50{,}000}{1{,}728} = \$28.94 \text{ per hour}$$

Chapter 13

1 The correct answer is: To establish how well something or somebody is doing in relation to a planned activity

Note that the question said 'the **main** aim'. Performance measurement may well be used to decide on bonus levels but this is not the main aim.

2 ROCE = [A] / [B] × 100%

Profit margin = [A] / [C] × 100%

3 The correct answer is: Sales ÷ capital employed

Asset turnover = sales ÷ capital employed. Net profit margin = net profit ÷ sales revenue

4 The correct answer is: False

Labour, direct expenses and overheads will be a greater proportion of total cost.

5

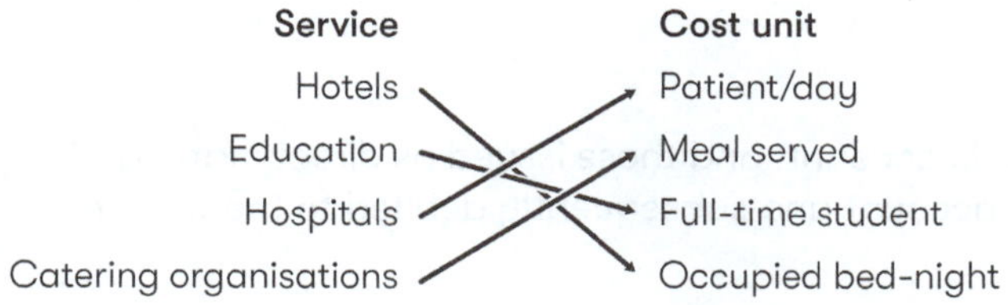

6 The correct answer is: (1), (2), (3) and (6)

7 | Total cost incurred in the period | / | Number of service units supplied in the period |

8 The correct answers are:

- Use of composite cost units
- High levels of indirect costs as a proportion of total cost

Service costing characteristics include composite cost units and high levels of indirect costs as a proportion of total cost. Not-for-profit organisations such as hospitals would not measure performance on profit so profit per patient would be inappropriate.

9 The correct answers are:

- High levels of indirect costs as a proportion of total cost
- Cost units are often intangible
- Use of composite cost units

In service costing it is difficult to identify many attributable direct costs. Many costs must be treated as **indirect costs** and **shared over several cost units**, therefore the first characteristic does apply. Many services are **intangible**; for example, a haircut or a cleaning service provide no physical, tangible product. Therefore the second characteristic does apply. **Composite cost units** such as passenger-mile or bed-night are often used in service costing, therefore the third characteristic does apply. The fourth characteristic does not apply because equivalent units are more often used in **costing for tangible products**.

10 The correct answers are:

- Patient/day
- Operating theatre hour
- Outpatient visit

All of the above would be **measurable** and would be **useful for control purposes**. A ward and an x-ray department are more likely to be used as **cost centres** for the purpose of cost collection and analysis.

Chapter 14

1

(1) DR Work in progress control account
CR Production overhead account

(2) DR Finished goods control account
CR Work in progress control account

2 The correct answers are:

- DR Raw materials $100,000
- CR Raw materials $75,000
- DR Work in progress $75,000

Costs incurred are debited to the materials account, and those issued as direct materials to production are credited to the materials account and subsequently debited to the work in progress account.

3

	True / False
(1) Total wages incurred during October was $110,000	False
(2) Indirect wages incurred during October was $7,000	True
(3) Wages accrued at the end of October were $2,000	False

(1) Total wages **paid** was $110,000.

(2) Indirect wages of $7,000 were charged to production overhead.

(3) Wages were prepaid at the end of October.

4 The correct answer is: False

Material usage variances are recorded in the WIP account.

5

	True / False
(1) Integrated systems conform to statutory requirements	True
(2) Integrated systems are preferable to two systems because they conform to statutory requirements	False
(3) Integrated systems reduce the number of account reconciliations	True
(4) Systems with separate cost and financial accounting systems can aid provision of internal management information	True

(2) This is one of the disadvantages of an integrated system. It must conform to statutory requirements but this is not necessarily useful for management purposes.

(3) Having one set of accounts instead of two eliminates the need to reconcile the two systems.

(4) As mentioned above, the integrated system must conform to statutory requirements. Internal management information does not need to conform to statutory requirement and in some cases it is more useful if it doesn't.

6 The correct answers are:

- Material usage variance
- Variable overhead efficiency variance
- Idle time variance

The material price variance is recorded in the stores control account. The labour rate variance is recorded in the wages control account. The sales variances do not appear in the books of account.

7 The correct answer is: DR Overhead control account; CR Stores control account

The cost of indirect materials issued is credited to the stores account and 'collected' in the overhead control account pending its absorption into work in progress. Therefore the correct answer is the third option.

8 The correct answer is: An account which records total cost as opposed to individual costs

9 The correct answer is: DR Work in progress account; CR Production overhead account

---

Chapter 15

1 The correct answer is: 25%

The data tells us that there was a machine breakdown on 120 days (480 – 360) out of a total of 480.

P(machine breakdown) = 120/480 × 100%

= 25%

You should have been able to eliminate the first option immediately since a probability of 0% = impossibility.

If you selected the third option, you calculated the probability of a machine breakdown as 120 out of a possible 365 days instead of 480 days.

If you selected the fourth option, you incorrectly calculated the probability that there was **not** a machine breakdown on any particular day.

2 The correct answer is: 0.25

Factory	Ratio of visits
North	1
South	2
West	1
	4

P(visiting North factory) = 1/4 = 0.25

If you didn't select the correct option, make sure that you are clear about how the correct answer has been arrived at. Remember to look at the **ratio** of visits since no actual numbers of visits are given.

3 What is the expected profit? $ 11,500

EV = (15,000 × 0.2) + (20,000 × 0.5) + (–5,000 × 0.3)

= 3,000 + 10,000 – 1,500

= 11,500

4 What is the expected profit? $ 3,671

Expected sales volume = (1,500 × 0.8) + (2,500 × 0.2) = 1,700

∴ Expected sales revenue = 1,700 × $6 = $10,200

Expected unit cost = ($2.30 × 0.65) + ($2.50 × 0.35) = $2.37

∴ Expected total variable costs = $2.37 × 1,700 = $4,029

Profit = sales – variable costs – fixed costs = \$10,200 – \$4,029 – \$2,500 = \$3,671

5 The correct answer is: $\sum px$

An expected value is the sum of the different possible outcomes (x) multiplied by their associated probability of occurrence (p).

6

		Most useful	Not as useful
(a)	Whether to change the logo painted on the window of 700 retail outlets	✔	
(b)	Whether to purchase machine X or machine Y		✔
(c)	Whether to launch product A		✔
(d)	Deciding on the optimum daily purchases of a perishable item	✔	

Expected values would be useful for decisions (a) and (d) because they are repeated several times.

Chapter 16

1

(1)

$$\frac{\sum x}{n}$$

(2)

$$\frac{\sum fx}{n} \text{ or } \frac{\sum fx}{\sum f}$$

2 The correct answer is: Mode

3 80.5

$$\text{Mean} = \frac{\text{Total}}{7}$$

So Total	= 7 × 133.5
	= 934.5
934.5	= 143 + 96 + x + 153.5 + 92.5 + y + 47
934.5	= 532 + x + y
y	= 4x
So 934.5	= 532 + x + 4x
5x	= 934.5 – 532
5x	= 402.5
x	= 80.5

4

Class interval	*Mid-point (Discrete data)*	*Mid-point (Continuous data)*
25 < 30	27	27.5
30 < 35	32	32.5
35 < 40	37	37.5
40 < 45	42	42.5
45 < 50	47	47.5
50 < 55	52	52.5
55 < 60	57	57.5
60 < 65	62	62.5

5 The mode of a grouped frequency distribution can be found from a(n) [histogram].

The median of a grouped frequency distribution can be found from a(n) [ogive].

6 What is the median age? [9 1/2]

6, 7, 8, 9, 10, 11, 12, 13

Median is 9½

7

(1) [Lower] quartile = Q1 = value [below] which 25% of the population fall.

(2) [Upper] quartile = Q3 = value [above] which 25% of the population fall.

8 The area under the curve of a normal distribution = [1] which represents [100] % of all probabilities.

9 (a) The correct answer is:

$$\frac{Q_3 - Q_1}{2}$$

(b) The semi-interquartile range is also known as the [Quartile deviation]

10 The upper quartile is at the point where 25% of the area under the curve is above this point.

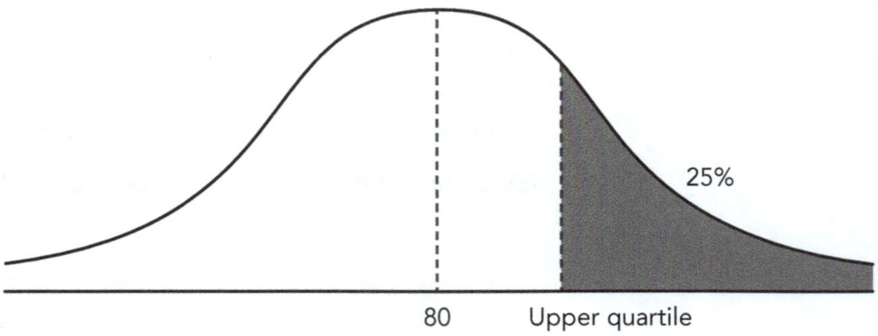

From the normal distribution table, the nearest value to 0.25 is 0.2486 which corresponds to a z value of 0.67.

If $z = 0.67$

$\mu = 80$

$\sigma = \sqrt{16 = 4}$

$$z = \frac{x-\sigma}{\sigma}$$

$$0.67 = \frac{x-80}{4}$$

$x - 80 = 4 \times 0.67$

$x = 2.68 + 80$

$= 82.68$

Chapter 17

1 Which option offers the best APR? Option 2

APR of Option 1 = $(1 + 0.011)^4 - 1$

= 0.0447

= 4.47%

APR of Option 2 = $(1 + 0.032)^2 - 1$

= 0.065

= 6.50%

Option 2 therefore offers the best APR.

2 What is the present value of the replacement cost of the machine? (To the nearest \$) \$ 3,252

$$\frac{25,000}{(1.085)^{25}}$$

3 If the NPV is \$22,000 at 9% and –\$4,000 at 10%, what is the IRR for the project? (To 2 decimal places) 9.85

$$IRR = a + \left[\frac{NPVa}{NPVa-NPVb}(b-a)\right]\%$$

$$= 9\% + \left[\frac{22,000}{(22,000 + 4,000)} \times 1\right]\%$$

$$= 9\% + 0.85\%$$

$$= 9.85\%$$

4 What is the present value of an annuity of $5,000 per annum discounted at 7% if it starts at the end of the third year and finishes at the end of the tenth year? 26,080

PV of annuity from year 3–10 = PV from year 1–10 – PV from year 1–2

= $5,000 × (7.024 – 1.808)

= $26,080

5 The correct answer is: Accept if the present value of future cash flows is positive

Accept the project if the net present value is positive.

6

(1) Included

(2) Not included (non-cash)

(3) Not included (past cost)

(4) Not included (included in the discount rate)

Appendix 1: Maths tables

Area under the normal curve

This table gives the area under the normal curve between the mean and the point Z standard deviations above the mean. The corresponding area for deviations below the mean can be found by symmetry.

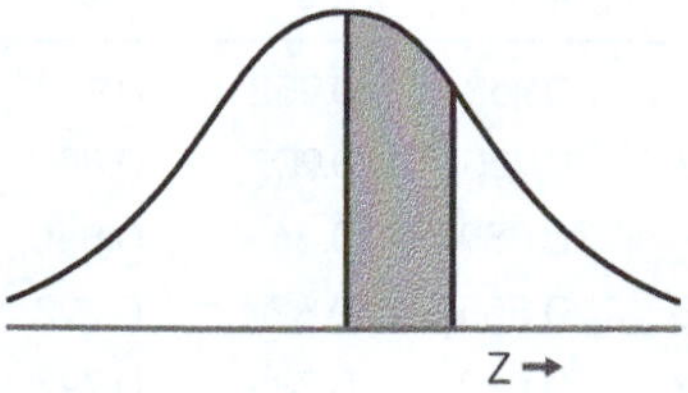

$Z = \frac{(x-\mu)}{\sigma}$	0.00	0.01	0.02	0.03	0.04	0.05	0.06	0.07	0.08	0.09
0.0	.0000	.0040	.0080	.0120	.0159	.0199	.0239	.0279	.0319	.0359
0.1	.0398	.0438	.0478	.0517	.0557	.0596	.0636	.0675	.0714	.0753
0.2	.0793	.0832	.0871	.0910	.0948	.0987	.1026	.1064	.1103	.1141
0.3	.1179	.1217	.1255	.1293	.1331	.1368	.1406	.1443	.1480	.1517
0.4	.1554	.1591	.1628	.1664	.1700	.1736	.1772	.1808	.1844	.1879
0.5	.1915	.1950	.1985	.2019	.2054	.2088	.2123	.2157	.2190	.2224
0.6	.2257	.2291	.2324	.2357	.2389	.2422	.2454	.2486	.2518	.2549
0.7	.2580	.2611	.2642	.2673	.2704	.2734	.2764	.2794	.2823	.2852
0.8	.2881	.2910	.2939	.2967	.2995	.3023	.3051	.3078	.3106	.3133
0.9	.3159	.3186	.3212	.3238	.3264	.3289	.3315	.3340	.3365	.3389
1.0	.3413	.3438	.3461	.3485	.3508	.3531	.3554	.3577	.3599	.3621
1.1	.3643	.3665	.3686	.3708	.3729	.3749	.3770	.3790	.3810	.3830
1.2	.3849	.3869	.3888	.3907	.3925	.3944	.3962	.3980	.3997	.4015
1.3	.4032	.4049	.4066	.4082	.4099	.4115	.4131	.4147	.4162	.4177
1.4	.4192	.4207	.4222	.4236	.4251	.4265	.4279	.4292	.4306	.4319
1.5	.4332	.4345	.4357	.4370	.4382	.4394	.4406	.4418	.4430	.4441
1.6	.4452	.4463	.4474	.4485	.4495	.4505	.4515	.4525	.4535	.4545
1.7	.4554	.4564	.4573	.4582	.4591	.4599	.4608	.4616	.4625	.4633
1.8	.4641	.4649	.4656	.4664	.4671	.4678	.4686	.4693	.4699	.4706
1.9	.4713	.4719	.4726	.4732	.4738	.4744	.4750	.4756	.4762	.4767
2.0	.4772	.4778	.4783	.4788	.4793	.4798	.4803	.4808	.4812	.4817
2.1	.4821	.4826	.4830	.4834	.4838	.4842	.4846	.4850	.4854	.4857
2.2	.4861	.4865	.4868	.4871	.4875	.4878	.4881	.4884	.4887	.4890
2.3	.4893	.4896	.4898	.4901	.4904	.4906	.4909	.4911	.4913	.4916
2.4	.4918	.4920	.4922	.4925	.4927	.4929	.4931	.4932	.4934	.4936
2.5	.4938	.4940	.4941	.4943	.4945	.4946	.4948	.4949	.4951	.4952
2.6	.4953	.4955	.4956	.4957	.4959	.4960	.4961	.4962	.4963	.4964
2.7	.4965	.4966	.4967	.4968	.4969	.4970	.4971	.4972	.4973	.4974
2.8	.4974	.4975	.4976	.4977	.4977	.4978	.4979	.4980	.4980	.4981
2.9	.4981	.4982	.4983	.4983	.4984	.4984	.4985	.4985	.4986	.4986
3.0	.49865	.4987	.4987	.4988	.4988	.4989	.4989	.4989	.4990	.4990
3.1	.49903	.4991	.4991	.4991	.4992	.4992	.4992	.4992	.4993	.4993
3.2	.49931	.4993	.4994	.4994	.4994	.4994	.4994	.4995	.4995	.4995
3.3	.49952	.4995	.4995	.4996	.4996	.4996	.4996	.4996	.4996	.4997
3.4	.49966	.4997	.4997	.4997	.4997	.4997	.4997	.4997	.4997	.4998
3.5	.49977									

PRESENT VALUE TABLE

Present value of £1 ie $(1 + r)^{-n}$ where r= interest rate, n= number of periods until payment or receipt.

Periods (n)	Interest rates (r) 1%	2%	3%	4%	5%	6%	7%	8%	9%	10%
1	0.990	0.980	0.971	0.962	0.952	0.943	0.935	0.926	0.917	0.909
2	0.980	0.961	0.943	0.925	0.907	0.890	0.873	0.857	0.842	0.826
3	0.971	0.942	0.915	0.889	0.864	0.840	0.816	0.794	0.772	0.751
4	0.961	0.924	0.888	0.855	0.823	0.792	0.763	0.735	0.708	0.683
5	0.951	0.906	0.863	0.822	0.784	0.747	0.713	0.681	0.650	0.621
6	0.942	0.888	0.837	0.790	0.746	0705	0.666	0.630	0.596	0.564
7	0.933	0.871	0.813	0.760	0.711	0.665	0.623	0.583	0.547	0.513
8	0.923	0.853	0.789	0.731	0.677	0.627	0.582	0.540	0.502	0.467
9	0.914	0.837	0.766	0.703	0.645	0.592	0.544	0.500	0.460	0.424
10	0.905	0.820	0.744	0.676	0.614	0.558	0.508	0.463	0.422	0.386
11	0.896	0.804	0.722	0.650	0.585	0.527	0.475	0.429	0.388	0.350
12	0.887	0.788	0.701	0.625	0.557	0.497	0.444	0.397	0.356	0.319
13	0.879	0.773	0.681	0.601	0.530	0.469	0.415	0.368	0.326	0.290
14	0.870	0.758	0.661	0.577	0.505	0.442	0.388	0.340	0.299	0.263
15	0.861	0.743	0.642	0.555	0.481	0.417	0.362	0.315	0.275	0.239
16	0.853	0.728	0.623	0.534	0.458	0.394	0.339	0.292	0.252	0.218
17	0.844	0.714	0.605	0.513	0.436	0.371	0.317	0.270	0.231	0.198
18	0.836	0.700	0.587	0.494	0.416	0.350	0.296	0.250	0.212	0.180
19	0.828	0.686	0.570	0.475	0.396	0.331	0.277	0.232	0.194	0.164
20	0.820	0.673	0.554	0.456	0.377	0.312	0.258	0.215	0.178	0.149

Periods (n)	Interest rates (r) 11%	12%	13%	14%	15%	16%	17%	18%	19%	20%
1	0.901	0.893	0.885	0.877	0.870	0.862	0.855	0.847	0.840	0.833
2	0.812	0.797	0.783	0.769	0.756	0.743	0.731	0.718	0.706	0.694
3	0.731	0.712	0.693	0.675	0.658	0.641	0.624	0.609	0.593	0.579
4	0.659	0.636	0.613	0.592	0.572	0.552	0.534	0.516	0.499	0.482
5	0.593	0.567	0.543	0.519	0.497	0.476	0.456	0.437	0.419	0.402
6	0.535	0.507	0.480	0.456	0.432	0.410	0.390	0.370	0.352	0.335
7	0.482	0.452	0.425	0.400	0.376	0.354	0.333	0.314	0.296	0.279
8	0.434	0.404	0.376	0.351	0.327	0.305	0.285	0.266	0.249	0.233
9	0.391	0.361	0.333	0.308	0.284	0.263	0.243	0.225	0.209	0.194
10	0.352	0.322	0.295	0.270	0.247	0.227	0.208	0.191	0.176	0.162
11	0.317	0.287	0.261	0.237	0.215	0.195	0.178	0.162	0.148	0.135
12	0.286	0.257	0.231	0.208	0.187	0.168	0.152	0.137	0.124	0.112
13	0.258	0.229	0.204	0.182	0.163	0.145	0.130	0.116	0.104	0.093
14	0.232	0.205	0.181	0.160	0.141	0.125	0.111	0.099	0.088	0.078
15	0.209	0.183	0.160	0.140	0.123	0.108	0.095	0.084	0.074	0.065
16	0.188	0.163	0.141	0.123	0.107	0.093	0.081	0.071	0.062	0.054
17	0.170	0.146	0.125	0.108	0.093	0.080	0.069	0.060	0.052	0.045
18	0.153	0.130	0.111	0.095	0.081	0.069	0.059	0.051	0.044	0.038
19	0.138	0.116	0.098	0.083	0.070	0.060	0.051	0.043	0.037	0.031
20	0.124	0.104	0.087	0.073	0.061	0.051	0.043	0.037	0.031	0.026

CUMULATIVE PRESENT VALUE TABLE

This table shows the present value of £1 per annum, receivable or payable at the end of each year for n years

$$\frac{1-(1+r)^{-n}}{r}$$

Periods (n)	Interest rates (r) 1%	2%	3%	4%	5%	6%	7%	8%	9%	10%
1	0.990	0.980	0.971	0.962	0.952	0.943	0.935	0.926	0.917	0.909
2	1.970	1.942	1.913	1.888	1.859	1.833	1.808	1.783	1.759	1.736
3	2.941	2.884	2.829	2.775	2.723	2.673	2.624	2.577	2.531	2.487
4	3.902	3.808	3.717	3.630	3.546	3.465	3.387	3.312	3.240	3.170
5	4.853	4.713	4.580	4.452	4.329	4.212	4.100	3.993	3.890	3.791
6	5.795	5.601	5.417	5.242	5.076	4.917	4.767	4.623	4.486	4.355
7	6.728	6.472	6.230	6.002	5.786	5.582	5.389	5.206	5.033	4.868
8	7.652	7.325	7.020	6.733	6.463	6.210	5.971	5.747	5.535	5.335
9	8.566	8.162	7.786	7.435	7.108	6.802	6.515	6.247	5.995	5.759
10	9.471	8.983	8.530	8.111	7.722	7.360	7.024	6.710	6.418	6.145
11	10.368	9.787	9.253	8.760	8.306	7.887	7.499	7.139	6.805	6.495
12	11.255	10.575	9.954	9.385	8.863	8.384	7.943	7.536	7.161	6.814
13	12.134	11.348	10.635	9.986	9.394	8.853	8.358	7.904	7.487	7.103
14	13.004	12.106	11.296	10.563	9.899	9.295	8.745	8.244	7.786	7.367
15	13.865	12.849	11.938	11.118	10.380	9.712	9.108	8.559	8.061	7.606
16	14.718	13.578	12.561	11.652	10.838	10.106	9.447	8.851	8.313	7.824
17	15.562	14.292	13.166	12.166	11.274	10.477	9.763	9.122	8.544	8.022
18	16.398	14.992	13.754	12.659	11.690	10.828	10.059	9.372	8.756	6.201
19	17.226	15.679	14.324	13.134	12.085	11.158	10.336	9.604	8.950	8.365
20	18.046	16.351	14.878	13.590	12.462	11.470	10.594	9.818	9.129	8.514

Linear Regression

The linear regression equation of y on x is given by:

$$Y = a + bX \text{ or } Y - \bar{Y} = b(X - \bar{X})$$

Where

$$b = \frac{\text{Co variance (XY)}}{\text{Variance (X)}} = \frac{n\sum XY - (\sum X)(\sum Y)}{n\sum X^2 - (\sum X)^2}$$

and

$$a = \bar{Y} - b\bar{X}$$

Periods (n)	Interest rates (r)									
	11%	12%	13%	14%	15%	16%	17%	18%	19%	20%
1	0.901	0.893	0.885	0.877	0.870	0.862	0.855	0.847	0.840	0.833
2	1.713	1.690	1.668	1.647	1.626	1.605	1.585	1.566	1.547	1.528
3	2.444	2.402	2.361	2.322	2.283	2.246	2.210	2.174	2.140	2.106
4	3.102	3.037	2.974	2.914	2.855	2.798	2.743	2.690	2.639	2.589
5	3.696	3.605	3.517	3.433	3.352	3.274	3.199	3.127	3.058	2.991
6	4.231	4.111	3.998	3.889	3.784	3.685	3.589	3.498	3.410	3.326
7	4.712	4.564	4.423	4.288	4.180	4.039	3.922	3.812	3.706	3.605
8	5.146	4.968	4.799	4.639	4.487	4.344	4.207	4.078	3.954	3.837
9	5.537	5.328	5.132	4.946	4.772	4.607	4.451	4.303	4.163	4.031
10	5.889	5.650	5.426	5.216	5.019	4.833	4 659	4.494	4.339	4.192
11	6.207	5.938	5.687	5.453	5.234	5.029	4.836	4.656	4.486	4.327
12	6.492	6.194	5.918	5.860	5.421	5.197	4.988	4.793	4.611	4.439
13	6.750	6.424	6.122	5.842	5.583	5.342	5.118	4.910	4.715	4.533
14	6.982	6.628	6.302	6.002	5.724	5.468	5.229	5.008	4.802	4.611
15	7.191	6.811	6.462	6.142	5.847	5.575	5.324	5.092	4.876	4.675
16	7.379	6.974	6.604	6.265	5.954	5.668	5.405	5.162	4.938	4.730
17	7.549	7.120	6.729	6.373	6.047	5.749	5.475	5.222	4.990	4.775
18	7.702	7.250	6.840	6.467	6.128	5.818	5.534	5.273	5.033	4.812
19	7.839	7.366	6.938	6.550	6.198	5.877	5.584	5.316	5.070	4.843
20	7.963	7.489	7.025	6.623	6.259	5.929	5.628	5.353	5.101	4.870

Index

Z

Bibliography

Chartered Institute of Management Accountants (2015) CIMA Code of Ethics. [Online] Available from: www.cimaglobal.com/Professionalism/Ethics/CIMA-code-of-ethics-for-professional-accountants/ [Accessed 31 October 2023].

CIMA (2005) CIMA Official Terminology. Oxford, CIMA Publishing.

CIMA (2016) About us. [Online] Available from: www.cimaglobal.com/About-us/ [Accessed 31 October 2023].

IFAC (2005) The Roles and Domain of the Professional Accountant in Business. [Online] Available from: www.ifac.org/system/files/publications/files/the-roles-and-domain-of-the.pdf [Accessed 31 October 2023].

International Accounting Standards Board (2012) IAS 2 Inventories. [Online] Available from: www.ifrs.org/IFRSs/Pages/IFRS.aspx [Accessed 31 October 2023].

Tell us what you think

Got comments or feedback on this book? Let us know.
Use your QR code reader:

Or, visit:
https://www.smartsurvey.co.uk/s/BAJPTT/

Need to get in touch with customer service?

www.bpp.com/request-support

Spotted an error?

https://learningmedia.bpp.com/pages/errata